# Birds
*of* Tropical
America

The Curious Naturalist Series

*Birds of Tropical America* by Steven Hilty
*Shark!* by R.D. Lawrence
*The Wind Birds* by Peter Matthiessen
*Nature's Everyday Mysteries* by Sy Montgomery
*A Natural History of Sex* by Adrian Forsyth

THE CURIOUS NATURALIST

# Birds
# *of* Tropical
# America

*A watcher's introduction to behavior,
breeding and diversity*

## STEVEN HILTY

*Illustrations by Mimi Hoppe Wolf*

CHAPTERS™

CHAPTERS PUBLISHING LTD., SHELBURNE, VERMONT 05482

Published by
Chapters Publishing Ltd.
2031 Shelburne Road
Shelburne, Vermont 05482

Library of Congress Cataloging-in-Publication Data
Hilty, Steven L.
    Birds of tropical America: a watcher's introduction to behavior, breed-
ing and diversity / Steven Hilty; illustrations by Mimi Hoppe Wolf.
        p.  cm. — (The Curious naturalist series)
Includes bibliographical references (p.   ) and index.
ISBN 1-881527-56-5 : $12.95
1. Birds—Latin America.  2. Rain forest fauna—Latin America.
I. Title.  II. Series
QL685.7.H54  1994
598.298—dc20                                                                94-22186


Trade distribution by
Firefly Books Ltd.
250 Sparks Avenue
Willowdale, Ontario
Canada M2H 2S4

Printed and bound in Canada by
Friesen Printers
Altona, Manitoba

Designed by Hans Teensma/Impress, Inc., Northampton, Massachusetts

Cover illustration: Mimi Hoppe Wolf

*For Margaret Bullock*

# Contents

# *Acknowledgments*

MARGARET BULLOCK encouraged this book from the beginning, and I am grateful to her for reading all the chapters and for her questions and criticisms that focused many sections. Her boundless curiosity was a delight. I thank John Blake, John Kricher, Van Remsen, Mark Robbins, Charles Schirone and an anonymous reader for comments on various chapters. I am indebted to Peter Jennings for his interest and for making it possible for me to finish writing, and to Beverly Hilty, who helped in so many ways. For travel opportunities and assistance, I thank Victor Emanuel and Victor Emanuel Nature Tours. At Chapters Publishing Ltd., I thank especially Barry Estabrook and Kim Werner for advice and skillful editing. This book borrows from the labors of many scientists, and without their work, much of this could not have been written. We are all indebted to them for light where there was none.

# Dreams Meet Reality in the American Tropics

## A Preface

OUR DESTINATION, following a grueling daylong hike, was supposed to be the ranger's house and headquarters of Colombia's Cueva de Los Guacharos National Park. In drizzling rain, I stared at the decrepit-looking cabin in the clearing in front of us. Something seemed wrong. Weeds and tall grass crowded the neglected yard.

"We have arrived!" our Colombian guide Rubén announced with an air of authority. He was already untying our two bulky packs from the mules.

"Are you sure this is the place?" I asked.

"Si Señor! This is the park guard's house."

I wasn't so sure. Some boards on the porch were broken, and I stepped over a gaping hole in the floor and peered inside. An old wood-burning stove leaned against one wall, a small wooden table with a broken leg against another. There was an old bench, rough-hewn and unpainted like the cabin, and an empty aguardiente bottle on the floor. Outside the window, I heard chipping notes of a small party of common bush-tanagers settling into a shrub for the night. A peculiar sensation—one of impending panic and confusion—flashed through my mind. I whirled around just as Rubén dropped the last bag on the ground, and with an ear-splitting yell, slapped the mules on the butt with a long harness strap. They bolted from the yard and disappeared down the trail into the forest.

"This place is abandoned! We'll be stranded! Quick! See if you can catch the mules," I yelled to my wife Beverly, but she was already on the run after them.

In a moment, Beverly returned, tugging on the reins of the mules, and with Rubén still protesting that this was our destination, I brushed him aside and began reloading the packs.

"We're going on," I said, though it was nearly nightfall and I had no idea how much farther ahead the park ranger's house might be—or even if Rubén had led us up the right trail. I hoped I sounded convincing.

We had arrived only the day before in the little Andean town of Palestina—just as the funeral ceremony of a shooting victim was taking place. The atmosphere was tense and solemn. Despite the town's unsmiling mood, a guide and mules were relatively easy to secure, but there was no hotel and no restaurant. We made do with some crackers, tins of tuna and soft drinks and were offered the use of a storage room for sleeping— sort of a tack room, *campesino*-style—with saddles, packs, feed bags, some benches and an assortment of chickens roosting overhead. Sleep was fitful, and long before dawn, we left with Rubén for the 16-mile hike to the park.

For the first few miles, the trail was dry and easy to walk. Dawn broke with a rush of bird song, and I stopped frequently to write notes and make tape recordings of these songs. As we switchbacked higher, the trail deteriorated, becoming steep, muddy and so stomped full of holes from mule trains that walking became extremely difficult. The trail also became slick, and I worried about falling. A flock of scaly-naped parrots wheeled overhead. Somewhere in the distance, a mountain-toucan was yelping but I barely looked up now as I strained onward, my legs burning and fatigue blurring my vision, hardly noticing the beautiful forested hills that now replaced pastures and clearings.

Beverly, riding one of the mules, was far ahead. We passed the last farmer's cabin sometime in midafternoon, and the trail continued upward. The scenery was fantastic; trees were gardens of orchids, mosses and bromeliads, and mixed-species flocks with dizzying assortments of colorful tanagers swirled overhead. But our guide Rubén, a man of these mountains, saw the rain-streaked skies and fading light of late afternoon and, perhaps watching our slow progress with apprehension, struck a bargain with his conscience and decided to abandon us by dropping our bags in front of an empty cabin high on a cloud-forest slope above Colombia's Magdalena Valley. Maybe he thought we would be too tired to notice this wasn't the place. Standing in the rain, exhausted, and staring at that decrepit little cabin, I almost didn't notice. It had been such a long walk that just completing the trip seemed almost too good to be true. And it was.

We stumbled forward in near darkness and squinted at a tiny point of light far across the valley. This was surely the park guard's place. I estimated it would take at least two more hours to reach the house for our progress was now slowed by the rain, and we had only a single small lamp to light the way. Ahead, there was a narrow wooden bridge suspended across a chasm so deep that, in the darkness and rain, we could not see the rushing water far below. I took a deep breath and started across.

Cueva de Los Guacharos—Cave of the Oilbirds—was the name given to this remote park, established in 1960 by the Colombian government to protect the country's largest colony of oilbirds. Over 5,000 pairs of these stranger-than-fiction birds crowd rocky ledges inside the massive cave entrance; hundreds more spill over onto the cliff face outside the cave entrance, each pair vying for a tiny piece of rock on which to sleep away the day or to lay their eggs. Leaving the safety of the cave at dusk, they boil out in a screaming, seething mass—thousands of them sounding their strange stream of clicks and fluttering off on three-foot-long wings into the shadowy clutches of the night. They are the only nocturnal fruit-eating birds in the world.

Oilbirds may be among the park's most famous inhabitants, but I was attracted to this remote park for other reasons as well. Fueled by tales of black tinamous, wattled guans, lyre-tailed nightjars and other species so rare they were little more than myth, I had come here to gather information on these and other little-known species for a forth-

TROPICAL RAINFOREST HABITATS ARE COMPLEX
AND PATCHILY DISTRIBUTED.

coming book on the birds of Colombia. This was one of many such expeditions I undertook to some of Colombia's most remote corners.

Such peripatetic behavior is not unusual among ornithologists, for even in northern latitudes, one must visit many habitats and geographical locations in order to see the birds in a region or country. In tropical latitudes, it is even more important to visit many areas because tropical birds, on average, have smaller distributions than do those in temperate latitudes. Thus, for an ornithologist wishing to learn something about the birds of a country like Colombia, which has approximately 1,700 species (all of North America, by comparison, has only about half that many), it is necessary to visit many different places.

We stumbled up the last remaining steps of the trail and onto the porch of the remote guard outpost. Fortunately, the last half kilometer of the trail was "corduroy"—a trail of sawed logs laid side by side across the trail. Trails constructed in this manner, often of palms because they resist rotting, are common in the Andes, and though slippery, they are an improvement over mud wallows churned up by the hooves of mules. Our guide remained for the obligatory cup of *agua panela* (hot water with a lump of brown cane sugar), which in a tradition of the Colombian Andes, is always offered to visitors. He then disappeared into the black and rainy night.

Early the next morning, I was out recording the songs of white-backed fire-eyes that lived in mossy thickets behind the park buildings. Over the next few weeks, working in the forest from dawn to dusk, I tape-recorded songs and obtained data on the habits and foraging behavior of many birds that lived in this cool, subtropical forest at 6,000 feet in elevation.

I was not birding here, for my pace would have been much too slow for those only interested in accumulating a long list. Instead, I tried to remain with each bird I saw for as long as possible, writing down, in a kind of scientific shorthand, everything that it did. What kind of habitat does it prefer? At what height above ground does it forage? How does it forage—by sallying forth to snap up prey from foliage, by reaching for prey from a perch, by hovering for small berries? Does it forage with mixed-species flocks? Is it shy or easy to observe? What are its field marks?

During the evening, I organized my notes in permanent notebooks. Tape recordings might be replayed and transcribed as well. Each day brought little discoveries—a new song, a behavior not previously noticed, perhaps a bird completely new to the area.

Gathering data for the birds of Colombia project spanned more than half a decade, and the fieldwork took me throughout Colombia. Often it was more an exercise in patience and perseverance than in exciting discoveries and clever data collection. Once, a friend and I were marooned for three days in a small town east of the Colombian Andes. Each day, we went to the little airport with buoyed spirits and anticipation, only to while away the day playing games, reading and drinking beer. At the end of the day, the response was always the same: "God willing the plane will come tomorrow."

Finally, of course, it did come—on the fourth day—and then, plagued with mechanical problems, it was barely able to leave. A large bucket placed under one engine to catch the dripping oil should have scared us off, but in the naiveté of our youth, we climbed aboard—eager for the chance to escape the confines of this dirty little town. The piston-driven engine finally coughed, then started, belching tremendous clouds of blue smoke that engulfed the plane. On the flight to Bogotá, I sat by the window, transfixed, as an oil slick grew to ominous proportions, covering first the side of the engine, and eventually half of the wing, with an ugly series of fused black streaks.

Today, I view delays in modern airports with a more sanguine perspective than some, as I am reminded of those wasted days of waiting and of the smiling face of an elderly lady that sold food, candy and drinks from a kiosk at that airport. During the long wait, we got to know her well—we were, in fact, among her most frequent customers.

One day, as temperatures soared within the little tin-roofed building where we waited, we must have looked particularly tired, sweaty and dejected because she looked at us with a face lined and brown beyond its years and said, "The United States is rich and it has everything. Why do you gringos come here? Is it because you want to learn how to suffer?"

She would never have understood my explanation. How could I tell her—someone whose daily income barely buys enough food for the next day—that I had traveled all the way to her country just to study birds?

I went to Colombia in 1971, a graduate student eager to begin research on tropical birds, and wound up spending 21 months there—15 at one locality in the Western Andes—before returning to the university. The site, a four-mile mule trip from the last road, was on a high ridge overlooking the Anchicayá Valley.

During those months, that ridge and valley were mine—in spirit if not actually in fact—for I worked there as a guest of the Corporación Autónoma del Valle del Cauca, an organization much like the Tennessee Valley Authority in the United States. They provided my wife and me with pack mules and a house, which we shared with a forest guard and one or more laborers. The house was rotten and cockroach-infested, but the tin roof kept out the rain, and the view of the cloud-filled valley just beyond the house was breathtaking.

Biological field research is partly an exercise in discipline. It is repetitive and sometimes tedious. Furthermore, the research results of field naturalists are often messier than those of their laboratory-bound counterparts who have the luxury of being able to control unwanted variables in an experiment. In a natural environment, a researcher's inability to control many variables often clouds the results. It is a problem that plagues even the most cleverly designed research, and it makes the findings of the many scientists whose work is discussed later in this book all the more remarkable.

Naturalists working in remote tropical areas must often contend with biting insects, sickness, hostile political environments and a lack of almost every conceivable modern convenience. Most naturalists accept these limitations in stride—perhaps even welcome the challenges that accompany them—for they offer a rare opportunity in our modern world to take charge of one's destiny. But within the last decade or so, excellent research facilities have become available in several neotropical locations. Consequently, some naturalists now see less of the pioneer than others when they look in the mirror.

There were many trips after Cueva de Los Guacharos—Mitú, Quibdó, Puerto Inídiro, Puerto Asís, Cúcuta, Barrancabermega, Fusagasugá, Isnós, Junín, Tumaco and so on—unfamiliar places with names strange and difficult to pronounce for English speakers. Some trips were more adventurous or more scientifically productive than others, but on each, I learned something about the birdlife of this magnificent country.

When I first began working in Colombia, I could identify few of the birds I saw. I carried notebooks full of written descriptions, crude sketches, even colored-pencil drawings back to museums and then spent hours sorting through trays of specimens trying to identify what I had seen. Sometimes a month or two passed before I would be able to check a bird's identification—only to discover I had failed to note some critical field mark. So, it was back into the field for another look—a far cry from today when modern guidebooks and tape recordings make most identifications possible almost immediately.

Once, in a moment of discouragement after a particularly tiring expedition, I wrote in my journal, "The thieves steal your equipment, the humidity ruins your film, the food makes you sick and the insects drive you crazy. Sometimes the people are cussed and you must always wait until mañana. The buses haul you like cattle, drive like maniacs and still they are late. I have returned so tired I couldn't eat and it's either pouring rain or a blizzard of dust. Worse still, the forest is disappearing so fast you have to run to catch it. But there are so many birds and so much to learn one could spend an eternity here."

These trips were eventually followed by a number of organized birding and natural history tours that I led to many parts of Colombia. This broadened my field experience, especially my field-identification skills, because questions are often hammered, rapid fire, at naturalist guides throughout the day. Some of these trips were better organized than others, but through it all, I felt that Colombia was one of the most fascinating places in which a naturalist could ever hope to work. It was not a perfect world, for dreams and reality were not always the same, but it was a place where a naturalist could easily allow himself to be seduced by great ornithological riches.

This book is about the lives of birds in the American Tropics. It is written for naturalists and travelers who want to know more than the names of tropical birds. In a sense, it was written by them, for it was the questions from hundreds of people that have traveled with me, when I was their naturalist and guide in the Neotropics, that defined the scope of this book.

Thousands of people now travel to tropical latitudes to see the rainforest and some of its remarkable birds and other wildlife. Most go for pleasure and curiosity, and a few go to study or conduct research; but in whatever capacity they travel, each will, by their visit, better understand the tropical rainforest and the world we share. All one needs is the curiosity to ask why, for that is where science begins.

But tropical environments are enormously complex and dynamic, and it is often difficult to answer even simple questions about tropical environments. Furthermore, the conclusions that scientists reach often lack generality. A bird may occur in several habitats and at different elevations, and in each place, it forages in different plants, eats different foods and interacts with a different community of competitors. Consequently, some of its behaviors and even its appearance may change.

To reconcile this complexity with our goal of understanding how some things work in tropical bird communities, there is an inherent risk of oversimplification. In this regard, readers should bear in mind the limitations of science and scientists, for all things will not be exactly as they are described in this book. And while many questions remain, much progress has been made in understanding the birds of tropical America.

# Avian Addresses
## Structure of a Rainforest Bird Community

B Y SPENDING several days with friends in the Manu rainforest in southeastern Peru, I was enjoying the opportunity to indulge myself—in this arguably the richest of all rainforests in the world for birds—by finding as many species as possible. But despite good fortune, there were some interesting gaps in my list after several dawn-to-dark days in the field. Where, for example, was the razor-billed curassow, the gray-cheeked nunlet, the white-shouldered antshrike and the Ihering's antwren? I knew that each of these species was there. The question was, where?

Back at the lodge one evening, I asked Paul Donahue, a naturalist who had spent many months at Manu. In addition to building observation platforms in some of the largest trees around and ferrying guests up and down on climbing ropes, Paul had spent months birding the trails. Producing a map of the more than 25 kilometers of trails surrounding the lodge, Paul began to plot bird locations for me with the precision of a military strategist. The razor-billed curassows were spending most of their time between the lodge and one of the canopy platforms to the southeast. Perhaps this area had more fruit on the forest floor at that time of year, but of course, that could change. And yes, he knew of two pairs of nunlets, one in vines near the river a kilometer away, the other pair right behind the lodge. Stabbing at the map with his pencil, he marked the location of an old tree-fall gap where he said I should find the white-shouldered antshrike. But he had found only one pair of Ihering's antwrens on the entire trail system. "They forage with a big mixed-canopy flock over on Tangrille Trail. That's 35 minutes of fast walking from here," Paul told me.

I studied the apparent randomness of the dots on Paul's map. Why were some species so spottily distributed when there appeared to be so much perfectly suitable habitat around? Pairs of birds were sometimes separated by nearly a kilometer, and they were almost certainly not using that much of the forest. It seemed to defy reason. Or did it? Perhaps the birds were telling me something by their locations.

Once inside a rainforest, it often looks the same no matter where you are or which way you look. Horror stories of people wandering away from trails and losing their way in rainforests as big as the State of Massachusetts are common enough to make anyone pause before charging blindly away from an established trail. But surprisingly, once you get over the initial euphoria of just being in a rainforest, its chaotic vegetative excesses become less intimidating. The mind begins to tame the anarchy of vegetation, transforming its various parts, like building blocks, into a network of interconnected but discrete habitats. Masses of green become a mosaic of microhabitats, some side by side, others stacked one above another from the forest floor to the canopy.

Rainforests offer the most complex array of microhabitats on earth for birds, but naturalists have barely scratched the surface of trying to understand how birds perceive and make use of these environments. What naturalists do know is that the organization of these communities is far from random.

Tropical birds are very sensitive to the distribution of vegetation and other features in their environment. They forage in very specific ways, which restricts where they can live, and most species are not uniformly distributed but clumped around certain features within the forest. It has to be that way to accommodate so many species. A 220-acre rainforest patch may contain nearly 250 species of breeding birds—five to six times the number in a temperate deciduous forest in North America. Another 75 species may also be present seasonally in a rainforest but not breed there. How is such a complex community of birds organized? Which species breed in which habitats and why? At what densities do they occur?

Hoping to answer some of these questions, Princeton ecologist John Terborgh headed a team of researchers that conducted a detailed tropical bird census in southern Peru in 1982. Terborgh wasn't the first in the New World to attempt such an undertaking—others had conducted censuses in Panama and French Guyana—but his was destined to be the largest and most exhaustive tropical bird census ever conducted. He assembled a team of five scientists, almost all of them with years of prior experience in southern Peru, and several with ongoing research projects within the census area.

One of the team's most amazing findings was that the diversity of birds at a single point within their census plot could exceed 160 species, an extraordinary number even though high bird diversity is characteristic of rainforests. What this means is that a skilled observer, at least theoretically, could stand in one place in that rainforest and, without taking a step, record more than 160 species whose foraging or breeding territories overlapped at that point.

Terborgh also found that this very high level of bird diversity did not occur throughout the forest. In some places, the diversity dropped by half. This same phenomenon can be experienced, in a less quantitative way, by almost anyone that goes birding in a tropical forest. Some sections of a forest, despite repeated visits, will be relatively devoid of birds. After a few days, you may begin to concentrate your walks in the more productive areas. Perhaps unknowingly, you will have uncovered a fundamental structural component of tropical rainforests—distribution patchiness.

All natural environments display this patchiness of species distribution, whether we examine the fauna living in a single tree or in an entire forest. A given acre of rainforest may contain only 100 to 200 species of trees out of a possible 500 in the area, and the trees in an area affect whether some birds choose to live there or not. Fruit-eating birds, in particular, are sensitive to the species of trees present. Tree-fall gaps, swampy or damp areas and floodplains provide numerous patches that are recognized by birds.

The distribution and age of tree-fall gaps will affect what birds are found in the forest and their abundance. A greater number of tree falls, or what ecologists call a high forest turnover, will result in a different distribution of habitat patches than stable areas where turnover is slower. This will, in turn, affect the composition of birds living there. A high-turnover forest, for instance, attracts species that use tree-fall gaps and edges rather than deep-shade birds that avoid sunlit gaps. A dense stand of saplings in a recent tree fall might, for example, attract a warbling antbird or rufous-tailed flatbill, while a tangle of canopy vines—often the only remaining evidence of a tree that fell long ago—would attract a fasciated antshrike and gray antbird.

Swampy or damp areas in a rainforest are larger-scale habitat patches than tree-fall gaps. Slight depressions of only a few inches in the forest floor are enough to receive runoff and hold water after rains. In these wet places, broad-leaved heliconia plants thrive, while in the higher and drier areas, ferns predominate. Permanently wet areas may host moriche palms and other water-loving trees.

This patchy distribution of plants that results from different rates of drainage within the forest is very important to some understory birds. Plumbeous antbirds, for example, seek the damp areas that support large heliconia thickets, while the ringed antpipit, a small semiterrestrial flycatcher, prefers drier, more open areas within the forest.

The floodplain itself reflects an even larger habitat patch within which differences in bird diversity can be seen. A river, as it meanders across the floodplain, sweeps away older forest on one bank and deposits sand on the other in a cycle that destroys one forest stage and allows another to emerge. Pioneering *Cecropia* trees and fig trees dominate the young side for a few years, producing a canopy that is open and bright. Beneath them, the understory is choked with heliconia and ginger thickets, which will eventually be replaced by a more diverse association of floodplain trees and one that, in turn, can support more kinds of birds. Floodplain forests, because of their large numbers of fig trees, and others with abundant fruit crops are likely to have many fruit-eating birds, especially barbets, honeycreepers and tanagers.

Floodplains, old and new, account for between 20 and 40 percent of the total land area in western Amazonia. In floodplain forest, which is known as *várzea* in the Amazon Basin, floods lasting several months each year result in high water marks that are clearly visible on most trees. Beyond this high-water zone, another broad change in the forest occurs. The low-lying flooded forest gradually gives way to *terra firme*, or upland forest. Here, the canopy is more clearly multilayered and closed, and the understory is darker and more open. This, the most bird-rich of all tropical habitats, contains many insect-eating species, such as woodpeckers, woodcreepers, furnariids and antbirds.

In temperate-latitude forests, most birders pay only token heed to the differences between floodplain and upland forest because only four or five species nest exclusively in floodplain forest in North America— the now-extinct ivory-billed woodpecker is probably the most notable of them. But the distinction between *terra firme* and *várzea* forest is important in the Tropics. Missing one of these large-scale habitats on your visit to the rainforest could mean missing from 30 to 40 percent of the birds.

In the census that Terborgh conducted in the rainforest of southern Peru, only about 10 percent of the birds occurred throughout the entire area. Not surprisingly, most of those that were found in all areas were large, wide-ranging species like raptors, parrots and colonial icterids, although a few small insect-eating species occurred throughout as well. The majority of species preferred specific habitats. The sirystes and white-lored tyrannulet, for example, favored the edges of tree-fall openings, while thrush-like antpittas occurred only in the tangle of saplings in young tree falls. Musician wrens and rusty-belted tapaculos like to sing from old logs, and their territories were located accordingly. The territories of each of these birds closely match the distribution of these particular features in the forest.

However, the locations of some birds with patchy distributions cannot always be determined by features like vines, tree falls and logs. I was reminded of this once when I went looking for a banded antbird. This enigmatic little bird inhabits the sun-flecked floor of Amazonian rainforests where it walks quietly, sneakily even, in an almost reptilian manner among the dry leaves. It tends to be rather patchy in occurrence, despite the presence of seemingly large areas of suitable forest separating some pairs.

Once, prior to a visit to the Cocha Cashu Biological Station in southeastern Peru, I questioned Ted Parker, an ornithologist with years of field experience in Peru, about this bird. Parker had previously spent three months carrying out a bird census there, and as it turned out, he knew the location of four pairs within the trail system. But he had not been there in five years and warned that at least half of the area was not used by any of these pairs. Furthermore, over the years, territories might have shifted.

So forewarned, and with his map coordinates in hand, I visited one of the spots, played a prerecorded tape and immediately a bird flew in at my feet. This was a remarkable testimony to the fidelity of this tiny bird to its home territory. But the question remained, why did it choose this area while leaving half of the forest unoccupied?

Since then, I have discovered many more pairs of banded antbirds in the Manu River Basin. Each time it's the same—a pair, or perhaps two pairs, that seem to be separated by a long distance from neighbors. Are the birds really using such large areas? Probably not, but no one yet knows why.

Mixed-species flocks are often patchily distributed within a rainforest. The species in an average understory flock defend only about 10 to 12 acres in the rainforest, while a canopy flock ranges over four times that much area. Because the size of understory flock territories are so much smaller, it might seem that these flocks would be most affected by patchy structures in the environment. This is not the case, however. Understory flocks usually occupy almost all of the space in the lower half of the forest, while large gaps between canopy-flock boundaries result in about a third of the forest canopy being unused.

Charles Munn, studying mixed-species flocks in the same area where Terborgh's census was conducted, observed that canopy flocks avoid areas where the canopy is discontinuous and broken up by many tree falls. Munn thought that canopy flocks might forage in areas where the forest canopy is relatively continuous in order to reduce their risk of exposure to predators when flying between trees, as well as to reduce the energetic cost of excess travel. But it is also possible that the forest understory simply looks more homogeneous to understory birds than the canopy does to its occupants because understory trees are much more numerous and more evenly distributed.

The causes of patchy bird distributions aren't always limited to structural differences in the rainforest. The way one species interacts with another can result in a mosaic of territories. When Nina Pierpont of Princeton University studied woodcreepers in Peru, she discovered that some species were restricted in their occurrence by aggressive interactions with closely related species. Some *Celeus* woodpeckers probably interact aggressively with each other, too, which results in a mosaic of nonoverlapping territories.

Two nunbird species at Manu similarly limit each other's distribution. The Manu Lodge is located more than a half mile from the river, but it is still on the floodplain. Consequently, from the river to the lodge, all of the nunbirds one sees are black-fronted because this species lives in floodplain forests and along river and lake edges. To find a white-fronted nunbird, visitors have to choose a trail that leads beyond the lodge, out of the floodplain and into high-ground forest. This pattern is virtually the same all over western Amazonia. But in Central America, where the black-fronted species is absent, the white-fronted nunbird occurs in all forested habitats.

Almost every naturalist notices that some areas in a rainforest are consistently devoid of birds, while other areas are more likely to be productive. Sometimes birders are tempted to blame their bad luck on a visit at the wrong time of day or on the weather, but could it be that there are real differences in the number of birds in some places in the forest?

Terborgh and his team certainly believe so. They found that species diversity was twice as high in some parts of the forest as in others, although there was little obvious difference in the appearance of the forest. The two poorest areas within the census area were adjacent to an oxbow lake, where several nesting colonies of caciques and oropendolas were located. Resident understory flocks roamed both areas, but no mixed-species canopy flocks used these sections of the forest. Because caciques and oropendolas are large and eat a wide variety of foods, their heavy use of these nearby canopy areas could have depleted insect and fruit abundance. The icterid colonies, then, may be like patches of unsuitable habitat—places to avoid by species that use the same foods. Distributions, however, are seldom determined by issues as simple as vines and thickets or the presence or absence of competing species like the icterids. A suite of factors is likely to determine the ultimate makeup of a bird community.

Inevitably in a discussion of birds with patchy distributions, the question of rarity comes up. Naturalists often discuss rarity as a function of how frequently or infrequently a species is seen. But the word rare has several ecological meanings, and each of them provides a different way to examine a species' status. It may include how abundant a bird is in its habitat, how restricted the habitat is and how large its geographical range is.

Carnivores are usually rare because they feed at the end of a food chain. Yet there are fewer jaguars than squirrels because jaguars' prey is less abundant than the nuts and seeds on which squirrels feast. Large birds are often considered rare for the same reason, although it may be perfectly normal for them to occur at very low densities.

For instance, harpy eagles eat squirrel monkeys, which eat insects, which eat leaves, which convert sunlight into energy. Consequently, harpies, which are at the top of the food chain, along with many hawks and eagles, are much less common than monkeys or insects or leaves. And while harpies occur at very low densities, they are not truly rare because they are found virtually throughout neotropical rainforests from Mexico to Argentina.

For the same reasons, the largest members in a guild or foraging category are usually the least common members of their foraging specialty. For example, the great potoo is the largest member of a group of nocturnal birds that sallies for flying insects. It eats primarily large moths, which are less numerous than small ones. Over its wide range, the great potoo is less numerous than its smaller and better-known relative, the common potoo. What proportion of rainforest birds fall into this category of rarity?

In the Manu rainforest, only about 9 percent of the breeding birds could be considered rare because they occur at low densities. Not surprisingly, raptors lead the list, accounting for more than half of the species judged to be rare for this reason. Parrots, large woodpeckers, ground-cuckoos, great potoos, long-billed woodcreepers and great jacamars are others at Manu that sit atop this chain of diminishing resources. All of these birds normally live at very low densities. As a result, naturalists see them only infrequently in the field. But almost all of these birds are widespread geographically.

On a global scale, these birds are not rare or in danger of disappearing. Nonetheless, they are often vulnerable to human interference. Most of them require very large tracts of rainforest in order to maintain viable breeding populations and are highly sensitive, as a group, to deforestation, which fragments their habitats into many small parcels.

The largest group of so-called rare species in most tropical rainforests consists of species that are common somewhere else. In Terborgh's census of 319 species, about 25 percent fell into this category of preferring some other habitat, such as early successional growth, floodplain forest, swamps, bamboo stands or something other than mature rainforest.

Some of these species are easy to pick out because they are among the most common and widespread neotropical birds; all of them are typical of disturbed and opened areas. Prominent on the list are the black vulture, pale-vented pigeon, lineated woodpecker, straight-billed woodcreeper, pale-legged hornero, great antshrike, white-browed antbird, yellow-breasted flycatcher and buff-throated saltator.

Some birders might call these species trash birds because they are common in secondary habitats and disturbed areas throughout western Amazonia. Yet the fact that these birds seem so common is probably due to the fact that the birders themselves are spending their time in "trashy" habitats. All of these birds are "rare" at Cocha Cashu because they do not thrive in mature, undisturbed rainforest.

Another meaning of the word rare may be applied to birds that are rare because of ecological specialization. Unlike species that are rare because they sit at a high trophic level in a food chain, these birds and animals may be rare because they have evolved specialized diets or utilize habitats that are rare or widely scattered. The white-shouldered antshrike is rare because it is found around certain old tree-fall gaps that have the right combination of cover and perhaps suitable nesting sites.

In tangled vegetation around the edge of the long oxbow lake that fronts the Manu Lodge, visitors occasionally see an agami heron. Agamis are beautiful herons, but their reclusive behavior and habit of remaining in the shadows beneath dense overhanging vegetation makes them difficult to find. Their long harpoonlike bills and combination of light and dark blue coloring that mimics both the shade and the occasional shaft of sunlight penetrating their lairs contribute to the artful deception of these shy fishermen.

Agamis aren't numerous and there may be only a pair or two on the entire lake. Their scarcity is partly due to the fact that they feed on fairly large fish, which themselves are two or three steps up the food chain ladder. But there may be other less obvious reasons for agamis' rarity. They only live where there is an abundance of overhanging vegetation that covers the muddy shore edge and hangs into the water—a restriction that greatly limits the amount of habitat available to them. If agami herons stalked their prey in the open, like most herons, they might be a good deal more numerous.

Sometimes the reasons for a bird's rarity can't be so easily pinned down. When Ted Parker was conducting the Cocha Cashu rainforest census, he was surprised one morning by an unfamiliar song coming from the *Heliconia* and ginger thickets in one of the low-lying sections of the forest that is prone to flooding during the wet season. As Parker listened to the strange song, the singer obviously on foot, he wondered if this could be the long lost rufous-fronted antthrush—a bird known from only a few specimens taken decades ago on a tributary farther downriver. His suspicions were correct, and the shy singer indeed proved to be this antthrush—a bird so rare and unknown to science that doubts had been raised about its very existence.

Many naturalists have visited the Manu wilderness since Parker first spent a dry season there in 1982, and because of his discovery, the bird has now become the focus of considerable attention. Within a few years, other naturalists found it at a half dozen other places along the Manu River, even right at the tiny jungle airstrip where well-heeled international travelers arrive, fresh from the thin air of Cuzco and eager for rain-forest adventure. When a few pairs were found near the Manu Lodge, visiting birders actually began to expect to see it. It seems unbelievable that this antthrush, whose whereabouts was unknown to science until a gifted young ornithologist found it a decade earlier, was now being taken for granted.

The expectations of birders notwithstanding, the rufous-fronted antthrush is a genuine rarity. In this enormous wilderness, the bird has been found only in a few rather widely scattered spots along the river.

Groups of three or four pairs of rufous-fronted antthrushes may occur close together, although they may be separated by several kilometers of rainforest from others of their kind. The entire river basin may shelter only a few hundred to a few thousand of these birds. No one knows. And we can only assume that it occurs nowhere else on our planet except in the upper drainage basin of the Madre de Dios and Manu River and nearby Tambopata River in southeastern Peru. Even if the rufous-fronted antthrush turns out to be much more numerous, naturalists will still consider it a rarity because of its very small geographical distribution. It is a classic example of yet another kind of rarity—one that is considered rare because it is confined to only one tiny area.

The reasons why the rufous-fronted antthrush is so rare can only be guessed. Certainly its preferred habitat is limited because the only place it has been found is in a very narrow strip of successional vegetation close to the river—areas that are damp, thick with mosquitoes that buzz in your ears and filled with rank-growing herbaceous plants that impede every step. Worse still for investigators, the places where the rufous-fronted antthrush lives are often among the first to flood when the rains begin and the last to dry out afterward, so its habitat remains isolated and inaccessible for much of the year. But the puzzle of the rufous-fronted antthrush's rarity may involve more than its patchy habitat.

Two other *Formicarius* antthrushes can be found in the Manu River Basin, and they are so similar in appearance and behavior to the rufous-fronted antthrush that ornithologists might suspect right away that all three of them compete for resources. One of them, the black-faced antthrush, is widespread in the Neotropics and lives in many kinds of forest habitats. Its loud whistled song soon becomes familiar to just about every visitor to New World tropical rainforests. In the Amazon Basin, the rufous-capped antthrush also occurs and takes slightly higher-ground forest. This tends to limit the black-faced antthrush to flood-plain zones, and there it runs head on into the rufous-fronted antthrush.

Where all three species occur together in floodplain forest, each seems to prefer areas with slightly different flood regimes. Occasionally, all three can be heard calling from the same place, though I've never heard them all in the same place at the same time. Perhaps the three defend largely nonoverlapping territories.

Is the rufous-fronted antthrush rare and local because it is an inferior competitor that only manages to hang on in a few *Heliconia* patches that are unwanted by its competitors, or is it a recent upstart on the scene and one that has yet to spread and make its mark? Whatever the reasons, it is a bona fide rarity: it is endemic to a single river system, its habitat is very restricted in distribution and it is unaccountably patchy even within its specialized habitat.

The rufous-fronted antthrush, like most endemic rarities, is vulnerable to even small amounts of habitat disturbance, and a new wild card has been thrown into its already uncertain distribution. Gold has been discovered downriver and within part of the tiny range of this bird. In the rush for gold, few in the mining business will concern themselves with the welfare of this curious and unprepossessing little bird, nor would they lament its loss if it stood in their way. Ironically, the economic impact of losing this bird, which may draw generations of tourists to the area, to say nothing of the loss of biological diversity, when balanced against the short-term gain of a few ounces of gold, could in the long run be a very poor trade indeed.

Tropical rainforests often give the impression of either being filled with birds or being absolutely empty. This can be attributed in part to mixed-species flocks, which move through the forest in waves. When a flock is present, every leaf and branch rustles with foraging birds, but in a twinkling they disappear, leaving the forest in silence.

With this kind of behavior, how does one even hazard a guess as to how many birds are in a rainforest? Terborgh's team of scientists combined several census techniques to estimate the number of birds in the rainforest at Cocha Cashu. Surprisingly, the total number of individual birds was rather similar to that in a temperate deciduous forests—around 955 pairs of birds per 220 acres compared to 1,000 pairs in a similar-sized area in New Hampshire. But this is about as far as the similarity goes.

The populations of the most common birds in the Peruvian rainforest are only about one-tenth the size of those in temperate forests, and less common rainforest species live at densities still lower than that. Furthermore, one-quarter of the birds in the census were represented by no more than a single pair.

Until Terborgh's study, few naturalists would have imagined that the average number of birds of each rainforest species is so low. All of this might seem discouraging to prospective visitors expecting to find the rainforest teeming with birds. The reality is, the rainforest is teeming with diversity, but not necessarily with great numbers of individuals. This is one of the first things that new visitors notice, because even after walking the same forest trail for several days, they continue to see new species.

Most tropical birds live at very low densities compared with those in temperate latitudes, and getting used to this can be a big shock to new visitors as well as a disappointment to those with only a few days to spend. But it also means that, even though a person may see rather few birds in any one day, new species will continue to appear for days to come. Finding birds in a rainforest can be slow, tedious work, and most veteran birders know that even after slogging up and down slippery trails and sweating in heat and high humidity for days, they will still add new species to their lists.

Some birds that occur at very low densities, such as raptors, macaws, ground-cuckoos and woodpeckers, have enormous foraging areas, so it can take days to catch up to them. Smaller birds may be rare because they seek out very specific habitats, like tree-fall gaps, swamps or *Heliconia* thickets, and the knowledge needed to locate these patchily distributed species can only be acquired by a combination of time and patience.

One noteworthy feature of tropical rainforest bird communities is the evenness of abundance of many species. Terborgh thinks that one reason for this is that a great many tropical forest birds are members of mixed-species flocks, and flock membership is generally limited to only a single pair of each species per flock. Thus, many species are present in identical numbers.

Tropical forests harbor nearly five times more big birds than temperate-latitude forests. This isn't difficult to verify, even by casual observation. A morning's walk in the spring or early summer in an eastern hardwood forest will produce many small passerine birds (especially songbirds), but with the exception of the occasional wild turkey, hawk or crow, few large birds. Species formerly present, such as the passenger pigeon and Carolina parakeet would have increased the total only slightly.

Why are there more large tropical birds than large temperate ones? This is, in part, due to the presence of large birds in several guilds in the Tropics that are absent in temperate latitudes. Tinamous, curassows, wood-quails and trumpeters all feed heavily on seeds and fallen fruits and have no counterparts in North America beyond the grouse and the wild turkey. Large-canopy fruit eaters like parrots, toucans and cotingas have no equivalents in temperate zones. But these are not the only guilds in which there are larger birds. Because insects are larger on average in the Tropics than in temperate regions, tropical insect-eating birds outweigh their temperate counterparts by over 50 percent.

Having grown up birding in temperate latitudes, I learned to rely on my ears to locate birds and on my eyes to spot movements. The hearing still serves me well when I walk into a tropical forest, but long ago I discovered that many tropical birds are not as active as temperate ones. An examination of the data from Terborgh's tropical-latitude and temperate-latitude censuses shows why.

The temperate-forest bird community is almost completely dominated by insect-eating passerines that actively pursue their prey. The same is true among tropical passerines—they are active searchers—but in a tropical forest, passerines are but a fraction of the total birds. Tropical birdlife is more evenly divided among seed eaters, fruit eaters and insect eaters.

In five tropical families—potoos, nightjars, motmots, jacamars and puffbirds—most of the birds employ an energy-conserving sit-and-wait strategy, moving only when an insect is spotted. In addition, parrots, cotingas and many fruit-eating birds alternate short feeding bouts with long periods of inactivity. This further contributes to the sense of quietness that is common in the rainforest.

This fundamental difference also has implications for humans in the rainforest. Indigenous hunters usually possess remarkable powers of concentration and have an excellent ability to spot motionless birds. It is a skill that serves them well when there is no food on the table. But most urban naturalists, like myself, find it difficult to muster the sustained concentration needed to consistently spot rainforest birds that are sitting quietly. This, combined with the difficulty of seeing birds in thick foliage, is enough to discourage many visitors who despair of seeing birds in mature rainforest.

As a result, many people concentrate much of their time along edge habitats, because birds inhabiting the edges of forest or woodlands are relatively easy to see. This is the domain of sallying species like flycatchers, which take advantage of the open spaces afforded by edge zones and are generally active and easier to see than their more patient allies inside the forest. Some birds position their territories so that part lies within an edge. Forest elaenias, their name notwithstanding, almost always include a tree-fall gap or an edge zone within their territory.

Yet, despite the widely held perception among birders that edge habitats somehow hold more species than the habitats they are adjacent to, this is not the case in tropical forests. Every edge habitat in Terborgh's rainforest census proved to have either the same number or fewer species than adjacent mature forested habitats. The areas of highest diversity were always well inside the mature forest, not along the forest edge.

Successional habitats, where trees have been blown down or otherwise destroyed, also seem to abound with birds. Like edges, these areas are open and well lighted, and birds are usually easy to see, so these areas appear richer than mature forest. But they aren't. Certain species are attracted to successional habitats of varying ages, but as a whole, successional and second-growth habitats contain considerably fewer kinds of birds than mature forests. In general, the more structurally diverse the habitat, the more likely it is to contain a higher diversity of birds.

In a temperate forest, keen birders often locate practically all of the breeding birds by listening carefully and recording the species they hear singing. In this manner, a census of the breeding birds can be made by plotting the locations of singing males on a map, and in a few days, it is possible to obtain a good estimate of the number and distribution of territorial male birds.

Most tropical birds sing regularly, too, especially at dawn, and learning bird songs in a tropical rainforest is essential to the success of anyone working there. Nevertheless, bird songs in the rainforest are a less reliable indicator of the number of birds than in a temperate forest for several reasons. Only about two-thirds of rainforest birds behave as if they have conventional territories, so the remainder of the species has to be estimated by some other means. Also, the census taker will run into problems even with conventional territory-holders. In temperate forests, it is usually only the male that sings and proclaims the territory jointly occupied by him and his mate. This is not the case in tropical latitudes, where many female birds sing territorial songs that are similar to those of their mates.

In the distance, an immaculate antbird's clear, descending series of *peer*-sounding whistles comes so rapidly it seems to be poured from a pitcher. The antbird's loud song carries well through the thick undergrowth. Is it a male or a female? The songs of the two sexes, like those of so many species of birds in the rainforest, are virtually identical. Only those with perfect pitch might recognize that the female's song is slightly higher. Many female antbirds sing as well as their mates do. So do female wood-quails, rails, doves, motmots, trogons, woodcreepers, ovenbirds and wrens.

The problem is even murkier for those species in which the males and females are identical. Both sexes of woodcreepers sing, and they also look alike. So for a tropical census of woodcreepers, naturalists may have to resort to counting the number of mixed-species flocks because there will be no more than a single pair of each species in the flock.

For species in which the pairs sing duets, however, it is usually easy enough to detect the presence of the pair. Wood-quails, wood-rails, nunbirds and the *Thryothorus* wrens all sing duets, and they are species that inhabit thick shrubbery and use duetting, among other things, to keep track of each other.

Aside from females that sing and complicate naturalists' census-taking procedures, there are other important tropical-temperate differences among conventional territory holders. Some rainforest birds, despite holding territories, sing very infrequently or confine their efforts to only a few minutes of predawn song. Puffbirds, wedge-billed woodcreepers, several gnateaters and *Tangara* tanagers are among a small but curious group of birds that sing very little or confine their singing to the briefest periods before dawn.

Many forest-dwelling puffbirds are so seldom heard that most naturalists are not able to identify their songs because, on the infrequent occasions when the birds are seen, they are inevitably sitting mute and immobile on a lookout. All puffbirds sing, but they generally aren't noted for their diligence. A collared puffbird may utter only three or four songs into the predawn darkness and then fall silent for the day. Despite their laconic habits, that may be enough, because collared puffbirds sing far earlier than most birds. Without interference from hundreds of competing avian and insect voices, the puffbirds' soft whistles float through the damp and shadowy rainforest dawn even as owls utter their last muffled hoots and nightjars flutter after errant moths. It may be that it is the quality of airtime, rather that the quantity of it, that is most important.

The territories of rainforest birds are large. While the wren and cardinal in my Kansas backyard seem to manage with only an acre or two, no rainforest birds could do with so little space. The amount of territory defended by birds in the rainforest of southeastern Peru varies from about 11 to more than 35 acres (in Central America it may be less). Many territories are far larger. Obviously, large birds have larger territories than small birds, but on average, tropical birds have territories that are about 10 times the size of temperate-forest bird territories.

This is a huge difference, but it isn't as remarkable as it might first appear. Temperate birds hold breeding territories for only a few weeks or months during the summer, a time when insects are at peak abundance. For a short period of time during the long sunny days of a temperate summer, the total productivity of many temperate habitats outstrips that of a rainforest.

Furthermore, North American breeding migrants that hold territories on their neotropical wintering grounds—and many of them do—often maintain only very small areas. A wood thrush or Kentucky warbler, for example, may spend most of its five-month to six-month winter tenure in Central America on a territory that is a small fraction of the size of that used by a tropical counterpart. But it is important to remember that wintering migrants are unmated and hold territories alone, and because they do not breed there, they require less from a territory than a tropical resident. Their tropical counterparts are stuck on the same property year in and year out, and their territories must be sufficient to see them through a lifetime.

In addition, many tropical insect eaters are quite specialized: they are limited to search-and-capture techniques that do not give them much latitude for opportunistic foraging. With this in mind, the large territories of tropical birds, in general, begin to seem more like a necessary insurance policy against occasional rough times.

Fully a third of tropical birds have dispensed with conventional breeding territories entirely. In temperate latitudes, monogamous male-female pairs on defended territories are the norm, and social breeding systems like those of acorn woodpeckers and scrub jays are exceptional. Not so in tropical latitudes where unconventional social systems are rampant. Alternative life-styles occur among species in a wide variety of families, but they are especially prevalent among nectar-eating and fruit-eating birds such as hummingbirds, cotingas, manakins, mourners and icterids, as well as the professional ant followers.

Multiple male display grounds, known as leks, are common and represent one of the most striking differences between temperate-latitude and tropical-latitude forests. Rainforests also harbor a number of communal breeding species including trumpeters, some toucans, *Melanerpes* and *Celeus* woodpeckers, nunbirds, *Campylorhynchus* wrens and jays.

Conventionally, ecologists have conducted bird censuses by working alone for relatively short periods of time on small temperate-forest plots. These methods, when applied to rainforest communities, have not been successful. With up to six times the number of breeding species and very low population densities for most species, the rainforest presents a challenge to ecologists.

The study of tropical bird communities is still in its infancy, but we must not lose sight of the progress that has already been made. I am constantly reminded of my own modest progress when I recall the frustration of my first day spent at a rainforest near Leticia, Colombia. Alone and armed only with a cheap pair of binoculars and a note pad, I wandered through the forest, eventually encountering several mixed-species flocks in the canopy. But at the end of the day, I positively identified just a single bird, a male pink-throated becard.

Today, rainforest community studies are large-scale efforts conducted by coordinated teams of experienced scientists. Yet the forest is still alien. Threads of mystery are untangled here and there, but caution is still the watchword when formulating generalizations. Things that seem clear in one place are often much less so somewhere else.

Many of the conclusions from the work of John Terborgh and his co-workers may prove to be only partially applicable to other neotropical forests. Yes, birds and animals do have addresses, but their addresses are usually not advertised, and the clues that lead us to them are subtle. Our eyes and ears are less attuned to the signals of the rainforest and the messages of its creatures than are the eyes and ears of those who spend their lives there. Nevertheless, each new discovery brings joy and understanding, and what could be more important?

# *Tropical Diversity*

## Why So Many Bird Species in Tropical Forests?

**M**OST BIRDERS are fanatical about keeping lists. They list birds they've seen in their backyards, their home state, their country and even the world. At one time, birders dreamed of seeing 600 species within the borders of the United States. The birding equivalent of the four-minute mile, this "six hundred club" was rarified air, the stuff of dreams, and those who achieved this mark were justly proud of their accomplishment. Today, with improved transportation, professional birding tours and birding hotlines, that goal has been pushed to 700 and is still climbing.

Birders eager for large life lists often find themselves in tropical latitudes, and with good reason. I have led a number of birding trips to Colombia, a country about the same size as the combined areas of Oklahoma and Texas. Twice, we recorded 750 species in three weeks—more birds than most people will see in a lifetime in the United States and Canada combined.

In 1982, two ornithologists, Scott Robinson and Ted Parker, set out to see as many birds as possible in a single day in a rainforest in southern Peru. Their astounding total of 324 species was reached by walking trails near their camp and paddling a small dugout canoe on a nearby lagoon. During the entire day, they ventured less than a mile from their camp.

These successes could be duplicated in other places, and they illustrate the richness of tropical rainforests. There are simply more species of birds in tropical regions, especially tropical rainforests, than in comparable temperate zones—and in most cases there are a lot more. Inevitably we must ask, why are there so many kinds of birds in tropical regions?

Most groups of plants and animals have the greatest number of species in equatorial latitudes, and their numbers gradually decline toward the poles. If we compared the number of breeding birds in areas of roughly equal size, we might find more than 800 breeding species in eastern Ecuador, 600 in Panama, 350 in northern Guatemala, 150 in southern Texas, 130 in Minnesota, 60 on the Hudson Bay and 26 on the north slope of Alaska. This trend is repeated again and again among organisms as varied as trees, butterflies, frogs, bats, even parasites.

Not all diversity trends are dictated by latitude, however, because there is variation in the richness between tropical regions. Wet tropical forests contain more species of birds than moist tropical forests, which are, in turn, more diverse than dry tropical forests. Amazonian rainforests contain more species than do those of Africa or Asia. A few square kilometers of rainforest in eastern Ecuador harbors more species than a similar area west of the Andes in Ecuador. Even within the Amazon rainforest itself, species diversity varies considerably. Rainforests of western Amazonia, because they are close to the Andes, are richer than those in the eastern part, and forests on alluvial soils are much richer than those on white sandy soils.

Of all the diversity patterns, the tropical-temperate gradient is perhaps the most intriguing and the most perplexing. Many theories, among them climate stability, geographical history, competition and predation, have been suggested to account for this gradient in species diversity. What has become clear is that differences are not caused by one single factor but by a combination of many things.

Distinguishing between the various factors has proved hard because several of them often vary in tandem, making it difficult to separate the contribution of any one of them. Take, for instance, the complexity of the habitat. Layers of foliage, as viewed from the ground up, are a measure of the complexity of a habitat. As one moves from pioneering grass and shrubs on a river sandbar into progressively more mature forest, each profile of foliage contains more and more layers of leaves, and the number of bird species also increases. But habitat complexity is just one of the many factors that influences the increase in bird species.

The vast grasslands, or llanos, of central Venezuela are a Mecca for birds and birders alike. The abundance of waterfowl and long-legged waders, the wide open horizons and the vast herds of cattle that now roam these plains are reminiscent of eastern Africa and the everglades. Walk out into the dusty grasslands in the dry season, and a streaky-looking yellowish pipit flushes at your feet and flies off with a sharp *chit-chit,* showing white outer tail feathers. Somewhere in the distance, an eastern meadowlark sings its familiar song, but here revealing a slight tropical accent. A turkey vulture tilts and teeters overhead. A pair of southern rough-winged swallows chases by, inscribing little zigzags and circles as they go, while at the edge of a distant marsh, a cocoi heron waits patiently in shallow water.

It is an association of birds that has a decidedly familiar ring to northern naturalists. These same birds, or their ecological equivalents, occur in temperate grasslands and marshes. If transported to a Kansas pastureland, the vulture and the meadowlark could probably travel incognito, unrecognized as tropical impostors among their peers. The rough-winged swallows are so similar to their northern cousins that they were once all considered to be the same species, and the cocoi heron is but a great blue heron dressed in formal black and white attire.

In the Venezuelan marsh, there are great egrets, green herons, snipes and skimmers, and they all look and behave much as they do in temperate marshes. So, too, do the whistling-ducks whose eyes are riveted on our every move as they stand frozen at attention with necks stretched tall. There are also kingfishers and terns—different species here, but they fill the same ecological role that their counterparts do in the North. All of this shouldn't be too surprising because grasslands and marshes are structurally simple, largely two-dimensional communities. Without the added dimension of vertical height, they offer birds only a limited number of ways to divide up a habitat or a set of resources.

Despite the similarities between these two bird populations, there are hints that even here, in this relatively simple tropical habitat, the comparison isn't so straightforward. In the grasslands, there are an ibis, a whistling heron, a lapwing, a thick-knee, a terrestrial flycatcher and several yellow-finches and sparrows. In the marshes, there are jabirus, tiger-herons, several ibises, a spinetail and more flycatchers. For most of these, it is difficult or impossible to pick out an obvious temperate counterpart.

Wandering into nearby gallery forest, the similarity between temperate and tropical bird populations begins to weaken. Gallery forests hug the banks of the sluggish rivers that meander across the flat tropical grasslands. Many Amazonian birds have spread northwestward, following these narrow forest corridors across the plains from the Orinoco to the Andes. As boulevards of safe passage, these gallery forests permit Amazonian species to rub shoulders with meadowlarks and pipits from the grasslands.

Stand by a shady stream bank and shy wood-rails scamper away on coral legs. Hoatzins—strange, disheveled, leaf-eating creatures, half bird, half spare parts—glare suspiciously and hiss before crashing off in a panic to the safety of denser foliage. A curassow, stately in repose and aloof in demeanor, quietly tiptoes up the bank where its white petticoats and black plumage dissolve into the shadows. Spinetails chatter in streamside shrubbery. A sunbittern bursts off the bank; its obelisk-shaped sunburst on each wing so closely resemble large eyes that one might recoil in surprise.

In the forest, numerous unfamiliar birds with no obvious northern counterparts range from the ground to the treetops—tinamous, woodcreepers, scythebills, jacamars, becards and a bewildering number of flycatchers. And rich as it seems, the gallery forest is but a distillation of the still greater diversity in the rainforests.

What began as a simple comparison between ecologically equivalent tropical-latitude and temperate-latitude birds in a grassland has now lost its relevance. In the rainforest, there is an onslaught of birds that have no temperate-latitude counterparts. Naturalists have wrestled with the problem of explaining increased tropical diversity for a century or more, but answers have proved elusive. Part of the problem stems from the fact that there are two major components to tropical diversity: the evolutionary events that produced so many species in the first place and the mechanisms that accommodate so many species in a tropical habitat.

The emergence of land bridges has allowed entire bird populations to mingle, enriching tropical and temperate latitudes alike. Ice ages and other climatic upheavals have affected not only polar but tropical regions as well, and they have probably resulted in repeated changes in the extent of forest and grassland in South America. This has provided many opportunities for isolation, recontact and eventual species buildup. Although understood only in broadest outline, these historical events affect what we see today.

These kinds of historical events probably aided my bird quests in Colombia because there the Andes split into three separate ranges, each of which offers many opportunities for species to evolve in isolation. It also might have aided Scott Robinson and Ted Parker on their record-setting day because their count, which was conducted in southeastern Peru, lies squarely within an area that is postulated to have been a Pleistocene forest refuge—an area where forest persisted even while surrounding forests were replaced by grasslands or light woodland. These regions of ancient forest, which are still being identified, are among the most species-rich in Amazonia.

In a more general sense, tropical latitudes may be richer in species simply because more of the earth's surface is located there. Bigger land areas provide more opportunities for species to evolve. This makes sense when we consider that the chance of a population becoming isolated is better in a large land area than in a small one. On a small landmass, there may be few chances for populations to remain separated from each other long enough for different species to evolve—a process biologists call speciation. On the other hand, large land areas, by virtue of their size, should provide more chances for long-term separation of populations because of the presence of more mountains, rivers and different types of vegetation.

Large land areas also buffer a species from extinction better than small land areas. Species on islands and small geographical landmasses are particularly vulnerable to chance events that can wipe them out.

Thus, the large surface area that is within the Tropics should result in more opportunities for speciation to occur and at the same time reduce the chances of species extinction.

Nevertheless, geography and history provide, at best, only incomplete answers as to why there are so many species in the Tropics. It is better to turn to ecological factors that directly affect tropical diversity because naturalists can see these in the field and measure their differences.

More than three decades ago, community ecologist Robert MacArthur of Princeton University made a serious attempt to get at the roots of tropical diversity. On the basis of his previous studies of wood warblers in the northeastern United States, MacArthur thought that structural features of the forest environment played an important role in determining the diversity of birds or animals found there. Quite simply, MacArthur believed that the more diverse the environment, the more kinds of birds it would support.

MacArthur was partially right. Tall, complex tropical forests do shelter more birds than temperate forests. But he was unable to fully account for the increase in bird species in the Tropics on the basis of forest structure alone. For nearly two decades after MacArthur, the problem of tropical diversity was largely ignored, dogged in part by the technical difficulty of censusing tropical birds. These were the very same problems that eventually ovdrwhelmed MacArthur's pioneering work in Panama.

A tropical bird census is a daunting task—just learning bird vocalizations alone takes years—and standard censusing techniques used in temperate latitudes, which rely heavily upon singing males in territories, are inadequate by themselves given the large number of birds with novel breeding systems in rainforests. The foraging and breeding territories of some tropical birds are very large or are used for only part of the year, so the standard 20-acre to 25-acre census plot, which is adequate to sample birds in a temperate forest, misses many tropical birds.

Against such odds, ecologist John Terborgh and several colleagues took on the task of examining the structure of rainforest bird communities and trying to uncover the ecological factors that permit so many birds to coexist in Amazonian rainforests. Their starting point was an inventory of the birds in a large floodplain bend of the Manu River in southern Peru.

Terborgh and his team reasoned that diet and behavior might offer clues as to how birds coexist. The researchers carefully recorded information on what birds ate and the search-and-capture techniques they used to obtain their food. Placing so much emphasis on food might seem to contradict the old saying, "to eat like a bird," but birds actually have high metabolisms and eat tremendous quantities of food for their size. Indeed, much of a bird's life is occupied with finding food or defending territories that contain food. So it shouldn't be surprising that food, and competition for it, is an important factor influencing the number of birds in any habitat.

Tropical forests offer many food resources not available year-round to temperate birds. Wet seasons and dry seasons produce fluctuations in the amount of food available to birds, but they are never as severe as seasonal changes occurring in temperate latitudes. This increased predictability of food availability makes it possible for many tropical birds to specialize.

Fruit is an obvious example. Most of the fruit produced in a temperate forest ripens and falls from late summer through the winter months, but little is available during the nesting season. In the rainforest, fruit is available year-round, and often there are many different kinds in both the canopy and the understory. Even during the leanest times, birds are able to find a dozen or more kinds of ripe fruit. In fact, fruit is reliable enough year-round in most rainforests that a few species, like the gray-winged trumpeter and some quail-doves, are able to subsist almost entirely upon fallen fruits that they pick up off the forest floor.

When Terborgh compared the rainforest birds at Manu with those breeding in a tall hardwood forest in South Carolina, which is one of the most structurally complex forests in eastern North America, the fruit advantage was clear. Excluding kingfishers, swallows and other species associated with water, Terborgh recorded a total of 319 forest bird species in the Manu rainforest census. Twenty-nine species ate only fruits, and many more included some fruit in their diets. In the Carolina hardwoods, no species lived entirely on fruit, and only seven fed seasonally on fruit.

Nectar, like fruit, is another important resource in tropical forests. Eight hummingbirds were resident year-round and many more were seasonal visitors to Manu, compared with only a single seasonal resident in the Carolina forest. Here, then, was solid evidence that some of the increase in tropical diversity was due to the presence of year-round foods in the Tropics that were lacking in temperate latitudes.

Seeds of immature fruits are available year-round in tropical latitudes, and they provide another opportunity for specialization that is largely unavailable in temperate latitudes. Parrots and parakeets are perhaps the most persistent immature-seed predators in the rainforest. Eighteen species of parrots, all but one of them present year-round, are significant predators on the seeds of a wide variety of immature and ripe fruits in the Manu rainforest.

Swarms of raiding army ants flush a bonanza of insects and small prey from the rainforest floor as they rampage through the leaf litter in search of prey. A band of cleansed forest lies in their wake, but it is the panic-stricken hordes fleeing the ants' onrush that attracts the ever-scrutinizing eyes of a uniquely tropical group of bird—the antbirds.

Some of these quarrelsome vagabonds have, over eons, become so persistently dependent upon ant raids to flush their quarry that they are now unable to find food for themselves anywhere else. Scientists have dubbed them professional ant followers, and their profession—unique to the Neotropics—is one that exists only with the help of the ants. Lurking over the ant swarms, these birds dart to the ground and snap up any luckless prey that escapes the voracious clutches of the ants.

At Manu, six professional army ant followers forage in this way, obtaining virtually all of their food thanks to ants. Additionally, several other species work part-time shifts in the vicinity of raiding ants. Army ants are common and widespread throughout humid parts of the American Tropics, but there are none in temperate latitudes that forage above ground, so they cannot be followed by birds.

The ant followers are commensals—they benefit from associating with another species, in this case the ants—but some lesser-known rain-forest inhabitants also ply a commensal trade, making use of other uniquely tropical resources. Double-toothed kites and black-fronted nunbirds regularly follow some kinds of monkeys in neotropical rain-forests, and both species forage in much the same way. They sit patiently, waiting for the monkeys to move through the foliage and flush insects and small vertebrates. When an insect or lizard is flushed, these birds drop down and grab it in a long swooping flight.

On the floor of the forest below these birds, there is another com-mensal bird-mammal association, though it is one that is less frequently observed. Several neotropical ground-cuckoos, which resemble their fa-mous desert-dwelling cousin the roadrunner of the American Southwest, follow herds of wild peccaries. Some peccary herds are truly awesome in size, numbering a hundred individuals or more, and the vertebrates and insects flushed by these animals are chased down by these nimble ground-cuckoos. When the peccaries move too far away—a herd may range over dozens of square miles—the wily cuckoos switch to following army ants in yet another commensal relationship.

Some resources are present in both tropical and temperate forests but are of much greater importance to birds in the Tropics. Curled dead leaves suspended in the rainforest are one such resource, since they often serve as favorite hiding places during the day for many insects.

At Manu, seven species of birds are dead-leaf specialists exclusively, and several other species spend significant amounts of time investigating dead leaves. Following mixed-species flocks, dead-leaf specialists move from one hanging dead leaf or cluster to the next, ignoring everything in between. Almost all of the specialists are foliage-gleaners or antwrens—two families that are not found outside of the American Tropics. These acrobatic birds fly from one dead leaf to the next and then, while bend-ing down or hanging straight down, peer inside the curled up leaf. Some species forage in the lower strata of the forest, some in the canopy and a few check mostly clusters of dead leaves that accumulate in the forks of branches.

Such extreme specialization is only possible in a tropical rainforest because leaves are replaced there at a low but relatively constant rate throughout the year. On the other hand, dead leaves are little more than an incidental and seasonal resource in temperate latitudes. Blue-winged and worm-eating warblers check them frequently and so do chickadees and titmice, but quantities of dead leaves are primarily available during the fall months, when insect abundance is declining, so the leaves are not an especially productive resource. But several temperate-latitude-breeding parulid warblers switch to dead-leaf searching once they return to tropical wintering grounds.

Vines are another structural resource that take on considerable importance in the Tropics. Vines and vine tangles are a prominent part of all mature rainforest communities, and like curled dead leaves, they represent a resource that is productive year-round. Tropical vine diversity and abundance far exceed that in temperate latitudes, due in part to the damage that freezing temperatures cause to the long, delicate plumbing of vines. Tropical vines are such an important part of the rainforest that ecologists consider the presence of large ones to be an indication of undisturbed rainforest.

Vine tangles may envelop entire tree canopies and tie large areas of forest together. It is among these vast tangles that several vine-specialist birds live. So ubiquitous are vines in tropical forests that vine-gleaning and vine-inhabiting specialists can be found in tropical dry forests as well as wet forests. Among them are fasciated antshrikes, gray antbirds, thrush-like wrens, long-billed gnatwrens and rose-breasted chats—all birds that spend their lives in or near the security of canopy vine tangles.

Epiphytes are plants that grow on top of other plants; they include mosses, ferns, orchids and woody shrubs. They comprise a large part of the total plant diversity in a tropical forest, and along with vines, they are a major part of what makes a rainforest look like a rainforest. In humid tropical forests, it is estimated that epiphytes account for between 35 and 65 percent of all plant species and an astounding 40 percent of the entire biomass in a rainforest. They are most abundant in cool cloud forests in the mountains of Central and South America. Here, trees disappear beneath carpets of epiphytes so dense that they cover every square inch of their hosts' surfaces, and forests become fairyland gardens of diversity.

In addition to adding structural complexity to the forest, the live and dead parts of epiphytes create innumerable microhabitats for invertebrates and small vertebrates that could not exist otherwise. The importance of epiphytes to the avian community is enormous. Birds visit their flowers for nectar, eat their fruits, glean food from their foliage and use them to shelter their nests.

The importance of epiphytes to bird diversity was revealed by a study conducted in Costa Rica which showed that epiphytes, including their fruits, nectar and foliage, were involved in a third of all foraging visits by all birds to cloud-forest trees. The white-throated mountain-gem and ochraceous wren used epiphytes on more than 90 percent of their foraging visits, and several species concentrated their foraging mainly on certain kinds of epiphytes. The mountain-gem visited only epiphytic ericaceous shrubs, a bush-tanager searched dead organic matter on epiphytes and mosses and two birds, the olive-striped flycatcher and golden-browed chlorophonia, fed heavily on mistletoe berries.

Large tank bromeliads are a prominent epiphyte on many tropical trees. The buffy tuftedcheek and streaked tuftedcheek, two foliage-gleaners, are tank-bromeliad specialists. The most endearing features of these two birds are their large, fluffy white cheek patches, which impart an almost feline expression. Tuftedcheeks are found high in cloud forests from Costa Rica to Bolivia, and both species spend most of their time rummaging in the debris that accumulates between the leaves of tank bromeliads. With cheeks flaring, these determined birds plunge into the midst of one bromeliad after another, spending up to a minute at each one before moving on.

Despite the presence of so many novel foraging resources within the Tropics, this does not completely account for the difference between temperate-latitude and tropical-latitude diversity. Terborgh and his team discovered that these area-specific foraging specialties that were unique to the Tropics year-round—fruit, nectar, immature seeds, army ants, dead leaves, vines and epiphytes—accounted for only about a third of the in-

creased diversity in a lowland rainforest when compared with rich hardwood forests in South Carolina. Evidently, there were still some pieces of
the puzzle missing.

Next, Terborgh turned to insect-eating birds, which account for
more than half of all birds in the rainforest. There are many more large
insects and insectlike creatures in the Tropics than in temperate latitudes,
and some are truly awesome to behold. I well recall a friend's absolute
disbelief when, as we were seated on a log having lunch in a rainforest in
Peru, he saw between his bare legs an insect that looked much like a
whip-scorpion with antennae that measured almost 24 inches from tip
to tip! Most rainforest visitors will see relatively few large insects, but
their presence in some numbers does present an opportunity for a foraging specialization not available to birds in temperate latitudes.

As a food resource, large insects have not gone unnoticed by tropical
birds. Seventeen percent of the Manu rainforest's diversity is composed
of birds that specialize on this uniquely tropical resource. Nearly all temperate birds feed on insects during the breeding seasons, but their prey is
much smaller in average size than in tropical latitudes.

In the Tropics, there are many large-billed and large-bodied birds
that are superbly equipped to capture and dispatch huge beetles, katydids
and even small vertebrates. Thomas Schoener, now at the University of
California at Davis, was the first to point out this tropical connection
between large bills and large insects. He showed that, for birds of comparable weight in tropical and temperate regions, the tropical species had
larger bills. Anis, motmots, puffbirds, nunbirds, the great jacamar and
even oropendolas are all well equipped to capture large insects. Except
for anis and oropendolas, they are, as a group, rather lethargic and are
content to sit and wait patiently for the one big meal to show up. All of
these birds are able to consume even very hard-bodied beetles, which
they thoroughly tenderize by pounding them against branches.

Large-insect specialists have few ecological counterparts in temperate-latitude forests, although wild turkeys and such generalists as crows
and jays may occasionally capture large-sized prey. In the Tropics, some
nocturnal birds can be counted among the large-insect specialists.

LARGE-BILLED TROPICAL BIRDS LIKE
CHESTNUT-CAPPED PUFFBIRDS SPECIALIZE
ON LARGE-INSECT PREY.

Potoos, which are the rather distant, oversized relatives of nighthawks and nightjars, specialize in capturing large night-flying insects, especially moths. It is also possible that the diversity of small tropical owls may be partly supported by large insects.

The remaining increase in Manu's bird population—a whopping 50 percent—seems to be the result of an increased number of species within each guild in the forest and possibly by some structural differences in the habitat. The word guild has been adopted by ecologists to define a group of birds or animals that share similar diets and behaviors. One guild, for example, might include all of the arboreal gleaning insect eaters in a forest, another the arboreal sallying insect eaters and so on.

The concept of a guild is useful because it allows ecologists to make comparisons between groups of ecologically similar species from different communities. When guilds from tropical and temperate forests are compared, the tropical guilds nearly always contain more species.

Even between simple guilds like aerial feeders, in which the physical space where birds forage is much the same in tropical and temperate regions, the tropical ones contain more species. The aerial insect feeders over an Amazonian rainforest, for example, may contain three species of kites, three nighthawks, five species of swifts and a martin, whereas over a temperate forest in eastern North America, one would find only a nighthawk, a swift, a martin and, perhaps locally, a kite. Ecologists attribute this excess of tropical species in each guild to a phenomenon they call increased species packing.

There are several possible reasons, all more or less related, for a tighter packing of species within tropical guilds of birds. One may be that birds are able to subdivide the physical space within a tropical forest more finely. This, in turn, may be related to the fact that most birds in tropical rainforests live at a much lower population densities than their temperate-latitude counterparts. The great height of trees and complex internal structure of a rainforest make it possible for birds to divide the forest more narrowly than is possible in temperate latitudes.

A good example of this fine partitioning of the forest is provided by antwrens of the genus *Myrmotherula*. These small, fidgety birds are very similar in size and shape and glean insects from leaves or twigs. In Amazonian rainforests, naturalists typically can find one antwren species living near the forest floor, several in the middle levels of the forest and three more in the canopy. By segregating vertically within the forest, their foraging zones are kept separate.

But vertical subdivision of the physical environment can be only part of the story, because most species still overlap with two or three competitors. A further partitioning of the environment is achieved by different search-and-capture methods. While one antwren searches leaves in the middle level of the forest, another searches twigs and branches and still another examines dead leaves. In this manner, the antwrens, by using different search-and-capture techniques at different heights within the forest, do not compete directly for the same food resources. Such a high degree of foraging specialization, which is typical of many birds in rich tropical environments, seems to be possible only within the complex structural environment of a rainforest, and this, in turn, allows many species to coexist.

There is another aspect of tropical diversity that cannot be directly measured in a single census area. From the air, the Amazonian rainforest may look like a relatively homogeneous carpet of greenery, but nothing could be further from the truth. Tropical habitats are often patchy in distribution; sometimes a particular habitat is separated from another similar one by miles of intervening rainforest.

Immense stands of bamboo dot the southwestern part of the Amazon Basin, but these clumps can be quite isolated from one another. Birders pay close attention to bamboo and, indeed, they should because up to 21 species of Amazonian birds are almost exclusively associated with bamboo.

Bamboo-specialist birds may forage among the leaves, drill into the canes, as in the case of the rufous-necked woodpecker, or pursue sallying and gleaning life-styles within the sheltering confines of the bamboo. Bamboo stands are a classic example of a habitat that is patchy in distribution but which contributes significantly to the overall species diversity of a region.

Groves of moriche palms are another habitat that, because of narrow environmental tolerances (the palms grow only in low-lying or permanently flooded areas), has a patchy distribution. Although palm trees are used as foraging sites and shelter by many birds, only a few species are wholly dependent upon them. The moriche palm is an exception to this general lack of specialization on palms: it is very attractive to a select group of birds.

Point-tailed palmcreepers spend their entire lives in these trees and will live nowhere else. Similarly, if a sulphury flycatcher is seen, moriche palms are undoubtedly nearby because this species rarely strays far from their vicinity. The moriche oriole's close association with this palm was recognized even by early ornithologists, hence its name, and palm-swifts build their long funnel-shaped nests in the pleats beneath the moriche palm's leaves. Red-bellied and red-shouldered macaws seek them out for roosting sites and also feed on their seeds.

As might be expected, the distributions of the birds that have linked their fates so closely to these palms are patchy too. In some areas, moriche palms are relatively numerous; in other areas, one may go dozens of miles without finding a single one.

Neither habitat—bamboo nor moriche palm—was included in Terborgh's Amazonian census at Manu. The nearest stands were far outside the census boundary. Yet these habitats, as well as tropical river islands, white sandy soil forests and many others, continue to enrich the overall diversity of tropical latitudes.

The great diversity of species in the Tropics is, more than anything else, what draws biologists back again and again. We are irresistibly pulled by the magic of the new and unexpected that the Tropics' great diversity brings. Yet when we stop to ask why there are so many species, a disarmingly simple question turns out to be more complex than we might ever have imagined. It is, in fact, a question with no single, simple answer.

As we sort through a half dozen or more antwrens in an Amazonian mixed-species flock, we watch their behavior carefully, hoping to spot differences in their manner of finding food, their general foraging height in the forest or the part of the tree that they prefer to search. These differences are the obvious ones that we can see. They may help us understand why so many species can share a patch of rainforest. But this answer is only part of a much larger question that has been millions of years in the making and will continue to fascinate and perhaps puzzle naturalists for some time to come.

# *Ghosts of Rainforests Past*
## Amazonian Biogeography

FROM THE COMFORT of an airplane cockpit a mile up, I looked down on trees that were green blurs. A splash of yellow or red color from a flowering tree, and perhaps a vulture—a dark speck teetering on fickle air currents far below—were the only reminders of the complexity of life passing beneath me. A wiggling, brown stream momentarily disrupted the otherwise seamless flow of forest.

From my aerial perspective, the Amazon Basin looked like a slightly rumpled rug of forest, unvarying and monotonous from end to end. But that was an illusion. The Amazon rainforest is as different from one end to the other as forests of the eastern United States are from those in the West. Ask any birder or naturalist why they go to different places in the Amazon Basin and the answer will be the same. They go because each area offers them the opportunity to see different birds and other wildlife.

Almost without realizing it, many birders become good biogeographers. Keeping a list of birds sighted in different areas is the first step toward understanding why birds—and all organisms for that matter—are distributed the way they are.

Suppose, for example, that someone wants to see as many Amazonian rainforest birds as possible. Where to go? A visit to Explorer's Inn in southeastern Peru would be a good place to start. With about 500 species in the area, you could spend months at this world-famous lodge, but no matter how long you stay, your list would never contain even half of the Amazonian rainforest's more than 1,100 species of birds. A visit to the Napo region of eastern Ecuador would add more new species to your list, and so would stops in southern Venezuela, Manaus, Belem and other areas in the Amazon Basin. Only after intensively birding many areas would you be likely to have a fairly complete list of the birds in that great river basin.

As an illustration of why you would have to visit so many areas to see most of the Amazon's birds, all you need to do is thumb through a few pages of range maps in a modern book on South American birds. The maps will reveal many curious distributions. Some bird species are found only north of the Amazon River, others only south of it. Still others are pushed against the Andes, hemmed between tributaries of the Amazon or confined to the headwaters region of a remote river. Globe-trotting birders intent on building life lists quickly grasp the implications of these scattered ranges. Yet the most fascinating aspects of these distributions may not be the challenge of visiting many far-flung locations to see these birds but the challenge of unraveling the causes of these distributions. Attempting to understand what past events might have produced such distributions adds a fascinating new dimension to the enjoyment of seeing birds.

Why aren't species uniformly spread over the Amazon? Why is a species found in one place while another related one occurs in seemingly similar habitat elsewhere? These are questions that biogeographers try to answer by putting together a puzzle that includes pieces from the past and the present, and they are the questions that we will be concerned with in this chapter.

All birds and animals reach an area by one of two ways: they evolve there or they immigrate to the region (on their own or by hitching a ride). The method by which birds and most animals are believed to evolve is called geographical speciation, and it is a very straightforward process.

First, a single population becomes divided into two distinct populations that are separated from one another so that individuals from the two can no longer interbreed. This separation could take place in a number of ways. A founding population might, for example, colonize a distant group of islands and then remain isolated there. The original ancestors from which the honeycreepers of Hawaii and the finches in the Galápagos evolved almost certainly arrived in just such a manner.

Subsequently, their offspring spread to adjacent islands, eventually resulting in a number of isolated populations. Mountains, glaciers or changes in sea level can split a population into two parts; rivers can change courses, stranding populations on opposite banks; and long-term climates can change the distribution of forests and grasslands, thus effectively isolating populations.

In the second step, members of the isolated populations develop new traits in response to local environmental or biological pressures, or even as a result of random genetic changes. Consequently, each new population is set on its own uncertain course of destiny.

The last step in speciation occurs when the separated sister populations eventually reestablish contact with each other, one or both of them extending their range to meet the other. If the two populations are sufficiently different by now, individuals from each population may no longer be able to interbreed—an indication that each population is functioning as an independent biological species. But the populations may still be so similar in their ecological requirements that they competitively rebuff each other where they meet. If this is the case, the two will be unable to overlap their ranges. Only if they differ substantially in some critical ecological requirement will their ranges eventually overlap.

This final step is of interest to biogeographers because the actual recontact may occur at any stage in the speciation process—sometimes before the populations are different enough to be considered separate species, sometimes long afterward. Birders also take interest in this last step because it can affect the total number of species on their lists if they unknowingly record two birds as distinct species even if they are not. How does one determine this? A good place to start is by understanding how the process of geographical speciation works.

The speciation process is not difficult to conceptualize in theory, but one of the biggest practical problems with the process is attempting to visualize how it might actually take place in nature. How, for example, are populations split apart and then later reunited? And for how long must the separations occur? There isn't an exact answer as to how long the separation must last, though some scientists believe it may be on the order of a few tens of thousands of years for certain species; others have argued that much longer periods of time are necessary.

The problem, then, is to visualize how such events might occur on a time scale that is relevant to the speciation of birds. Geologic events such as mountain-building and the separation of continents may split populations, but they are too slow and not reversible so they don't contribute to the overall buildup of species in an area. As rivers change courses, they, too, can isolate a species on the opposite bank, but most rivers are rather "leaky barriers" and many birds eventually cross them, either on island stepping-stones or in narrow headwaters regions.

One class of geologic events, however, does occur on a time scale that is neither too short nor too long for speciation. The worldwide climatic changes that are driven by slow changes in the oscillation of the earth's orbit seem almost tailor-made for producing the long-term yet reversible changes in the environment that are needed for geographical speciation.

Geologists now believe that a series of cyclical changes in the earth's orbit, known as the Milankovich Cycles after the Czech mathematician who described them, were responsible for the numerous advances and retreats of the glaciers during the Pleistocene epoch. According to Milankovich, there are four kinds of cycles, varying from around 22,000 to nearly a half million years each, that result from various alignments of the planets with the earth and from the inherent wobble of the earth on its axis. At times, these cycles distort the earth's orbit from circular to elliptical, causing slowly occurring and very long-term climatic changes that result in the onset or cessation of glaciation.

The changes in temperature and rainfall that these cycles produce are not large, but only a small change is needed to tip the balance in favor of a warmer or cooler cycle that will gradually change one habitat into another. The length of these cycles falls comfortably within the time period scientists believe is necessary for speciation to occur, and, furthermore, they produce reversible changes in the distribution of habitats such as forest and grassland—a necessary requisite for the completion of the speciation process.

Jurgen Haffer, a German geologist working in Colorado, was the first person to take into account Pleistocene climatic changes in his analysis of the distributions of South American birds. Haffer believes that the rainforests of South America cycled through several periods of expansion and contraction during the Pleistocene epoch, and that during these contractions, the forest was often fragmented into isolated units that he calls refugia. This repeated forest breakup, Haffer argues, provided the mechanism that produced the many unusual and often small and localized ranges of birds that one sees today in South America. His hypothesis provided a revolutionary way for biologists to discuss speciation and diversity in South America.

Haffer's interpretation of speciation in South America stretches back at least two million years, to the dawn of the Pleistocene epoch, and perhaps as far back as six million years. This is an important turning point in geologic history because, at about this time, the newly emerging Andes, stretching like a great green wall from the Caribbean to Tierra del Fuego, began changing the climate of the western Amazon Basin in a most dramatic and important fashion. Acting as a blockade to the westward flow of trade-assisted winds and clouds moving across the continent, the high Andes corralled masses of rain clouds over a broad arc of western Amazonia. This, in effect, switched on the great rain machine of the Amazon Basin, and forests spread far to the north and south and in an unbroken carpet eastward to the Atlantic.

If a modern-day birder could travel back in time and walk these late Tertiary and early Pleistocene forests, he or she would probably be hopelessly lost in an attempt to identify birds. There would be only a few birds recognizable using current birding books, and even many of the genera would be unfamiliar to our intrepid time traveler. And if our birder trudging through Pleistocene forests had the luxury of a guidebook to Amazonian birds of that period, it would probably be a good deal thinner than one today, for much of the diversity that we find so marvelous is believed to have had its origins in the turbulent climate and environmental changes of the Pleistocene epoch.

A majority of modern species of Amazonian birds either evolved during the late Tertiary period and early Pleistocene epoch or have undergone some evolutionary change since the beginning of that period. We can only imagine, then, what songs and calls issued from the depths of these early forests. Were ancestors of present-day antbirds lurking in the shadows? Were manakins dancing and screaming pihas screaming? And from what origin did the mysterious melodies of the musician wren spring? Were hoatzins peering suspiciously about and nibbling succulent buds in these ancient swamps?

Haffer points out that the amount of rainfall is largely responsible for the distribution of forests and grasslands that we see in the tropical latitudes. Forests grow where rainfall is heaviest, and grasslands and other arid habitats, which tend to occur around the fringes of the Amazon Basin, along various coastal areas and in scattered mountain valleys, predominate where rainfall is lower and more seasonal in distribution. The rainfall threshold is about 60 inches. Above this amount, forest usually grows; below this, grassland or scrub replaces the forest.

What is needed, then, to drive the geographic speciation process to completion is a series of climatic events that can shift the rainfall above and below this threshold and thus reversibly alter the distribution of forest and grassland. Could the periods of Pleistocene glaciation affect rainfall? Haffer thinks they did. It has long been known that northern glaciations resulted in massive floral and faunal upheavals in temperate latitudes, but it was tacitly assumed that tropical latitudes were relatively unaffected. This viewpoint now seems to be incorrect. Tropical latitudes were repeatedly affected by climatic swings similar to but less intense than those that buried Iowa and Wisconsin and other northern regions under miles of ice.

As glaciers advanced in polar regions and in the Andes, enormous amounts of water were locked up as ice. Sea levels dropped, and a general lowering of the earth's temperature—pollen samples from peat bogs in Andean lakes indicate average temperatures were 4 to 6 degrees Celsius lower at times—reduced evaporation and resulted in lower rainfall.

A decline of only about 20 to 25 percent in rainfall would be enough to shift large areas of rainforest below the 60-inch threshold and thus cause them to be replaced by grassland. Rainforests survived as isolated forest islands in areas of higher rainfall, and their animal populations were likewise isolated.

The hard evidence for cyclical changes in the extent of forest and grassland comes from pollen samples, and so far these are mostly from peat bogs in the Andes, not from the Amazon itself. Pollen is the currency of the paleobotanist because it is hard and easily fossilized. Carried by wind and water and buried in the damp ooze of bogs, pollen deposits laid down over centuries leave a record that is built up layer by layer. From drilled core samples in old bogs, the plant pollens can be identified and their approximate age determined. The various layers, thus mapped, give scientists a picture of the vegetation history of the area.

If, as hypothesized, the dominant vegetation of Amazonia, and indeed of all the Neotropics, swung from forest to grassland and then back to forest again over periods of tens to hundreds of thousands of years, it is not difficult to visualize the dramatic effect this must have had on wildlife. Most birds are adapted to a particular habitat and are dependent upon it for survival. Rainforest birds, for example, cannot survive outside of the forest, nor can savanna birds survive in the forest.

Changes that occurred during the Pleistocene epoch provided perfect conditions for the evolution of many species. During dry periods, birds unable to adapt to changing conditions either disappeared or became imprisoned in widely scattered islands of forest. Later, when humid conditions returned, rainforest expanded again, more or less replacing the grassland, and formerly isolated populations came back into contact. Each glacial advance and retreat may have lasted 30,000 to 100,000 years or more—long enough, in many cases, for new species to evolve.

Modern-day evidence to support the occurrence of such speciation lies buried in a seemingly chaotic jumble of bird distributions that begin to make sense only when we plot them on maps and compare them to each other. Haffer mapped the distributions of many closely related species of birds, in such varied groups as toucans, jacamars, parrots, cotingas and manakins. The nonoverlapping ranges of pairs or groups of closely related species—called a superspecies in technical jargon—are strikingly similar to the proposed forest refugia. The plotted ranges of each of these superspecies fill the Amazon Basin like a series of gigantic, interlocking pieces in a jigsaw puzzle and suggest that, at some time in the past, the populations were isolated but have since expanded and now meet. Because in many cases this happened before differentiation proceeded very far, we find many populations in the Amazon whose ranges meet but do not overlap—a sign that they are probably so similar that they cannot coexist. So here, we already get an inkling of why there are so few species that are widespread across Amazonia even though today the basin is covered with forest from end to end.

The manakins with blue crowns of the genus *Pipra* provide a classic example of how forest fragmentation may have broken up a formerly widespread population. Currently, taxonomists recognize four species and two distinct subspecies of manakins with blue crowns. They are all similar in appearance: they are black-bodied with varying amounts of blue or white on their crowns and rumps. The ranges of the species abut, but they do not overlap—an indication that the species are still so similar they are ecologically incompatible.

Large rivers contribute to the isolation of two of these species: the opal-crowned and snow-capped manakins. Both are now trapped south of the broad lower end of the Amazon River, and they are kept apart from each other by the north-south running Tapajós River. A third, the white-fronted manakin, occurs in the Guianas. The fourth and most widespread, the blue-crowned manakin, occupies western Amazonia, while a vocally distinct race of it lies isolated to the west of the Andes in western Colombia and Central America. Hybrids between any of the species are rare, except between the blue-crowned manakin (*Pipra coronata*) of western Amazonia and a green-bodied southern form of it known as *Pipra coronata exquisita*.

Haffer also examined the zones between proposed forest refugia, or contact zones, because these are the places where new lineages, spreading out with the advancing forest, should have come into contact with sister populations spreading from other refugia. Haffer located a number of these hybridization zones just where he predicted they would be—between the forest refugia. The large number of species whose range boundaries coincided with these recontact or hybridization zones indicated to Haffer that entire bird populations had merged in that area where a previous barrier, such as a grassland, had existed.

One such zone runs approximately northwest-southeast through southern Venezuela to the Amazon River. This zone marks the boundary between so many species that even though today the former barrier, probably a grassland, is obliterated by almost uninterrupted forest, closely related species meet here and still act as if a boundary exists—an invisible wall of genetic incompatibility maintained by many pairs of closely related species. Thus, the ghosts of the Pleistocene epoch still linger, haunting us with curious range distributions and challenging us to rummage in the attics of ancient rainforests for answers to modern-day problems.

Remnants of some of these former grasslands still persist today, scattered across southern Venezuela and adjacent parts of Brazil and the Guianas. A fine example of such a contact zone runs eastward through southeastern Venezuela, Guyana and Surinam. Three large grasslands, the Grand Savanna in southeastern Venezuela, the Rupununi in adjacent Guyana and the Sipaliwini in southern Surinam, are present-day remnants of the once broad corridor of savanna isolating coastal Guianan forests from those in the central Amazon valley.

It is believed that today, because these grasslands are much smaller, they are no longer a barrier, having been bridged by vast tracts of forest in many places. But the past lives on in the form of numerous bird distributions that still terminate along this now largely invisible line. Biogeographers refer to species north of this ancient barrier as Guianan species, those to the south as Amazonian—references to their ancestral affinities. Birders note these regional differences, too, even in casual conversation, although some may scarcely realize the historical implications that such a statement carries.

If geographic speciation is complete, species are able to overlap without interbreeding. It seems that this level of differentiation is reached more easily among insect-eating birds than among fruit-eating species. Closely related, coexisting species are relatively common among insect-eating birds in the Tropics but infrequent among fruit eaters. There are reasons for this. Fruit-eating birds are more mobile than insect eaters because their food is widely scattered. This results in better gene flow and hence fewer opportunities for populations to remain isolated. Secondly, there are simply more opportunities for specialization on insects than on fruit, and hence a greater likelihood that ecological differentiation can be achieved. Many insect-eating species, such as antshrikes, antwrens, foliage-gleaners, flycatchers and tanagers, although similar in appearance, are able to coexist because they differ ecologically. This also helps explain why it is more difficult for birders to identify the many look-alike species of insect-eating birds than fruit-eating birds.

Anyone who has ever watched a mixed-species flock in the Amazonian rainforest can attest to the difficulty of identifying the many similar-looking insect-eating birds flitting overhead in the foliage. There could be half a dozen species of *Myrmotherula* antwrens, all coexisting in the same forest flock. Not only are they similar in size and shape, but many of them are also similar in color—basic gray with a black throat and white shoulder dots. Some antwrens inhabit the canopy, others the understory. Typically, they are foraging specialists—they search for prey in very specific places such as hanging dead leaves or vines or the outer foliage of the canopy.

Such close packing of species doesn't often occur among fruit-eating birds. A fruit tree may attract many kinds of birds, such as guans, parrots, parakeets, toucans, trogons, flycatchers, thrushes, tanagers and even woodpeckers, but an observer is more likely to be struck by the distinctiveness of the birds rather than by their similarities.

It is the less advanced stages in the geographical speciation process that seem to drive so many birders to exasperation (and some professional ornithologists as well for that matter). These are the situations in which varying amounts of hybridization still take place in contact zones.

Several examples such as myrtle and Audubon's warblers and Baltimore and Bullock's orioles are familiar to North American birders. These populations came back into contact, because of the retreat of the last glaciation, before they were reproductively isolated, and they now interbreed, sometimes freely, sometimes to a very limited extent, in regions where the two populations are in contact.

Neotropical regions are filled with similar examples. Two manakins renowned for their snapping sounds and dazzling high-speed displays meet in northwestern Colombia. The two differ only in the color of their neck collars. The one in western Colombia is golden, the other, which ranges from northern Colombia to Trinidad and southward into the Amazon, has a white collar. They meet and interbreed in a very small zone near the northern end of the western Andes. At some display grounds where the two occur together, one can see both white-collared and yellow-collared birds, as well as intermediate ones, performing together.

Are the hybrids capable of producing fertile, viable offspring? Is the zone of contact stable? There are few good answers to these and related questions, and in such borderline cases, ornithologists may not agree on how to classify these two birds. Consequently, they are treated as either separate species or a single species.

The distribution of two Amazonian toucans also falls into a murky category like that of the manakins, although the scale of interbreeding is measured in hundreds of miles rather than the width of a dancing court. Both Cuvier's and red-billed toucans are usually found on bird checklists, and most birders list their sightings of these species separately. Together, these two birds span the breadth of the Amazon Basin. Pure Cuvier's populations are found near the Andes and pure red-billed populations are found in the Guianas and eastern Brazil. But in a fairly broad area from southern Venezuela to the Amazon River and southward, they hybridize extensively, and honest ornithologists would be hard-pressed to assign a name to some of the individuals they see. Such gray areas are difficult to reconcile with the rigid taxonomy we seem compelled to impose on birds and other organisms in field guides.

Until recently, naturalists and birders usually saw these toucans in the western part of the Amazon Basin or in Surinam—the two end points of their ranges and the regions where they look most different. Determining which was which was easy. But time and political events have a way of changing human travel patterns. Venezuela relaxed its restrictions on travel in its southern frontier state of Amazonas. As new tourist facilities appeared in southern Venezuela, birders and naturalists walked, unaware, into the midst of a hybrid zone. It wasn't long before some "ghosts of the past" began to appear. Suddenly the toucans didn't "look" right, or at least they didn't look like the books said they should. What are they? And now everyone knows what Haffer knew all along.

In the western Andes of Colombia, there are two lovely *Ramphocelus* tanagers, both a lustrous and velvety black. One has a glistening lemon-colored rump and lives in the Pacific lowlands and western foothills; the other has an equally glistening scarlet rump and lives in the Cauca Valley and in the foothills on the eastern side of the same range of the Andes. They are (or were) separated by the vast forested flanks of the Andes, for neither of these birds enters far into primary forest.

Curiously, if not for the intervention of man, this story might end right here, for although obviously related, these birds looked quite different and were classified as separate species. But deforestation in the Andes created avenues of expansion for both species, and in time, the two forms met in a number of river valleys on the western Andean slopes. Where they met, scarlet-rumped and lemon-rumped birds interbred producing orange-rumped birds that are now predominant in these valleys.

However inadvertent, this man-made experiment in speciation brings to light a problem inherent in applying the speciation concept uniformly. There are, no doubt, many species pairs like these tanagers—geographically isolated from each other and perhaps masquerading as species in textbooks. They are, nevertheless, unable to pass the test of reproductive autonomy. All that we can do in such a situation is to compare the degree of differences between such populations with their closest relatives that have passed or flunked the test of free interbreeding.

The important thing that we must keep in mind is that birds are dynamic, evolving organisms, not static machines, and they are slowly but continually changing in response to a multitude of physical and biological pressures. In our lifetime, we see only a snapshot of each species; it is far too short a time to witness evolutionary change, but by examining many species in different stages of speciation, we can begin to imagine a continuum that reflects an entire species cycle. Small wonder, then, that we often have difficulty trying to neatly file away every bird into the same kind of taxonomic cubbyhole.

Haffer's Pleistocene refuge theory is seductive because it offers a simple and elegant mechanism by which geographical speciation can operate. It also provides at least a partial explanation of how tropical latitudes build such diverse faunas. Evidence supporting the refuge hypothesis has been claimed for organisms as diverse as butterflies, lizards and frogs. But despite its appeal, the refuge hypothesis remains controversial. A number of scientists have voiced dissenting opinions, suggesting that there are other possible interpretations of Haffer's data and that it is possible to achieve similar speciation without recourse to explanations of forest fragmentation.

According to one hypothesis, proposed even before Haffer's, the formation of major rivers in the Amazon Basin fragmented ranges of widespread species and then acted as barriers to gene flow, thus serving to isolate populations. More recently, biologist Angelo Capparella has rekindled interest in the river barrier hypothesis, noting that, because the ranges of so many Amazonian birds are delineated by large rivers, more attention should be paid to the role of rivers as a principal cause of speciation and high species buildup in the Amazon.

Capparella's argument is persuasive because it does not require changes in habitats—as yet unproved in the Amazon Basin. Furthermore, it does not entirely refute Haffer, who was also aware that rivers were at least secondarily important as barriers to gene flow. Capparella, however, emphasizes rivers rather than forest refugia as a principal cause of Amazonian speciation.

Until evidence from pollen samples is found that might support the proposed vegetation changes in Amazonia, the refuge hypothesis remains elegant but open to challenge. New advances in molecular biology may soon make it possible to test Haffer's ideas in another way. Capitalizing upon the assumption that rates of genetic change are fairly constant over time, biologists are now attempting to measure amounts of change in DNA sequences and directly compare those of various related ancestral lines.

Two biologists, Joel Cracraft of the University of Illinois and Richard Prum of the University of Kansas, have already attempted this kind of analysis using some of the very toucans studied by Haffer. While several splits in the toucan ancestral tree have been identified, the molecular techniques are not yet sophisticated enough to precisely date the divergence of the various ancestral lines. Some could have been divided by the rise of the Andes, and other separations could have occurred later. If these separations can eventually be correlated with periods of glaciation and forest breakup, Haffer's thesis will be stronger than ever.

South America has many birds with small overlapping ranges—about 50 times as many as in North America—and they are distinctly clumped in distribution. Cracraft, noticing this clustering of species, called these areas endemic centers—regions containing many species found nowhere else. Cracraft placed no restrictions on the size of the range of the birds he included within his endemic centers, nor did he try to correlate their location with past events, as Haffer had done. Still, his maps of endemic centers matched, at least in lowland South America, many of the forest refugia areas postulated by Haffer, lending support to the idea that past events have helped shape present distributions.

Cracraft's endemic centers and Haffer's forest refugia are regions of unusually high species diversity. Why should we be concerned with these locations or with the locations of their ancient ancestors and where they met in the past? Knowing the location of these regions is valuable for more than birding excursions because these areas have a high number of endemic species. Knowledge of these areas is of great value to conservationists and biologists interested in preserving biological diversity.

Refugia, zones of secondary contact, river barriers and concepts like endemic centers are valuable tools that can help us understand the world in which we live, and they can help us in our efforts to preserve it. If we ignore them and the messages they send from a history, only dimly perceived at best, ghosts of rainforests past may indeed return to haunt us and future generations.

# High-Andean Genealogy
## Unraveling Ice Age Secrets

THE ANDES stretch in a long, narrow band for nearly 4,000 miles from Venezuela to Tierra del Fuego. More than half of this distance lies within tropical latitudes. But to visitors arriving with visions of gently waving palm trees and balmy weather, the high Andes must seem anything but tropical. The air there is desperately thin, solar radiation is intense and temperatures, though sometimes hot during the day, often drop below freezing at night. Climatically, it is an extraordinarily harsh environment, yet almost 250 species of birds are known to breed above tree line in the Andes. Of these species, 166 of them breed nowhere else.

From the lovely old colonial city of Popayán in Colombia, I boarded a *por puesto* bus bound eastward across the central range of the Andes. My destination, a zone of páramo vegetation above tree line, was just over three hours away. Few of my fellow bus passengers would have dreamed of stopping there, for no one lived in that cold, bleak region, though it is home to some of the Andes' most interesting, if enigmatic, birds. Most of the birds that we think of as quintessentially tropical—parrots, toucans, motmots, jacamars and so forth—do not occur there. They live at elevations thousands of feet lower, in steamy, lowland jungles where the temperature is warmer and food more certain.

For more than two hours, the bus labored upward, the driver, with casual machismo and a radio blaring cumbia music, swerved to avoid oncoming trucks on blind curves, chain smoked and carried on a non-stop banter with several passengers. I gazed across enormous chasms that dropped away, unobstructed, for thousands of feet. They began inches from where our wheels bit the gravel. Patches of dark woodland clung to steep slopes—survivors of a landscape now mostly tamed by machetes, cows and potato fields. A blue-capped tanager dashed across the road and dived headlong into a thicket just before it was engulfed by the enormous cloud of dust churned up by our bus.

Above tree line in the Andes, there are two dominant types of vegetation: from Venezuela to Ecuador, it is a boggy grassland called páramo; from Peru southward, the grassland is drier and ecologists use the term puna.

To most visitors, páramo is a somewhat mysterious and water-soaked land of swirling mists, cold drizzling rains and foreboding skies. To someone trying to cross it on foot, it can be hell. The weather changes with maddening frequency. Brilliant sunny skies turn to fog and mist in minutes and then back again, usually many times every day. Hiking cross-country can be impossibly difficult in the soggy páramo for vast areas are virtually floating bogs of moss, grass and cushion plants—a hazard to experienced hikers and treacherous and potentially fatal to the unwary.

Puna is higher, drier and colder and also friendlier to humans. At night, the puna is very cold because its dry air loses heat quickly, but days are often sunny and pleasant, and the puna's dry grasslands are home to most of the proud and distinctive highland Indians variously united at one time or another within the Inca empire. The puna's once vast grasslands have been abused through the centuries by human occupation and overgrazing, but bleak as they are, the puna is an infinitely more agreeable environment for human occupants than the páramo. It is no accident that the great Inca empire flourished here rather than northward in the páramo.

My bus was more than two hours east of Popayán and gaining altitude with every lurching curve. The top third of the driver's windshield was covered by a woven tapestry adorned along its lower edge with dozens of dangling, fuzzy balls. His necktie, still knotted and at the ready, hung from the rearview mirror. With each curve, the necktie swayed in front of an immobile statue of the Virgin Mary mounted on the dash. I half expected to see the Virgin's eyes roll upward with motion sickness. An assortment of colorful cartoonlike stickers on subjects ranging from sex to safe driving filled most of the remaining window space. I wondered how he saw through all the stuff.

I looked at a crumpled piece of paper showing a hastily sketched map of Puracé National Park, my destination. Puracé lies mostly within páramo and it is a showpiece park—not for its roads or facilities, for they are almost nonexistent, but because it preserves one of the finest examples of páramo in existence. Spectacled bears and mountain tapir roam its wilder parts, as well as the tiny páramo deer, so shy that local legend says they have been known to die of fright at the sight of a human.

The páramo is one of the most distinctive-looking plant communities in the world, and during the rainy season, when most plants flower, it is also one of the most beautiful, comparable to such famous landscapes as the rhododendrons in the Himalayas or the lobelias atop African volcanos. Flowers of many kinds carpet its slopes and provide an incredible contrast between the forests below and the treeless land above.

My destination within Puracé Park was a large but shallow lagoon. Silvery grebes and several ducks usually inhabit the lagoon, but more importantly, the surrounding vegetation is a vast showcase of páramo plants, and it is the only páramo of its kind that is accessible by road within this huge park. The air grew colder and we burst into a fairy-tale landscape of giant cushion plants, strange lobelia-like sunflowers called *Espeletia* and patches of darkly mysterious elfin woodland little higher than a person's head. I almost imagined I could see gremlins and elves in the mossy depths of these miniature woodlands. It was the sort of topsy-turvy land only Lewis Carroll could have imagined. The skies were clear and the páramo's wetness sparkled in the morning sunlight. It was a magical moment.

The páramo is home to many distinctive birds whose names are unfamiliar to most naturalists—sapphirewings, pufflegs, cinclodes, tit-spinetails, thistletails, canasteros, chat-tyrants and so on. These fascinating birds thrive in the numbing cold and perpetual dampness that grips these remote mountaintops. I wondered who the ancestors of these hardy birds are? How did these birds reach this land, which is so other-worldly and utterly alien from the rainforests below? How long have they been there?

When biogeographers ask where an avifauna came from or how old it is, they usually start by examining two kinds of evidence—historical evidence, which comes from fossils and from geological and paleobotani-cal data, and modern evidence, which they get by studying distribution patterns of present-day birds. Because birds are so fragile, few have been left in the fossil record. As a result, biogeographers often rely on geologists and the plant pollen records studied by paleobotanists to learn about the history of physical and environmental changes. Modern evidence, by contrast, is obtained from field observations and from specimens in museum collections.

In the past two decades, biogeographers Francois Vuilleumier and Jon Fjeldsa, working independently and building upon the studies of earlier scientists, have reexamined the origins of high-Andean birds. Their work tells us a good deal about the probable course of events that has led to the birds we see today in the páramo and puna. The story begins a long time ago.

Perhaps ten million years ago, in Miocene times, the emerging Andes stood barely 4,000 to 6,000 feet high. At that time, the young Andes were covered with tropical-forest vegetation and populated by birds derived from lower elevations. Mountain-building continued into the Pleistocene epoch, and eventually, a cold alpine grassland—the fore-runner of modern-day páramo and puna—developed in areas above the tree line. This high grassland stretched the length of the Andes, and in southern latitudes, it occurred at a lower and lower elevation until it eventually merged with the cold, windy plains of southern Patagonia.

During the latter half of the Pleistocene epoch, perhaps beginning two million years ago, the earth's climate began a series of chilling temperature oscillations that plunged vast areas of North America and Eurasia into one agonizing ice age after another. Cold glacial episodes alternated with warmer interglacials. Entire floras and faunas were pushed southward by advancing glaciers that destroyed everything in their paths.

The inevitable extinction of many organisms was followed by recolonization and speciation during warmer episodes. The last major glaciation began as recently as about 25,000 years ago and ended a mere 11,000 years ago.

It was believed, until recently, that tropical latitudes were relatively unaffected by Pleistocene climatic events in polar regions. This promoted the idea that the Tropics have been stable for a long time. Scientists now know that Andean highlands experienced ice ages of their own. These tropical ice ages were not brought on by northern glaciers that pushed southward into tropical latitudes but, rather, by glaciers that developed high in the Andes themselves as a result of the general cooling of the world's atmosphere. Evidence of three of the four glacial episodes that affected North America and Eurasia have been found in the Andes. Some geologists believe the Andes were spared the first glacial advance that occurred in North America because they were not high enough at the time to develop an ice cap.

The wet alpinelike páramo regions of Venezuela, Colombia and Ecuador and the drier puna grasslands of Peru, Bolivia, northern Argentina and northern Chile probably did not appear until after the first major northern-hemisphere glaciation, which occurred about one to two million years ago. In geologic time, then, páramo and puna grasslands are of very recent origin and so are the birds that inhabit them.

Páramo is wettest and best developed in Colombia's eastern and central Andes. There, it is characterized by extensive quaking bogs, tall bunch grass and ground-hugging cushion plants. One of the most characteristic páramo plants is the *Espeletia* (known in Spanish as *frailejón*), a genus of plants belonging to the sunflower family. More than 75 species occur from Venezuela to Peru. With straplike, downy-soft leaves that grow in whorls or rosette patterns and trunks two meters high and as thick as a human body, these plants impart a distinctive, otherworldly appearance to the region. Páramo vegetation first appears on mountain slopes at about 10,000 feet and continues to the snow line. It is often separated from other mountaintop páramos by intervening cloud forests or dry valleys at lower elevation. Consequently, páramo occurs as a series of vegetation islands down the northern backbone of the Andes.

Farther south, dry puna grasslands spread out across vast high plateaus known collectively as the altiplano. Unlike the islands of páramo vegetation, puna grassland extends more or less unbroken from Peru to northern Argentina and Chile. Generally arid and sparsely vegetated, the puna receives its annual rainfall during a well-defined wet season. Consequently, most vegetative growth in the puna takes place during the warmer, rainy months, while páramo plants grow almost year-round but very slowly and under near-freezing conditions.

The extent of páramo and puna has changed many times since their first appearances. During warm interglacials, like the one we are presently experiencing, páramos were isolated from one another by great areas of mountain forest, much like islands in the ocean. During colder glacial episodes, vegetation zones were pushed to lower and lower elevations. Gradually these former páramo islands increased in size and grew closer together. Ultimately, some became connected to neighboring ones, permitting birds and other organisms to intermingle.

Where the páramo and puna vegetation communities meet along the eastern slope of the Andes in Peru, gross visual differences between these two plant communities begin to blur. Here, both habitats share many plants with each other, but they have little in common with the mountain forests immediately below them or with the low grasslands of northern South America or the scrublands of Brazil. Instead, páramo and puna share a majority of their plants with the Patagonian steppes to the south.

In his studies of high-Andean birds, biogeographer Vuilleumier, of the American Museum of Natural History, found that páramo and puna birds have three main origins. The largest proportion of these birds, about 38 percent, originated in or very near the páramo and puna itself as a result of local speciation from high-country ancestors. A second important group, which makes up about 25 percent of these birds, can be traced directly to ancestors in Patagonia. The remainder are mostly widespread species or colonists that have come from elsewhere in South America or North America or are of unknown origin.

To see how Vuilleumier reached his conclusions, it is necessary to re-view some of the clues that biogeographers use. A biogeographer may begin by looking at the number of endemics—species, genera or families that occur nowhere else. Biogeographers believe it takes a long time for large numbers of endemic species, genera and families to accumulate. When Vuilleumier found that there was not a single endemic family and only about four endemic genera (a wader, two hummingbirds and a finch) out of a total of 84 genera breeding in the high Andes, this suggested to him that the birdlife there was of recent origin.

Vuilleumier did find that about 29 percent of the species of birds in the páramo and puna were endemic. This number is high but still considerably lower than the endemism usually found on old oceanic islands. If páramo mountaintops are as isolated as old islands, then the number of endemics should have been higher. Because they weren't, Vuilleumier concluded that the páramo-puna birdlife has not been strongly isolated in the past, nor is it so today. Consequently, the number of endemic birds that we see in the high Andes today is probably the result of local speciation that has occurred fairly recently and of frequent immigrations of species followed by differentiation, rather than a result of long periods of isolation that would be necessary for many endemic genera and families to evolve.

The problem now is how to determine which high-Andean species originated as a result of local speciation and which are more likely to have been derived from past immigrations. Answering each of these problems involves different approaches. An estimate of how much speciation has occurred locally can be obtained by estimating the number of what biologists call allopatric and sympatric species present today. In allopatry, two or more closely related species have nonoverlapping ranges; in sympatry, two or more overlap in range.

The charming little bearded helmetcrest, a hummingbird that is found in the páramos of Colombia and Venezuela, illustrates how it is possible to obtain several distinct populations from a single local ancestor without any immigration from outside areas. Currently, the helmetcrest is found in the páramos of four isolated mountain ranges: the Santa

Marta Mountains, the central and eastern Andes of Colombia and the Andes of Venezuela. The birds in each area look only slightly different, having tail stripes that vary in width and color and different colored feathers on the beard and forehead. Though ornithologists once considered them separate species, they are now believed to be merely well-differentiated forms of a single species.

It is relatively easy to visualize a sequence of events that might have led to the situation we see today. During a cold glacial episode, all life zones would have been displaced to lower elevations, resulting in a single helmetcrest ancestor occupying a large and more or less continuously connected band of páramos in Venezuela and Colombia. Thousands of years later, as the climate slowly warmed, the glaciers would have retreated and the páramo zone would have moved upward, eventually persisting only on the tops of a few isolated mountain ranges. Unless the helmetcrest was able to adapt to a new environment, it would have become restricted to the dwindling areas of páramo, surviving not as a single widely distributed population but as several isolated populations.

Today's four separate helmetcrest populations have probably existed since the end of the last ice age, or for about 10,000 years or so—long enough for the populations to begin taking on characteristics of their own. And what happens next? Supposing the earth's climate cools once again, the cycle will be repeated. Páramos will be pushed downward and the four isolates may come into secondary contact. What happens at this point depends upon the degree of differentiation—the sister populations might interbreed, or if they are different enough, they might not, in which case two or more sister species would now occupy the range of the former ancestral species. The four helmetcrest populations in Colombia and Venezuela are but a snapshot in time of a process whose final chapter may not be played out for thousands of years, if ever. We can glimpse this final chapter, however, by examining other species—older in origin perhaps—that are now sympatric.

This final stage in speciation occurs when two formerly isolated populations expand their range and overlap each other without interbreeding. The bar-winged and stout-billed cinclodes are such a species pair, and their close ancestral relationship isn't hard to spot. They are much alike—dull brown with a broad, pale wing band and dirty white underparts—and naturalists have to look closely to tell them apart. Only careful scrutiny reveals that the stout-billed species has a longer and heavier bill and is slightly larger. Such hair-splitting differences would hardly seem worth mentioning but they are critical differences that separate these two species. With its larger bill, the stout-billed cinclodes is able to forage in damp and muddy places, especially around water, where it probes and digs for prey items that are probably difficult for its smaller relative to obtain.

The importance of identifying allopatric and sympatric species is that they are simply stages in a process of speciation that occurs locally. Consequently, it gives biogeographers a way of determining how many species have evolved locally—in this case, within the páramo and puna biomes or close to them.

Determining whether the presence of a species is due to local speciation or immigration is often done by directly comparing lists of species and genera from different areas. If a species has been derived through local speciation, it is not likely to have closely related species in other areas, whereas, if its origin is through immigration, it *should* have closely related relatives in other areas. Using this method to compare the páramopuna birds with those in other geographical areas, Vuilleumier concluded that Patagonia was the most important source of immigrants colonizing the high Andes.

The bird connection with Patagonia is most obvious in the puna of Argentina, Bolivia and Peru. There, the number of shared species is much higher than it is farther northward. This shouldn't be surprising because, for one thing, the puna is much closer to Patagonia than the páramo. Secondly, the ancestral lines of many modern high-elevation species were present on the Patagonian steppes even before the final uplift of the Andes, and these birds were already adapted to the seasonal and unpredictable Patagonian climate. For those birds, an expansion into the climatically similar puna would have been easy. But northward, in the páramos of northern Ecuador, Colombia and Venezuela, there is a nearly 50 percent reduction in the number of Patagonian species. The páramo, like a pathway of stepping-stones, has acted as a filter, slowing the dispersion of some Patagonian species northward and at the same time causing local extinctions of others when they became trapped on shrinking páramo islands.

The origins of some high-Andean birds are difficult to trace because it is often impossible to separate the tangled influences of ecology, history and chance—all of which have influenced and continue to influence present-day distributions. Immigrants may include widespread species like the black-crowned night-heron, barn owl and house wren. These birds occur in the high Andes, but they are successful colonists in so many kinds of habitats that their presence there tells a biogeographer little about their origin.

Large water birds tend to be good colonists, too, because their habitats are not very stable and because of their mobility. A lake or marsh can easily dry up or flood, forcing birds to move away. Consequently, unless there are very large barriers that restrict their movement, most water birds don't show the kinds of complex geographic variation that biogeographers like to see when they look for patterns to help them reconstruct historical events.

The páramo and puna support numerous aquatic and raptorial birds whose origins are somewhat obscure. Several high-Andean birds are also widespread in North America, among them the least bittern, American coot, northern harrier, short-eared owl and eastern meadowlark. Several genera, on the other hand, may have originated in North America and subsequently spread southward, including a grebe (*Podiceps*), several ducks (*Oxyura*), an avocet (*Recurvirostra*) and the flickers (*Colaptes*). Great horned owls are widespread in open areas of both North and South America as are various species of harriers. Stiff-tailed ruddy ducks (*Oxyura*) are found at both ends of the high Andes but not in the middle, and the cinnamon teal has a similar distribution, so these species could have had a southern or a northern origin.

Which birds evolved in North America and then spread southward or vice versa? Were they pushed southward during one of the glacial episodes, leaving some of their kind trapped on high-Andean summits when the climate moderated? For some species, it may never be possible to determine with certainty what occurred.

Despite the difficulties associated with tracing the distributions of aquatic birds, Swedish ornithologist Jon Fjeldsa believed that the nearest relatives of most high-Andean water birds were in the Argentine lowlands. From bird lists, Fjeldsa plotted the location of regions he called core areas, based on the premise that if one area has more species in a particular group than another, then the one with the highest number of species probably represents the original or oldest refuge and is the center for later outward dispersal. When Fjeldsa compared the high-Andean water bird fauna with places with the most relatives, he found that the strongest links were between the high Andes and southern South America. Most Andean water birds had relatives in the lowlands of Argentina or in the southern foothill plateaus. In fact, the high-Andean birds were little more than a subset of the larger and more diverse pampas-Patagonian water bird populations.

Some Patagonian water birds make use of the highlands as molting or staging areas and even occasionally breed there. This gives us a good clue as to how the Andean habitats may have been colonized originally. The connection with southern relatives becomes progressively weaker northward through the páramos, and at the latitude of Bogotá, the wetland birdlife seems to have been drawn from many different areas with no single area predominating.

One of the things that impressed me when I visited the páramo and puna was that most of the high-Andean land birds belonged to only a few families—mainly hummingbirds, furnariids, flycatchers and finches. Hummingbirds have successfully colonized some of the highest habitable regions of the Andes. The Chimborazo hummingbird is regularly found at elevations exceeding 15,000 feet, and some thornbills occur nearly as high. Yet the grip of these species on this environment is often tenuous. Many of them retreat down into wooded ravines during storms or when flowers are scarce. Although they are one of the dominant families in the páramo and puna, they have managed only a toehold there in compari-

son to their rich diversity at somewhat lower elevations. Furnariids thrive
in open habitats and are proportionally much better represented in both
the páramo-puna and Patagonian regions than anywhere else in South
America—an indication that many of them have been open country
birds for a very long time.

How and why were some ancestral lines in each of the four families
able to achieve such a dominance in the high-Andean grasslands? This is
not a question that can be easily tested scientifically, and we can only
speculate on their success based on their distribution and abundance
today. Two families, the furnariids and flycatchers, are suboscine passeri-
formes—old ancestral lineages—and that may be the key to their success.

The ancestors of modern furnariids and flycatchers probably evolved
in South America well before their more modern songbird counterparts
appeared in Central America. By the time a land bridge permitted North
and Central American songbirds to invade South America in numbers,
the suboscines (non-songbirds) were already successfully occupying insect-eating niches all across the continent.

At this time, one or more furnariid groups and the tyrannid ground-
tyrants had already adapted to terrestrial life in the open country of
southern South America, and many foraging niches were already locked
up, so to speak. This was especially true for the niches of insect-eating
birds, which were probably already very finely divided before oscines appeared on the scene. Consequently, the songbird lineages were more successful at exploiting fruit-eating and seed-eating niches.

A few thrushes, a pipit and a wren ancestor colonized the high grasslands, but by far the most successful songbird colonists above the timber-
line in the Andes were seed-eating birds. The original ancestors of such
groups as the sierra-finches (*Phrygilus*), yellow-finches (*Sicalis*), seedeaters
(*Catamenia* and one *Sporophila*) and the siskins (*Spinus*) could have
come from almost anywhere. They share a number of attributes that
preadapted them to high grasslands. They form flocks readily and wander widely, so they would probably not have had difficulty reaching isolated highland areas nor using widely scattered food resources. Virtually

all of them can subsist nicely on a diet of seeds, buds and vegetable matter, and these resources would not be difficult to secure in the high grasslands.

Reconstructing a picture of how the present high-Andean birdlife evolved is clearly not an easy task. There are often very few clues and frequently many ambiguities. Sifting among cryptic fragments of evidence that stretch back several million years, a biogeographer must use information from many scientific disciplines to piece together a slowly unfolding saga of biotic change.

Some of the high-Andean birds must have originated from ancestors living in forests and valleys nearby. Many more appear to have been pioneers from the Patagonian steppeland—species already adapted to the environment they encountered in the open highlands. Doubtless, a few are colonists from North America or from other lowland areas in South America, and perhaps as many as a quarter are the result of speciation within the high Andes themselves.

On my way back to the warmer and more hospitable confines of Popayán, amidst yet another hair-raising bus adventure, I could only look back and marvel at the hardiness of these high-Andean birds, living where winter comes almost every night and sometimes lasts all day as well. I also could take satisfaction in knowing where they may have come from and why their bloodlines serve them so well in this environment, a place where others of less hardy stock cannot survive.

# *Tropical Travelers*
## Migration Within the Tropics

E ach spring in North America, legions of birders and naturalists temporarily flee their jobs, families and friends to renew the rites of spring with one of the oldest and most abiding mysteries in the animal kingdom. From High Island to Point Pelee and from Central Park to the Salton Sea, people from every walk of life escape to marshes and woodlands to witness spring bird migration. The phenomenon of migration is endlessly fascinating and mysterious. Who could fail to be in awe of a bird weighing barely an ounce—the weight of a few pennies in your pocket—flying, in a few short weeks, from Central America to Canada?

Many ornithologists would agree that the abundance of food in temperate latitudes is an important factor in a long-distance migratory strategy. Recall for a moment the almost overnight transformation in spring as fields, marshes and forests seem to burst with life. For a few brief weeks in a temperate spring and summer, the abundance of food is greater than anything available in tropical latitudes. Summer's abundance (as well as winter's dearth) of food is a compelling argument justifying long-distance migration.

But what about birds that carry out their migrations without ever leaving neotropical latitudes? Are they also responding to seasonal changes in food within their environments? When and to where do they migrate, and for how long?

In a worldwide context, migrations range in distance, from very local to transcontinental, and in time, from irregular to predictable. Sedentary nonmigratory birds and migratory birds should not be thought of as distinct groups but as end points of a continuum because they are linked by a spectrum of species between these extremes. This chapter discusses those species that lie on the short-distance end of the spectrum—those species whose migrations occur within tropical latitudes. Understanding them requires thinking about bird migration differently, perhaps even casting aside some long-cherished ideas we may have about migration.

Tropical migrations are most likely to be short-distance ones. They are more often about going up and down mountains than crossing oceans and continents, and they are more about finding enough food to ride out the hard times than about cashing in on the good times. If transcontinental migrants are gamblers, accepting the risks inherent in long migrations in return for a potential jackpot of reproductive success in the end, then both resident and short-term migrant tropical birds are reproductive conservatives.

These birds lay very small clutches of eggs and put a minimum of energy into each nesting attempt. Nest failures are frequent, but most tropical birds will have many more opportunities to succeed because they live to an old age. With this in mind, it may be difficult to understand why birds that spend their entire lives in tropical latitudes need to migrate at all. Why would such icons of tropical birdlife as parrots, toucans, quetzals, bellbirds and hummingbirds migrate? And if so, where would they go? Such questions may seem quaint to naturalists today, but that has not always been the case.

An appreciation of tropical migration has been slow to come. The fact that it has lagged so far behind our knowledge of temperate-latitude migrations can be traced, in part, to the northern bias of many ornithologists and to the fact that there have been very few tropical ornithologists. Most ornithologists grow up in northern latitudes and are educated at northern universities. If their interests lead them into tropical environments, their visits are usually short—perhaps only a few weeks or months at a time—hardly enough time to notice the subtle comings and goings of many tropical birds.

One of the first naturalists to discuss short-distance tropical migration was Alexander Skutch, whose long residence in Central America and careful observations revealed seasonal migrations in tropical birds as varied as quetzals and white-ruffed manakins. Later, James Karr, then at the University of Illinois, began mist-netting birds in the lowlands of Panama. Karr documented seasonal migrations of tropical species in grassland and open habitats and small-scale seasonal migrations even among some forest understory birds.

In 1974, John O'Neill and Ted Parker of Louisiana State University camped near tree line in the Andes of Peru where a snowstorm caught them by surprise. This storm brought to light yet another kind of migratory behavior. The next morning, as they emerged from their tent and stepped into a snowy landscape, they noticed several birds moving down the valley to elevations well below where they were camped. Later, they discovered ground-tyrants, sierra-finches and several insect-eating furnariids—all species typical of much higher elevations—near their camp. The storm passed quickly, and in a day or two, these storm-driven refugees from the grasslands far above tree line had mostly disappeared; they were already working their way back up to the high country. But O'Neill and Parker knew they had witnessed a short-term altitudinal migration—a highly unpredictable phenomenon—of major proportion.

The observations of Skutch, Karr, O'Neill, Parker and others helped ornithologists reorient their thinking about sedentary tropical birds, suggesting that short-distance migrations of various types might be an integral part of the dynamics of many tropical habitats. Since then, naturalists have gradually gained an appreciation of the extent of tropical migrations, although major questions remain.

Easily recognized intratropical bird migrations are the exception rather than the rule. When fork-tailed flycatchers migrate across the Amazon Basin from breeding grounds immediately southward, they gather in great roosting flocks along rivers and in clearings. Flocks of hundreds or thousands may descend for the night and then take off again at dawn. During these brief but spectacular trans-Amazonian passages, they could scarcely be missed. Migrating kettles of plumbeous kites and swallow-tailed kites are easy to spot, too, and if we regularly checked oilbird colonies in caves, their seasonal departure and return could easily be verified. But, for the most part, tropical migrations take place so quietly we are never aware of them.

In a rainforest, few clues tell us a migration might be underway. Through the year, we are not likely to notice much change in temperature or day length. Differences between rainy and dry seasons may be slight—few trees lose their leaves or grow them back at the same time, no seasonal burst of flowering marks the changing seasons and there may be no chorus of new songs to draw attention to the arriving migrants. In short, none of the clues that we consciously or unconsciously use to mark the important migratory periods in temperate latitudes seem to be present in the Tropics.

Quetzals and bellbirds are symptomatic of the difficulties of studying tropical migration. Although Skutch first noted the annual departure of quetzals from the highlands of Costa Rica in the 1940s, their annual migrations to lower elevations during the latter part of the wet season have been widely recognized and discussed in scientific communities only recently. Three-wattled bellbirds breed in the same cloud forests as the quetzal, and their annual migration takes them down mountain valleys and out into the lowland rainforests of eastern Nicaragua and Costa Rica—sometimes all the way to the coast.

Until recently, much of the area was inaccessible, so their migrations went virtually unnoticed by naturalists. These are short-distance migrations—perhaps a few miles or a few hundred miles. The quetzal and the bellbird breed in mountain cloud forests during drier months of the year. Later, when the rains arrive in earnest and the abundance of fruit declines, they vacate their highland territories and move downslope in search of warmer and drier environments and better foraging areas. We may not be accustomed to thinking of quetzals and bellbirds as migratory birds, but their annual pilgrimages, which may span nearly as much vertical as horizontal distance, are an adaptation to different seasonal resources, just as is that of the blackburnian warbler who spends half the year in a Colombian coffee plantation and the other half in a Canadian spruce-fir forest.

When Bette Loiselle and John Blake, now at the University of

RESPLENDENT QUETZALS BREED IN CENTRAL
AMERICAN CLOUD FORESTS AND MIGRATE
TO LOWER ELEVATIONS DURING THE
RAINIEST MONTHS.

Missouri at St. Louis, began looking closely at seasonal movements of birds on the Caribbean slope of Costa Rica, they discovered a much more dynamic bird community than anyone had previously suspected. Catching birds in mist nets at predetermined spots year-round, these two scientists discovered migrations among many fruit-eating birds previously thought to be resident. Furthermore, the arrival times of most of these tropical migrants were closely timed to coincide with an abundance of the fruits that these birds preferred.

At the La Selva Biological Station near Puerto Viejo, the number of fruit-eating birds in the forest understory was highest when fruit was most abundant. At the same time, similar kinds of fruits were scarce at higher elevations—a correlation that led Loiselle and Blake to conclude that the elevational migrations of these species were responses to the changing seasonal abundances of fruit.

Without long-term systematic work like that carried out by Blake and Loiselle, the migrations of many tropical birds would rarely be noticed. For example, if you looked carefully, you could probably find a red-capped manakin—at least a displaying male—almost any day of the year in the rainforest at the La Selva Biological Station in northeastern Costa Rica. But Loiselle's and Blake's netting samples showed a threefold increase in the number of these manakins during January and February, while at the same time, none were captured at a site 400 meters higher and a few kilometers away in the foothills.

One might wonder how such increases could have been overlooked by the many naturalists that have worked in the La Selva rainforest. But consider for a moment how difficult it is to see even one or two of these manakins, especially females and immatures, on a morning's walk in the rainforest. If it weren't for occasional calls given by the males on their favorite display perches—and the calls, which sound like static on your radio, aren't especially conspicuous—a birder might easily spend days in the forest without ever seeing one of these birds.

Sometimes only some individuals within a bird population migrate, so an influx or exodus of migrants merely adds to or subtracts from a resident population. The red-capped manakins studied by Loiselle and

Blake are just such a tropical example. But these kinds of migrations are difficult to pin down, and even with decades of observations and armies of observers in North America, much remains to be learned. Sleuthing out examples in the rainforest requires even more patience and geographical detective work.

On my first few visits to the Colombian Amazon, I noticed that there were many more tropical kingbirds along the banks of the rivers during June and July than in January and February, but I didn't know why. For several years, I attributed this difference to the presence of young birds during the middle of the year. Later, I learned that almost the entire population of tropical kingbirds south of the Amazon Basin is migratory. During the austral winter months of April through September, birds from southern Brazil, Paraguay and northern Argentina pull back northward into Amazonia. The "extra" kingbirds I was seeing in June and July were southern-latitude migrants that temporarily infiltrate the ranks of the local residents each year. Beyond the resolution of this migratory puzzle, there is the larger question of how many other migrants remain undiscovered. Kingbirds are conspicuous and easily counted, but many tropical species are not.

Tropical bird migrations lack the synchrony that marks migrations in temperate latitudes. In North America, we are accustomed to seeing migrants chiefly during the spring and fall, and they come principally from two sources. One group arrives from southern latitudes to breed; the other group arrives from boreal regions, either passing southward in the fall and returning in the spring or staying for the winter months. But tropical-latitude migrations aren't so clear cut. Birds that breed in the mountains during the driest months may move lower to warmer and drier zones where more food is available during the rainiest months. Many tropical hummingbirds, however, do just the opposite—they move up into the mountains during the wet season to nest and down into the lowlands during the dry months.

The complexity of intratropical migrations is perhaps nowhere better revealed than at the Cocha Cashu Biological Station in southeastern Peru. Lying in the floodplain of the Manu River and separated from the last Andean foothills by a distance of about 20 miles, the birdlife around this remote biological station has been the subject of close scrutiny. Cocha Cashu's distance from the Andes is not great, but to a bird traveling through the rainforest, this must represent a journey of considerable risk. Nevertheless, highland breeding birds like emerald toucanets and fawn-breasted tanagers find their way into lowland forests. There, they mingle with another set of short-distance migrants like sungrebes, greater anis and black-throated mangos that are seasonal visitors or breeders from other lowland areas.

Manu's rainforest also hosts several well-known north-temperate breeders during the northern winter months, among them eastern kingbirds and sulphur-bellied flycatchers. During the opposite season—the austral winter months—a much larger number of south-temperate breeding birds arrive. They include the greenish elaenia, gray elaenia, brown-crested flycatcher, crowned slaty-flycatcher and rufous casiornis. Superimposed upon these are an undetermined number of birds that migrate or wander seasonally in search of fruit or nectar. Old oxbow lagoons, some of them partially grass-filled, dot the Manu's floodplain, and they also receive their share of migrants, including doraditos from the austral region, seedeaters that wander in search of grass seeds and water birds that use these lagoons for a few months to decades. Is this the monotonously unvarying Tropics that early naturalists wrote about?

Once in western Colombia, my wife Beverly described a bird to me that I was unable to identify. We had been working for several months in the area, and I wondered how anything so distinct could have escaped our notice for so long. A few days later, the mystery bird showed up in one of our mist nets. It was an adult black solitaire, a little-known Pacific Andean endemic that at the time was only known to occur to the south of where we were working.

Over the next few weeks, a curious thing happened. We began to see them almost daily, sometimes several in a day. Then the solitaires vanished, only to reappear again for a few days almost six months later. Both times, the birds were seen feeding on the berries of melastome shrubs, and their passage coincided with the two annual peaks in the abundance of small fruits. Were these solitaires following a migratory path along the contour of the Andes rather than up or down slopes? Was fruit scarcity where these birds occurred a possible cause of the migration? The answers to these questions are unknown.

How common are short-distance migrations in the American Tropics? According to Gary Stiles, at least 75 species of birds in Costa Rica's new Braulio Carrillo National Park, which lies on the Caribbean slope, are migratory. This represents about 20 percent of the birds in the park. Furthermore, in the country as a whole, he estimates that at least half of the birdlife shows evidence of seasonal movement.

No other neotropical areas have been studied as intensively as Costa Rica. The local migrations between the mountains and the lowlands that have been unearthed in Costa Rica are probably typical of Central America in general. They also characterize the fringes of the Tropics that lie along the southern border of the Amazon Basin and the Andes of Bolivia and northern Argentina. The extent of migration within the equatorial heart of the Andes—the Andes that run through Colombia, Ecuador and northern Peru—is not as well documented. Is it as extreme as that nearer the edges of the Tropics? No one really knows.

Equatorial and relatively nonseasonal parts of the American Tropics should harbor fewer tropical migrants than more seasonal areas. Nevertheless, short-distance migrants are part of the dynamics of even very wet equatorial tropical forests.

In eastern Peru, short-distance migrations were well known to Louisiana State University graduate students David Pearson and Dan Tallman, who conducted research programs there in the late 1960s and early 1970s. Pearson noted three sources for these short-distance migrants; some were local, others were from the nearby Andes and several, such as aracaris, parrots and flycatchers, he believed, were following concentrations of fruiting trees.

At Pearson's Yarinacocha study site, which lies almost squarely in the center of the eastern Peruvian lowlands, he noticed that short-tailed parrots, blue-headed parrots and pale-mandibled aracaris were present only during the early rainy season when fruit was most abundant. None of these species was previously known to be a short-distance migrant, yet all three were present for only a few months of the year.

Any distribution map constructed on the basis of information at the time would have portrayed these birds as permanent residents throughout their range, yet their true distribution may prove to be far more complex. As the distributions and behaviors of tropical birds become better understood, simplistic distributions inked in black on a map will be replaced by more realistic multilayered ones that show seasonal distributions and migratory routes similar to those now found in modern field guides to birds in North America and Europe.

Pearson also worked at Limoncocha, a mission operated for many years by the Institute of Linguistics in eastern Ecuador. The mission is about 600 miles northwest of Yarinacocha. Here, close to the equator, the rainfall is much higher and less seasonal than at Yarinacocha—conditions that should smooth out seasonal differences in fruit and insect abundance.

Yet, at Limoncocha too, Pearson found that some species were present for only part of the year. Mealy parrots, for example, showed a distinct fondness for certain fruits and left when those were not available. The swallow-tanager, a highly migratory bird throughout its vast neotropical range, was present for a few months. Several edge and open-habitat birds showed an unusual pattern of partial migratory behavior. Among them were Picui and plain-breasted ground-doves, yellow-headed caracaras, red-breasted blackbirds, several seedeaters and grassquits. All are colonists that rapidly invade deforested areas. Initially they appeared to nest and then migrate away until the following breeding season, but after a number of years, as the populations of these birds increased or as the extent of deforestation increased and stabilized, most of these species gradually became established permanently, and migration was no longer evident.

During my 15 months of residence in a rain-drenched region of western Colombia, I found that about 17 percent of the nearly 250 species of tropical breeding birds at this site were short-distance migrants. More species of hummingbirds than of any other family were migratory. Only 10 of the 22 hummingbirds were resident—mostly forest-dwelling hermits and aggressive species or short- or medium-bill-length species that could change feeding roles quickly. This high degree of mobility is not unusual. More surprising is the fact that the other short-distance migrants were drawn from so many different taxa—parrots, pigeons, quetzals, cotingas, flycatchers, thrushes and tanagers. But there were no exclusively insect-eating species among them.

Short-distance tropical migrants are generally birds that experience temporary or seasonal food shortages. Birds that face a reduction in their food have two choices. They can switch to eating different foods or they can migrate. Some birds do switch, although there is a limit to just how far even the most generalized foragers can go. Birds that normally eat both fruit and insects may be able to switch to one or the other for short periods of time, though many tropical birds are locked into relatively specialized foraging niches. Those lacking the ability to switch diets are candidates for migration when hard times arrive.

Hard times are more likely to affect fruit and nectar eaters than insect eaters because the abundance of fruit and nectar is more variable seasonally than that of insects. This is why most short-distance migrants in neotropical forests are fruit-eating or nectar-eating birds. Contrary to what one might expect, there is not necessarily an abundance of fruits and flowers throughout the year in tropical latitudes. Where rainfall is seasonal, plants respond by timing their peaks of flowering and fruiting to the most favorable times of the year for pollinators or for seed distribution and germination. The result may be that peaks and troughs in the abundance of flowers and fruits occur.

When James Karr studied bird community structure in the lowlands of Panama, he found a surprisingly high proportion of migratory birds in the three habitats he was studying—grasslands, mature forest and shrubby second growth. Elaenias, seedeaters and other birds in the grassland and shrub habitats were especially seasonal in their occurrence.

Karr also found that, although the complex structure of the mature forest acted as a buffer against the effects of seasonality and thus offered a more stable environment in terms of food resources, only in the lower stratum of the tall, mature forest, the most protected and unvarying environment, did most birds stay at home. There, climatic variables like wind speed, humidity and temperature are relatively constant all year, and hermit hummingbirds and insect eaters like antbirds, spinetails, foliage-gleaners and leaftossers remained on territory year-round.

On the other hand, grassland birds and those of the forest canopy and second-growth areas were more likely to confront seasonal changes in their environment and varying food supplies. Seedeaters, canopy hummingbirds and fruit eaters of the canopy, edge and second-growth regions, in particular, were likely to be absent for weeks or months each year.

Karr had, in fact, uncovered the second important factor that predisposes tropical birds to migrate—the habitat where they live. Fruit, for example, is more abundant but also more seasonal in occurrence in canopy, edge and second-growth habitats than in the forest undergrowth, and fruit-eating birds of these habitats are more likely to migrate than ones that live in the more buffered environment of the forest understory.

Tropical grassland birds often have migratory life-styles. Those on Karr's grassland study plots just east of the Panama Canal Zone were no exception. Seedeaters disappeared around the end of the rainy season and did not return again until after the next rainy season was underway. Their numbers increased dramatically—nearly fourteenfold in one area—during the rainy months of July through September when the grasses were seeding. This is a pattern repeated throughout tropical grasslands.

Seed-eating birds are attracted to large grass seed crops, and migratory or nomadic behavior is an adaptation that allows them to exploit these widely scattered and unpredictably occurring resources. The seed crops of few plants are less certain than those of bamboo. Although widely distributed at high elevations in Central America, the Andes and southeastern Brazil and in the lowlands from southeastern Peru to southern Brazil, bamboos are, in a reproductive sense, the ultimate gamblers. They die after flowering, thus risking a lifetime of waiting for one final fling at reproductive glory. As a consequence, bamboo seeds are not a predictable food resource unless an organism has the mobility to search far and wide for the occasional seeding patch.

Only a few seed-eating birds have adapted their breeding schedules to the short-lived and unpredictable seed crops of bamboo. The large reproductive payoff that these birds gain by waiting for lavish seed crops is countered by unpredictable breeding locations, inexact schedules and a highly migratory, gypsylike life-style. This specialized group of birds includes some of the most enigmatic species in the Neotropics, among them the purple-winged ground-dove, barred parakeet, slate-colored seedeater and slaty finch.

Perhaps the ultimate in unusual migratory behavior is shown by a few species of birds that inhabit tropical grasslands immediately south of the Amazon Basin. These species are fire-followers, and in their opportunistic migratory behavior and highly local distributions, they recall the bamboo seed followers. Tropical grasslands are usually maintained, in part, by fire. No longer the disaster they were once thought to be, fires are now viewed as not only beneficial but necessary to the natural maintenance cycle of grasslands because they remove invading trees and woody growth and invigorate soils with new ash. The fire-following birds, which include both seed eaters and insect eaters, seek out these recently burned grasslands for breeding.

Ornithologist John Bates and several associates of a research expedition with Louisiana State University censused and collected birds in a number of grasslands in west central Brazil and eastern Bolivia. Known as campos, these grasslands range from completely open habitats to those with varying amounts of treelet and shrub cover. Fires sweep through all of these campos, though some burn more frequently than others.

Bates discovered that the campo miner, a drab-looking, terrestrial bird with a rather short tail and long bill, avoided tall grass but quickly located burned grasslands where it set up territories almost immediately and began breeding. Within a few days after a fire swept one grassland, at least nine birds were observed displaying over the charred landscape. Blue finches and coal-crested finches are also attracted to fires, and like the miner, they may migrate long distances to reach new burns. But, unlike the miner, these species are more attracted to burned campos with trees and shrubs, and these birds may remain there for several years, even after the vegetation has partly regenerated.

Unfortunately, through a combination of natural and human-influenced causes, many campos now burn every year. Campos that survive four to five years without burning are increasingly rare. In one such area in eastern Bolivia, Bates found a small population of rufous-sided pygmy-tyrants—a bird that was practically unknown to modern science. He and others soon discovered that the pygmy-tyrant thrived only in grasslands that had escaped burning for several years and that were being invaded by trees and shrubs.

The pygmy-tyrant's scarceness was linked not so much to the loss of campo grasslands in general as to the loss of critical older stages of campo. When campos burn, pygmy-tyrants disappear without a trace, presumably migrating away in search of new areas. Unfortunately, suitable campos in Brazil are increasingly rare for they are burned and plowed today at a rate that may exceed the loss of tallgrass prairies in North America a century ago.

Narrowly adapted behaviors have not worked in favor of many birds in the modern world. A reproductive strategy tied so closely to an event as unpredictable as bamboo flowering or a natural grassland fire requires an enormous geographical area for success. Today, deforestation in the Andes and in the coastal mountains of Brazil, where most of the bamboo specialists are concentrated, and the almost complete conversion of campo grasslands to wheat fields and other agricultural pursuits has fragmented and greatly reduced the amount of suitable habitat. Some of these birds may have already wandered beyond the point of no return; they are truly among those species known as the living dead—species that still exist but which have no viable ecological future because there is no longer sufficient habitat or food resources to maintain a stable population.

Migratory behavior has also evolved in various tropical aquatic habitats that become inhospitable during part of the year. Few places in the

American Tropics change so dramatically in appearance from rainy to dry seasons as the table-flat grasslands of Venezuela and Colombia, and the pantanal of Brazil. As lagoons and marshes bake into checkered expanses of dry, cracking mud, waterfowl and long-legged waders congregate in increasing numbers at a diminishing number of pools, yet when the rains return, water spreads in a shallow veneer across a landscape that now seems like the ultimate paradise for wading and aquatic birds. And it is, but perhaps not in the way one would think.

The 26 species of large waders in the llanos display many foraging specialties, not all of which are compatible at all times to the varying water levels and prey densities encountered during the year. Consequently, some wading birds migrate away from these areas for varying lengths of time each year.

Scarlet ibises disappear almost entirely during the rainy season, migrating to estuarine habitats along the northern shores of Colombia and Venezuela. Little blue herons and rufescent tiger-herons move locally, and even the normally ubiquitous great egret migrates, its numbers falling by nearly two-thirds when the water gets too deep. Bitterns also concentrate in favorable marshes, and many crakes and gallinules vacate the llanos completely during the dry season. Although long legs and long-reaching necks are adaptations that enable aquatic birds to function in seasonally changing water levels, their ability to migrate, at least locally, is perhaps most important for it permits these birds to take advantage of seasonally changing food abundances.

In the high Peruvian Andes, aquatic species of shallow lagoons and marshes migrate to the Pacific seacoast during the April-to-September dry season. At this time of the year, water levels in high lagoons drop precipitously, and open water and marshes may freeze during cold nights. Puna ibises, Andean lapwings and Andean gulls regularly appear on the Pacific coast at this time of year, and a dozen other puna water birds appear on the Peruvian coast in small numbers—a locality they share with another well-known group of migrants, those from the Austral region of Argentina and Chile.

Migratory behavior in birds has undoubtedly evolved over time and for many purposes. Species that migrate to temperate latitudes make up only one facet of bird migration, though it is the one that is most familiar to many of us. The diversity and complexity of migratory behavior only reaffirms how little we yet know about bird migration. But this will change. As naturalists increasingly take a world view of environments and look to tropical latitudes, and as world public interest focuses more on tropical latitudes, migratory birds will inevitably come under closer scrutiny. The mantle of mystery surrounding migration, especially short-distance tropical migrations, has been disturbed only a little, but as we peek inside, we see a tropical birdlife that is dynamic beyond our wildest dreams of only a short time ago.

# The Clubbiest of Clubs

## Life in a Mixed-Species Flock

THE RAINFOREST was hot and sultry. I had walked for more than an hour when the trail I was following began to climb a long, low hill. My shirt was damp with perspiration and I sat at the side of the trail to rest. Except for the monotonous drone of insects overhead, not a sound could be heard—the forest seemed absolutely devoid of birds. Where were they?

A faint chip note in the distance caught my attention, and I was instantly on my feet and moving ahead to listen. There were more chipping notes and a movement in the canopy trees. The calls were closer. I moved forward and suddenly saw birds everywhere from eye level to the tops of the tallest trees. They were moving fast and it was difficult to see any of them well.

A small flycatcher darted out and perched in the open. In a second, it vanished but I saw a woodcreeper hitching up a trunk directly behind it. The loud calls of a shrike-tanager overhead diverted my attention from the creeper, but the instant I focused my binoculars on the shrike-tanager, it flew. I looked back at the creeper. It was gone. By then, birds were streaming out of a large canopy tree over my head, and I hadn't managed a good look at any of them. There was a rufous tail poking out from behind vines and trash. A foliage-gleaner . . . but what kind? It moved and I caught glimpses of it between leaves. It flew. More dark forms darted across the trail—laggards hurrying along to catch up—and that's the last I saw of the flock. The forest was quiet again. Frustrating. Exhilarating. Challenging. A fairly typical birding morning in a tropical rainforest.

Experienced birders and naturalists seek out mixed-species flocks, as they are called, because of the many kinds of birds they can see in them, but it requires a lot of concentration to remain with a fast-moving mixed-species flock in the rainforest. There is constant leapfrogging as some birds fly ahead and then are left behind by others rushing past.

The flock seems to generate an energy of its own—it is as if every bird in the forest is caught up in the maelstrom of activity. There are woodcreepers running up trunks, foliage-gleaners rummaging in trash, greenlets hanging from leaf tips and brightly colored tanagers flitting through high foliage. As if driven by an impetuous urge to join the action, birds forage and move at a furious rate.

Sometimes all we see are maddening glimpses of birds at neck-breaking angles high overhead. For human observers, it is not unlike what a bird of prey must experience as it attempts to single out an individual from among a highly synchronized, twisting, turning flock of shorebirds or starlings. The moment we lift our binoculars, motion elsewhere distracts our attention. For the unacquainted, there may be few opportunities to see any bird well enough to obtain its field marks before the flock moves away.

In northern latitudes, many small forest birds gather in mixed-species flocks during the winter months. In the deciduous forests of eastern North America, chickadees, titmice, creepers and woodpeckers flock together, and in piñon pines in the southwest, it may be bridled titmice and bushtits. In grasslands, the groups may consist of sparrows and longspurs. But all of these flocks quickly disband when the breeding season arrives. In contrast, the drama of mixed-species flocks in tropical forests is played out every day all year long. And the most complex bird flocks of all occur in the vast rainforests of the western Amazon Basin, where as many as 70 species and more than 100 individuals may travel together.

Flocks may include temporary associations of individuals that are drawn together by food such as a fruiting tree, a fire, an army-ant swarm or an emerging colony of termites. At the other extreme, they include complex, multispecies groups of insect-eating birds that forage together every day throughout their lives. It is these latter birds that are the theme of this chapter.

Mixed-species flocks are found in all kinds of forests from sea level to tree line. Yet, despite the pervasiveness of flocking in tropical forests, the reasons why unrelated birds from many different families choose to form flocks and forage together have been difficult to pin down. Are flock associations in tropical forests stable over time? What are the benefits of participation in a mixed-species flock, and are the benefits the same for each species? What are the costs associated with flocking? What kind of behavior allows some species to participate in flocks but not others?

Finding reason amidst the chaos and confusion of a mixed-species flock in the rainforest may seem beyond the ability of any biologist faced with tropical heat, insects and hundreds of hyperactive little birds that flit in treetop jungle foliage nearly 200 feet overhead. Yet in 1976, Princeton student Charles Munn, armed with courage and a generous supply of determination, went to the wilds of eastern Peru and set about just such a task. He began to tease apart the components of the most complex mixed-species flocks on earth in an attempt to find out why so many birds associated with one another and what the benefits were.

Munn used mist nets strung at various heights to capture and color-mark birds, and he used a number of ingenious models of birds and insects that he fired into the midst of flocks with slingshots to experimentally document the reactions of certain species to predators and prey. His almost superhuman efforts revealed unsuspected drama and suspense among flock members, and he helped unravel some of the mysteries surrounding the costs and benefits of joining mixed-species flocks.

Anyone who has watched a mixed-species flock in the forest canopy knows how frustrating it can be to see the birds in them, and of the neck pains and fatigue that accompany holding binoculars steady while trying to look straight up even for a few minutes. Because of this, I have sometimes resorted to lying down flat on my back on the forest floor, in defiance of chiggers, ants and other crawling and biting things, in order to more easily observe a canopy bird flock.

But not all flocks are high overhead. There are, broadly speaking, two kinds of mixed-species flocks in tropical rainforests—one in the forest canopy and another in the understory. Fortunately, the two flocks tend to move independently of each other, and this is why naturalists breathe a sigh of relief when they encounter an understory flock. Many of the birds forage from near eye-level to only about 50 feet up.

In the Amazonian forests where Munn worked, flocks usually contain five to ten pairs of birds—the core species—and another fifty or so species that join for varying lengths of time each day. The part-time joiners usually move among several flocks during the course of the day. The five to ten core pairs, on the other hand, occur on territories that overlap exactly, so the territory of any pair is the same as the territory of the flock as a whole.

These core species spend every day of their lives together. No new outsiders may join until a flock member of that species dies or deserts the collective flock territory, thus leaving an opening to be filled. It is, in a sense, much like an exclusive social club whose members, once admitted, enjoy the benefits of life membership and also bear whatever costs there may be.

Young birds wander widely through the forest, searching for a vacancy. This period of youthful wandering is the most hazardous of their lives, as it is perhaps for most animals, including humans, for they are obliged to forage without the benefits of parental assistance and flock association. Many young birds, through naiveté and inexperience, ultimately fall to predators before they are able to join the safety of a flock. Mixed-species flocks, then, truly are the clubbiest of clubs, and all individuals of core species strive to gain membership.

Canopy-dwelling forest birds usually have much larger territories than understory birds, and the territory of a canopy flock may overlap that of up to four understory flocks. Sometimes both groups will forage together. When this happens, it is a birder's dream come true, and perhaps his or her worst nightmare, too, because the forest suddenly becomes alive with birds from top to bottom, but so much happens all at once that it is impossible to see more than a small portion of the action.

When a hawk glides in toward a mixed-species flock, you might ex-

pect that all eyes would instantly spot its approach. Eventually, most individuals would probably see it, but in a world where even a split-second
delay could spell the difference between life and death, there is a premium placed on sharp eyes and quick reaction. Many birds may have
their heads buried in foliage the moment a hawk appears, or they may be
myopically examining cracks and crevices only an inch away from their
beaks and won't be in good positions to spot incoming predators. By the
time they spot the hawk, it may be too late to react.

Munn noticed that two species in the flocks—the white-winged
shrike-tanager in the canopy and the bluish-slate antshrike in the understory—perform an invaluable role as flock sentinels, and their frequent
loud calls help species stay oriented within the flock. Perched on open
branches in the center of the flock, it was invariably one of these two
Argus-eyed birds that was first to spot incoming hawks and sound the
alarm.

The sentinels profit, too, by the activities of other flock species,
which act as unwitting beaters for them. From their perches, the shrike-
tanager and antshrike waited for hard-working species such as woodcreepers and foliage-gleaners to flush prey that the sentinels then chased
and usually captured. Neither sentinel steals food directly from the
mouths of other birds, but because of their longer wings and tails, they
are both fast-flying and are usually the winners in any contest for flushed
prey.

But if the outcome of the chase between a sentinel and another bird
seems in doubt, a most remarkable thing may happen. The sentinel, in
what appears to be a conscious attempt at deceit, may utter a false alarm
call in an attempt to divert the attention of its competitor. Because these
chases last no more than a second or two, even the slightest hesitation,
prompted by an alarm, is usually enough to tip the balance in favor of
the sentinel reaching the prey first.

Examples of such lying are rare in nature. Crying wolf too often, of
course, could lead to a lack of response, but the penalty for ignoring an
alarm, if it turned out to be true, is very high in a forest with seven or
more kinds of bird-eating hawks. Consequently, mixed-flock species

seem to be willing to pay the cost of an occasional missed prey item as part of the benefit of having a sentinel on hand. Unless flock members happen to be in a place where they have a good view, they always play it safe and dive for cover at the first sound of an alarm. For the sentinels, the benefit of flock participation translates into increased feeding opportunities, while the cost of flock association may be little more than the energy required to signal danger.

Sometimes birds that use beaters also become pirates, stealing prey directly from their beaters. Birders that have visited Central or South America have probably seen antbirds following roving swarms of army ants. For an antbird, finding a swarm of raiding army ants is as good as finding a meal ticket because the birds benefit from the abundance of terrified prey flushed by the ants. The ants, by all accounts, are losers in the arrangement because a portion of their prey is pirated by the antbirds—literally snatched from their jaws by these avian pirates.

In other relationships between birds and beaters, there are winners but no real losers. In the grasslands of northern South America, cattle tyrants ride the backs of slow-moving capybaras and watch for insects disturbed by these rodents as they amble from grassy fields to water holes. Other alliances include anis and cattle egrets that follow cattle, ground-cuckoos that follow forest-dwelling peccaries and kits and nunbirds that follow monkeys.

Naturalists have long suspected that increased foraging efficiency is another advantage to flocking, although initially one might be led to just the opposite conclusion—with so many birds madly foraging together, they might seem to compete with each other and perhaps get in each other's way. Evaluating the food-finding efficiency of birds in and out of mixed-species flocks is no easy task, and no one prior to Charles Munn had attempted such a comprehensive analysis of mixed-species flocks in a lowland rainforest. Using several ingenious techniques, however, Munn discovered that both sentinels as well as their flock associates find food more efficiently in mixed-species flocks than when foraging away from them.

The bluish-slate antshrike normally commutes between its nest and the flock even when feeding its young, but occasionally antshrikes are unable to locate their flock and must forage on their own. Munn noticed that when they must do so, the antshrikes greatly increase their rate of movement—working harder to compensate for the absence of their flock mates. And just as the sentinels profit from associating with flocks, it is equally important for other flock species to associate with sentinels. When sentinels are absent from the flock, antwrens and woodcreepers move into thicker cover, spend more time checking for danger and find significantly less prey than when the sentinels are present.

Flocking probably increases the foraging efficiency of a bird by reducing the duplication of effort, which seems inevitable if every species forages independently. If all the birds in a flock foraged alone, each bird would not know where the others had been, and therefore it might waste time searching an area that other species had already picked over. Testing such a hypothesis is difficult although the concept is appealing and not unlike that used in the corporate world. Rather than sending its salespeople out at random to sell a product, a company organizes its sales force so that each salesperson visits only a certain area and doesn't attempt to solicit customers outside of this area. For the seller, this prevents unnecessary duplication of effort and competition with other sales representatives. And like sales territories, the common flock boundary of the core species helps ensure that duplication of effort is minimized.

Perhaps more important, every species in the flock has its own unique method of looking for and capturing prey. One species of woodcreeper, for example, may hitch up a trunk while another climbs high bare limbs, another checks moss clumps and another checks the outer foliage, palm fronds and so on. As a result of such closely meshed specializations, each species captures some kinds of prey better or in a different place than other species. In flocks with many closely related birds, some may forage in almost identical ways, but they may keep apart by staying at different heights in the forest.

Most birds that forage in mixed-species flocks are insect eaters, specializing on a variety of prey ranging from leafhoppers to large caterpillars and katydids. In the lowland rainforest flocks in Peru, Charles Munn was able to group flock members into several broad foraging categories. In his flocks, there were 15 species of grayish- or buff-colored antwrens and antvireos that scan foliage by hopping quickly along small branches and among tangles and lunging at the prey they spot. There were also 23 species of brownish-colored woodcreepers, foliage-gleaners and spine-tails. The creepers focus myopically on bark surfaces while the foliage-gleaners and spinetails are more preoccupied with rummaging in the vine tangles and piles of trash that accumulate around epiphytes and in vines. Some species forage at eye-level, others somewhat higher and still others in the canopy.

Each flock also contains a few kinds of flycatchers that sally for prey. Besides these, there are jacamars, nunbirds, barbets, woodpeckers, antbirds, wrens, tanagers and orioles. Some flock birds are excessively active—even when judged by such acknowledged standards of hyperactivity as North American wood-warblers—while others are methodical and selective in their search for arthropods. Woodcreepers hitch up trunks and along limbs, carefully inspecting the bark surface as they go. They are textbook studies in the careful, methodical, leave-no-stone-unturned approach to foraging. An antwren, on the other hand, may fidget and hop among dozens of twigs, limbs and patches of foliage, giving each only a moment's glance. Jacamars, while giving the impression of high energy because they whip their heads around rapidly, watching for fast-flying insects like dragonflies and butterflies, usually do not move far from their favorite tree-fall gap. They may join flocks briefly as they pass through, but they are unable to follow them.

Andean cloud forests shelter mixed-species flocks of some of the most colorful and energetic small birds in the world. Moving along steep forested slopes and towering canyon rims, these flocks forage among giant mossy trees and tiny fruiting shrubs alike, traipsing from one to the other, then back again with scarcely a pause in their frantic schedules.

Like flecks and swirls of color amidst green-mantled mountain slopes, these flocks are ephemeral eddies of life, all chips and chatter and animated bits of brightness one moment, then shadowy silhouettes in gray-white fog the next. They are in constant motion like their lowland counterparts, but they are also very different. There are no sentinels among them. How do these sprightly groups of birds manage so well without sharp-eyed sentinels?

The roster of bird-eating raptors—blood-thirsty accipiters and for-est-falcons—is almost as long in the Andes as it is in the lowlands, so the flocks must surely stay vigilant. Moreover, every flock contains its share of foliage-gleaners, woodcreepers and flycatchers whose foraging behav-ior places them at risk of sneak attacks. But the large number of tanagers in these mountain flocks is a key ingredient missing from lowland groups. A dozen or more kinds of tanagers and tanager allies may ac-count for more than half of all the individuals in every Andean flock. No one knows for sure just what role they play in predator detection in flocks, but their collective vigilance may be an important reason why specialized sentinels have not evolved in the Andes.

I spent a year studying small tanagers in Colombia's Andes. Day after day, I recorded what they ate, what they did and where they went. I was primarily interested in the *Tangara* group, but I also ended up with an intimate look at the lives of several others. These birds lead high-energy lives, and in their pell-mell rush from one fruiting tree to the next, they sometimes overlook insect fare. Leaves, moss-draped branches and bare twigs shelter countless insects, but such places often receive only a super-ficial once-over by *Tangara*. In a burst of activity, a few twigs are scanned, but attention spans are short and the birds quickly move on.

Daily foraging routes are dictated not by random wanderings in search of insects but by the distribution of fruiting shrubs and trees. The routes are constantly adjusted to include newly discovered fruiting trees while old routes are abandoned just as readily when fruit crops are ex-hausted. Tanagers, of course, can fill up on fruits and berries quickly so they remain relatively vigilant at all times. Checking for danger, which they do almost incessantly, does not greatly reduce foraging efficiency. Even without sentinels, there are so many individuals on the alert that every flock member enjoys the benefits of group vigilance.

When animal behaviorists first became interested in mixed-species flocks, there was a tendency among them to search for the one most important advantage of flocking. It is clear now that there is no single, universal answer that explains why birds participate in mixed-species flocks. Rather, naturalists must look for possible benefits that each bird obtains by joining a mixed-species flock. These benefits may include protection from predators, availability of beaters, opportunities for piracy and increased foraging efficiency. For each species, the benefits may be different and they may vary with the circumstances. Offsetting benefits are costs, and only when benefits outweigh costs is one likely to find birds in mixed-species flocks.

Naturalists learn to look for links between costs and benefits when they study animal behavior. In mixed-species flocks, for example, a woodcreeper with its head thrust amidst epiphytes on a mossy limb is all the more remarkable to us because we see its behavior put into a new perspective. The creeper is enjoying the benefits of flocking—protection from predators and an ability to forage with fewer interruptions. This is made possible by the watchful vigilance of a sentinel like the shrike-tanager whose cries, whether true or false, the creeper cannot afford to ignore. At the same time, the woodcreeper incurs certain costs in the form of occasional prey items lost to the sentinels and the time that it loses heeding false alarms.

An observant naturalist might point out that in a survey of rainforest birds, fewer than half participate in mixed-species flocks. If flocking is good for woodcreepers, antwrens and foliage-gleaners, why isn't it good for all forest species? Are the costs of participation in mixed-species flocks too high for some birds? Ornithologist William Buskirk, while a graduate student at the University of California, was interested in the question of why many tropical forest birds do not join mixed-species flocks.

Searching for answers, Buskirk surveyed flocking birds in the mountains around Monteverde in Costa Rica. He soon discovered that forest birds that do not associate with mixed-species flocks fall generally into one of three categories: terrestrial birds, sit-and-wait foragers and hummingbirds. Buskirk reasoned that these birds don't need to forage with other species because their behavior, and in some cases their habitat as well, reduces their vulnerability to predators. These very traits also make it almost impossible for the birds to forage and at the same time keep up with the rapid pace of mixed-species flocks.

Terrestrial birds are obvious logistical mismatches for arboreal flocking birds. They forage by walking or hopping on the ground; some flip over leaves, pick or scratch in leaf litter, eat fallen seeds or fruit or follow army ants, but none move rapidly enough to keep up with mixed-species flocks. Nor do they need to. Aided by large eyes that adjust instantly to changing light levels near the rainforest floor and with somber colors that render them nearly invisible in this dark and shadowy zone, such birds are elusive targets. Furthermore, they operate in a world where safety is rarely more than a split-second away—shrubs, logs and leafy tangles provide ample cover.

Sit-and-wait foragers like jacamars and puffbirds are unable to participate in mixed-species flocks, except serendipitously as the flock passes them by, because these birds move very infrequently. Like the terrestrial group, their foraging behavior is incompatible with rapidly moving birds in mixed-species flocks. Sit-and-wait foragers perch quietly and are virtually motionless for long periods of time, waiting mostly for large insects. Their constant vigilance is an asset. Like the sentinels that double as sharp-eyed lookouts in mixed-species flocks, sit-and-wait foragers are difficult for predators to surprise, so they may not benefit greatly from flock association.

Foraging hummingbirds are virtually predator-proof, secure in their unrivaled aerobatic flight. They are paradigms of vigilance and alertness both at rest and in flight, and their small size and rapid, evasive movements almost eliminate the possibility of any threat from bird-eating hawks. These attributes have freed hummingbirds from dependency on mixed-species flocks and are a major reason why, among New World nectar eaters, hummingbirds alone have been able to evolve novel foraging strategies, such as nectar traplining and flower defense.

Manakins generally fall within the category of sit-and-wait foragers, too, though many of their attributes parallel those of hummingbirds. They are very small birds and aerobatic fliers that are adept at hovering.

Furthermore, manakins frequently feed on berries at scattered understory shrubs, and these usually don't have enough fruit to attract many birds or the attention of predators that might lie in wait. This helps explains why manakins are unusual in their ability to eat fruit and still remain solitary.

When not feeding, manakins sit quietly and remain vigilant. Consequently, away from their courtship grounds, manakins (especially females) are very inconspicuous and easily overlooked; on a walk through the rainforest, you are not likely to see many manakins, except for perhaps a group of males on a display arena. But a sample of birds caught in mist nets usually reveals manakins, especially duller female and subadult ones, to be among the commonest birds in the forest.

Some of the first birds a visitor is likely to see on a holiday to the rainforest are flocks of parrots and parakeets. In pairs and various-sized groups of their own species, they noisily crisscross morning and evening skies on commutes that carry them to all points on the compass. All New World parrots and parakeets fly in flocks of their own kind. It is a behavior so characteristic of these birds that one might scarcely pause to question why. Yet, this seemingly trivial point is somewhat troublesome to naturalists trying to explain the advantages of mixed-species flocking.

Scientists hadn't previously considered the distribution of food resources to be an important factor in flock structure until William Buskirk found a strong correlation between the way food is distributed and whether birds join mixed-species flocks or flocks of their own species. The birds that most often join mixed-species flocks are ones whose food is well dispersed. Insects are usually dispersed, and so is most animal prey as well as the flowers of plants that bloom at scattered intervals throughout the year. Birds that consume food which is scattered have to disperse to find it, and these are the very conditions under which they are most vulnerable to predation. Such species clearly benefit by associating with other species.

Parrots and parakeets, on the other hand, eat mostly fruit or fruit seeds—decidedly clumped food resources—and, arguably, they might not need to join flocks. They probably associate in flocks for the same reasons that seabirds, swallows, bees and other organisms that utilize clumped resources do—flocks are a good way to share information about food. For parrots and their kind, extra eyes help locate fruiting trees and help watch for predators. Flight calls and the almost constant banter between flying birds and those in fruit trees facilitates information exchange.

So why don't we see mixed-species flocks of parrots and parakeets? The answer seems to lie with both the distribution of fruit and the great range of sizes of fruit and seeds that are available. Unlike Andean tanager flocks, in which most of the birds are relatively similar in size and can share the same fruits and berries, parrots differ greatly in body size and in the size of their beaks—from enormous gaudy macaws down to sparrow-sized parrotlets. As a result of this size difference, the birds eat different kinds of fruits. In addition to the mismatch of fruits they prefer, the fruiting trees they seek are likely to be widely scattered. This results in greatly different commuting times between roosts and feeding trees. Macaws regularly travel many miles each way, and pairs or small groups scatter over vast areas. Tiny parrotlets, on the other hand, may subsist on small fruits they find nearby or they may gather in large, high-flying flocks that cover immense distances in search of certain fruit crops.

Seeing a mixed-species flock brings excitement and energy to our forest walk. It provides us, as naturalists, with an opportunity to see many kinds of birds, but it offers us more than the opportunity to increase our lists. Mixed-species flocks are dynamic and stable partnerships of individuals. They can tell us much about how the lives of their members are organized. And there is another lesson, too—nearly lost perhaps—in the frantic pace of their lives, because as we watch individuals within these flocks struggle to communicate, to separate truth from lie and to benefit from an association that also imposes certain tolls, we are reminded of just how much these mirror our own struggles in life.

# *Antbirds Don't Eat Ants*

## Rhythms and Rituals at Ant Swarms

FAINT NOTES alerted us to a group of birds following army ants in the undergrowth. We moved forward slowly, our eyes straining to see movements in the dim understory light. Several dark forms chirred and scolded loudly, then instantly vanished into the undergrowth.

We stood quietly in the humid stillness of the rainforest. Perspiration traced little rivulets down our foreheads and backs. There was no sound except the drone of cicadas overhead and the faint patter of untold thousands of ants racing through the leaf litter. I knew the antbirds would be back, and eventually some of them did return to forage, warily keeping an eye on us and staying behind foliage.

The forest floor was covered with several hundred thousand ants racing in every direction. I now counted nearly 20 antbirds of several species. Activity was frantic. Antbirds were pivoting around saplings and lunging after prey in dazzling displays of gymnastic skill. They postured aggressively toward each other to maintain or gain better foraging positions over this shifting, swirling world of ants. Outright attacks on competitors were commonplace.

We stood transfixed, watching one of the great dramas of life and death that is played out thousands of times every day in the vast tropical rainforests of the New World. There in eastern Ecuador, as we peered through layers of foliage to catch glimpses of these strange, shadowy birds, I explained to the group of mostly North American birders assembled with me why these birds were following army ants.

"But don't antbirds eat ants?" someone asked.

"No, antbirds don't eat ants. In fact, very few organisms do because the ants' high formic-acid content makes them extremely unpalatable."

It was an innocent question, and I surely must have expected the next question.

"Well, why are they called antbirds?"

The answer is, of course, that they follow ants. But in fact, only a few antbirds follow ants, and for the most part, they follow just one or two kinds of ants known as army ants. It was a question that clearly called for more explanation.

Antbirds are a large family of birds, the Formicariidae—literally the antbird family (*formic* in Latin means ant)—although ornithologists now believe the family may actually consist of two families, one arboreal, the other largely terrestrial. Nevertheless, all of them live in the neotropical region, between southern Mexico and northern Argentina, but they are most numerous and certainly most diverse in the humid lowlands of Amazonia.

Among the more than 240 species of antbirds, fewer than 30 are associated with ants, and these latter only follow columns of army ants that are out on hunting raids. The remaining antbirds, most of which have little to do with ants, have radiated into a wide variety of habitats. Almost everywhere one goes in the Neotropics there are a few antbirds to be seen, even in regions far above tree line in the Andes. A square mile of Amazonian rainforest might harbor 40 or 50 species, though it would take days, even weeks, to find them all.

The species that biologists call professional, or obligate, ant-following antbirds associate with only a few kinds of army ants, but they obtain almost all of their food by capturing prey flushed by these carnivorous insects. To understand what motivates these birds, one also needs to understand how the ants operate, for the lives of the two are inextricably entwined.

The species most favored by professional ant-following birds is *Eciton burchelli*, a large blackish ant with a light rusty brown abdomen and long legs. This is the army ant most likely to be encountered by visitors to the New World Tropics, and its raids, along with the attendant birds, are one of *the* characteristic features of neotropical rainforests.

There are few sights in the American Tropics that leave a greater impression on visitors than a closeup look at a raiding swarm of army ants. In a big army ant raid, a half million ants may blacken the forest floor as they race over every square inch of leaf and bark surface, under logs, in brush piles, even up into trees. As they race back and forth, not a leaf or crack or cranny is left untouched. Any arthropod or small vertebrate that does not flee is immediately attacked by hordes of viciously biting ants.

Even humans are not immune to these raids. "Stand still!" I admonished a companion who was beginning to shift uneasily in his tracks as thousands of ants raced over his feet and through the leaf litter where he stood. "They won't bite through your socks and they probably won't crawl more than a foot or two up your pant legs!" With pants tucked inside his socks, he would be quite safe from the ants' vicious bites, though I know the experience is unnerving.

Around army ant swarms, one quickly learns to step over the columns of ants so as not to disrupt the chemical trails they follow. Such disruption sends this blind army racing around in all directions, including up one's legs. But standing very still, often for 10 or 15 minutes, is a necessary part of observing professional ant-following birds.

A raid starts when ants begin to leave their bivouac, or swarm. The bivouac is composed of several hundred thousand workers linked together in a ball-shaped mass large enough to fill a bushel basket. A single queen and thousands of immature ants are buried deep inside. The bivouac is almost always located in an area of heavily shaded forest. It may be beneath the buttress of a tree, under a log, in a brush pile or in a tree hole many feet above ground.

Raids often start around dawn. At first, the movement looks uncoordinated, but the lines coalesce into a single large column that grows longer and longer. Soon a veritable river of ants, sometimes 50 abreast, begins pouring out of the bivouac. Workers race ahead a short distance, then turn back and are immediately replaced by others that press ahead still farther in a continual leap-frogging pattern. Little obstacles and gaps in their path are spanned by tiny ant bridges, formed on the spot by workers that link their tarsal claws together. By this time, professional ant-following antbirds are usually on hand, watching alertly and awaiting the start of the raid. If the raid is late, the antbirds may wait for hours, spending their time loafing, preening and bickering among themselves.

Most prey is flushed and captured near the front of the swarm. Behind, the slowly advancing front is an interconnected and constantly changing network of ant columns that ultimately form into a single trail leading back to the ant bivouac. The raid progresses, perhaps advancing 200 yards in the course of a day's rambling, perhaps only 50 yards. Almost always, the route is serpentine and with much backing and filling as columns fracture and pursue separate directions and then later dissolve back into the main swarm.

When the queen is laying eggs—up to 300,000 in the course of a few days—and until the eggs hatch, relatively little energy is needed by the colony. During this period, which may last two to three weeks, energy needs are low, and the colony stays in the same place each night. On some days, they may not raid at all. However, once the eggs hatch, the growing larvae require more energy, and the swarm enters a nomadic phase. This also may last up to three weeks.

Now, the swarm seeks a new campsite at the conclusion of each day's raid. The larvae are transported to the new camp, right along with the remains of the day's booty. For the antbirds, this is the period of time when the ant swarms are most reliable as a source of food. The hungry larvae are growing rapidly, and food demands keep the swarm constantly on the move searching for prey.

When the larvae form cocoons, raiding activity diminishes and once again the colony enters a stationary phase for up to three weeks. During this period, a new batch of eggs is laid by the queen. This stay-at-home phase continues until the eggs hatch. At about the same time the eggs hatch, tens of thousands of new sister workers begin to emerge from the cocoons of the previous generation. With larvae and new workers to feed, the colony is forced to take up its wandering ways once again, and the nomadic phase begins anew.

The cycle is unvarying. A colony spends two to three weeks at the same location each night. Then abruptly, the colony begins a two- to three-week nomadic phase, moving to a new location each night. The fact that the cycle continues year in and year out without interruption is important because it has allowed a highly specialized subset of antbirds to evolve. These are the professional army ant followers, which depend wholly upon raiding army ants for their food.

The importance of the ants to the professional ant-following antbirds and to a few species of woodcreepers that make their living almost entirely at ant raids is that the ants act as beaters, flushing a veritable smorgasbord of prey. Anything that can crawl, walk, hop or fly is certain to do so in order to escape the vicious bites and stings of the ants. Even large animals are not immune to the ant's bites and will move out of the way.

Small prey attempting to flee, including anything from cockroaches and katydids to scorpions, millipedes, even anoles and frogs, are caught in a viselike pincher attack from which only a lucky few escape. While vicious, fast-moving ants attack from below, predatory ant-following birds lurk above them, patiently waiting for a movement.

For birds, the advantage of feeding over an army ant swarm is that a lot of easy-to-catch prey is flushed by the ants. But there is a downside. Some days the ants don't go out on a raid, and sometimes even when they do, they don't flush enough prey to make it worthwhile for the birds. And even worse, there are a lot of competitors, such as other antbirds, willing to risk a scuffle in order to get a piece of the action.

Antbirds seem to be aware of their vulnerability around swarms— the constant hubbub of activity, bickering and occasional songs could not fail to attract the attention of predators—and they are often excessively wary and flee in an instant at the approach of a human. But if an observer is patient, which means waiting very quietly at the edge of the ant swarm, the antbirds will return, and within 30 minutes or so, they usually begin to settle down and resume normal foraging behavior. It is at this point that the curtains are drawn on some of the best rainforest theater in the Neotropics, for this is when we can watch these birds at length and perhaps reflect on how they have come to be and on the remarkable life-styles they pursue.

The evolution of army ant following probably began opportunisti-cally. Just as many tropical forest birds today make occasional use of the swarm's activities as a food resource, the early ancestors of today's profes-sional ant followers surely visited ant swarms too. Gradually, morpholog-ical and behavioral modifications evolved that enabled them to exploit this resource more efficiently than their competitors. Ultimately, for a few species, it became a way of life.

The anatomy and behavior of ant followers has evolved in response to the problems of competing in an intensely specialized avian microso-ciety. These birds are supremely able to exploit the resource-rich environ-ment over an army-ant swarm, but their extreme degree of specialization has made them vulnerable. Most professional ant followers are so com-pletely dependent upon the raiding activities of the ants for their food that it is unlikely they could survive if they failed to locate ant swarms or were prevented from foraging at them. And, neither the ants nor the antbirds could subsist without the giant lowland forests in which both roam.

Extreme anatomical and behavioral specialization usually comes with a price. Specializations may increase reproductive fitness, but the price can be steep indeed if it is at the expense of an organism's ability to adapt to changing environments. But several anatomical specializations give professional ant followers a leg up, so to speak, over the numerous species that occasionally attend ant raids. Any species that can monopo-lize the perches near the front and center of an ant raid, where most prey is flushed, will have an advantage over competitors perched higher and farther away. Here, professional ant followers excel, for they have espe-cially well-developed leg muscles and large strong feet, which enable them to easily jump between close perches and to cling to small vertical saplings with ease. This is an obvious advantage because they spend a lot of time waiting just above the ants, and suitable horizontal perches are often not available.

Studying bicolored antbirds in Panama, ornithologist Ed Willis no-ticed that the two outer toes of this species are slightly fused at the base.

This forms an enlarged sole area for gripping. The grip is further enhanced by minute projections on the sole of the foot, which when pressed down help them hold onto slippery surfaces. When the foot is relaxed, the sole slips easily and the birds can rotate quickly on their perches. Adaptations like special "track shoes" and overdeveloped leg muscles, which facilitate quick jumps out of the "starting block," give professional ant followers a competitive edge in the tumultuous, rough-and-tumble world above ant swarms.

Most ant followers are not strong fliers. Adapted for life in the forest undergrowth, there is little need for strong or fast flight. Foraging over ants, they frequently move to nearby saplings by jumping or by wing-assisted hops. If danger appears, they freeze or dive for the protection of a nearby thicket. So reluctant are most ant-following antbirds to leave the protection of the forest that large rivers, even roads, present major barriers to dispersal.

Willis, who spent thousands of hours watching ocellated antbirds, seldom saw them cross open areas. Large rivers, especially in the Amazon Basin, are barriers to dispersal and gene flow, although some antbirds eventually get across by island-hopping or by simply becoming stranded on the opposite bank when the river changes course.

But for a few, the rivers are probably permanent barriers. Over time, these species may evolve in isolation—permanently separated from a neighboring population just across a river. Three modern-day examples from Amazonia illustrate just how effective a river barrier can be. White-breasted antbirds (*Rhegmatorhina hoffmannsi*) live on the east bank of the Madeira River in Brazil but have never been found on the west bank. Harlequin antbirds (*Rhegmatorhina berlepschi*) occur on the west bank of the lower Tapajós River in Brazil but are unable to cross the Tapajós to the east or the Amazon to the north. White-throated antbirds (*Gymnopithys salvini*) are found right up to the south bank of the Amazon River in Brazil and Peru but do not cross the river into Colombia.

The inability of small forest birds like ant followers to cross even small open spaces makes them particularly vulnerable to the activities of

THE BICOLORED ANTBIRD (CENTER) AND
OCELLATED ANTBIRD (LOWER RIGHT) FOLLOW
AN ARMY ANT RAID IN LOWER CENTRAL
AMERICA. THE SPOTTED ANTBIRD (EXTREME
RIGHT) AND BARRED WOODCREEPER (LEFT)
ALSO FREQUENTLY FOLLOW ARMY ANT SWARMS.

humans. A new road, much like a river, creates a gap in the forest. Subsequent clearing of forest along the road then creates an even larger, more formidable barrier. In time, the fates of the populations are sealed. Broken into a multitude of isolated and increasingly smaller groupings that become more and more vulnerable, ultimately some populations become so small they are no longer viable. It happens so slowly, so quietly, that it is seldom noticed.

Barro Colorado Island in the Panama Canal Zone is a low mountaintop. It became an island between 1911 and 1914 when the surrounding valley was flooded to form the canal. When Ed Willis began studying ocellated antbirds in 1961, there were still about 45 birds on this island. Today there are none.

Nearly all professional ant-following birds have large bare areas of skin encircling their eyes. Sometimes this skin is colorful—red, pink or blue. The eye patch is so distinctive that it is the first thing that most observers notice about these antbirds. Five Amazonian *Rhegmatorhina* antbirds share a particularly bold, goggle-eyed appearance due to their bare eye patches, and it shows up in many other ant followers, including familiar species like the bicolored and ocellated antbird. It is also found in the chestnut-backed and plumbeous antbirds and in a few others that are only part-time followers of army ants. Are these bare eye patches used in sexual display, or do they possibly function as early warning devices to feel stray ants near their eyes?

In musing about colored eye patches, we are in the world of speculation, but much of the fun of biology is in speculation. Wondering the what ifs as we watch the antics of nomadic little birds in their shadowy forest floor world, one cannot help but wonder about many aspects of their curious life-styles. How, for example, do nesting ant followers cope with a food supply that is so unpredictable? Is it possible for birds to follow a nomadic food resource and still nest in the traditional way? Ed Willis, no doubt, wondered about just this problem when he set out to study these birds years ago. He was determined to turn speculation into fact.

The ants, of course, are nomadic, but the antbirds are tied to one place for at least as long as it takes to nest. If nests fail, and many do, then renestings could restrict the birds to one place for much longer. But chance events occasionally result in an absence of nearby ant swarms, leaving the bird pair with no choice except to trespass across a neighbor's area to reach a distant swarm. For many insect-eating birds, this would be next to impossible because of the risk of harassment and outright attack from highly territorial and intolerant neighbors.

The ephemeral and unpredictable occurrence of army ant raids clearly does not permit obligate ant followers to use such a strict territorial system. At an ant raid, so much prey is flushed that it often represents far more than any individual or pair could eat. Furthermore, because of the continual movement and fluid nature of the ant swarm, the prey that the ants flush represents an extremely elusive resource to defend. In a few days, ants can move far beyond an area that a pair of birds would be capable of defending. Therefore, the antbirds have no recourse but to become more tolerant of trespassing neighbors and adopt a modified system of territoriality in which nesting areas do not overlap but foraging areas overlap completely.

This difference in social organization between obligate ant followers and other insect-eating birds, including other antbirds, is one of the most striking consequences of following army ants. But not all ant followers have evolved the same modified social and territorial systems. The three species studied most intensively by Ed Willis—the spotted, bicolored and ocellated antbirds—each have somewhat different systems. The social and breeding systems of all three have probably evolved from classical territoriality, and together they form a continuum: that of the little spotted antbird, which also forages away from swarms, has evolved the least and that of the large ocellated antbird has evolved the most.

Spotted antbirds are the smallest of this trio of professional ant followers, and they are frequently driven away from swarms by bigger birds. Even when they aren't, they are usually banished to the poorest foraging places at the rear of the swarm. Consequently, spotted antbirds often forage in pairs at small swarms or away from swarms entirely. Their simple territorial system resembles a classically defended territory, though persistent trespassers are grudgingly tolerated.

The social and breeding behavior of the bicolored antbird is intermediate in complexity, and it is typical of how many ant followers have solved the problem of a fixed nest site and a moving food supply. Bicolored antbirds are nomadic when young, and after pairing, they may continue to wander for several months. Once a nest site is chosen, birds restrict their foraging activities to within about 400 meters of the nest— an area that should contain, on average, at least one *E. burchelli* ant swarm.

But bicolored antbirds may visit swarms a kilometer apart in the course of a morning. All pairs, as well as unmated birds, trespass freely over nesting areas. Large, active swarms may attract two, three or even four pairs of these birds as well as unmated male birds that might have wandered in.

But as pairs or individuals wander, an important change in the dominance hierarchy occurs. The dominant bicolored antbird pair at the swarm is *always* the pair that nests in that vicinity. If this pair is absent, the dominant pair is likely to be a close neighbor. The closer a pair is to its nesting area, the more likely it is to dominate other birds present at the ant swarm.

Groups of competing bicolored antbirds, which may contain pairs from several nesting areas as well as unmated wandering birds, follow swarms throughout the year. The same birds may follow the same ant swarm for several days, or the composition of the group may vary from day to day or during the day. Pairs may leave to follow another swarm, or low-ranking submissive birds, failing to secure a favorable position at the swarm, may abandon it in favor of another. Occasionally, all the birds may leave en masse and switch to another swarm. Whenever changes occur, there are corresponding adjustments in the social hierarchy. Normally these are accompanied by a complex array of postures, vocalizations and outright attacks as the pecking order is realigned.

The loose territoriality shown by bicolored antbirds offers several advantages over strict territoriality, where all intruders are excluded. It permits the dominant pair to take the most favorable foraging site near the center of the swarm when the swarm is close to their nesting area. This is particularly advantageous when the pair is breeding. On the other hand, the dominant pair is also permitted to trespass freely and is able to forage far from its nesting area—an advantage when no ant swarms are nearby or when arthropod populations in the forest litter are low. Furthermore, because most ant swarms flush more prey than a single pair of antbirds can eat, more birds are able to take advantage of a swarm. This, in combination with the small size of the nesting territories, permits much higher population densities than would be possible if each pair attempted to defend a large, exclusive foraging territory.

The territorial system of the ocellated antbird is considerably more complex. Ocellateds are larger than bicolored or spotted antbirds and easily elbow them aside at ant swarms. Like the bicolored, they have an area in the vicinity of their nest where they are always dominant over neighboring pairs, but here the similarity ends. Young ocellated antbirds continue to associate with their parents even after they are fully independent. This association leads to one of the most complex familial societies known among birds.

A patrilineal clan develops in ocellated antbirds. Young males bring females from outside the clan and generally remain within the sphere of influence of the clan. Large clans may include eight or more individuals from at least three generations. Although a clan's members sometimes quarrel, they bunch together in disputes against a neighboring clan—behavior that will surely bring to mind parallels in our own species.

Willis's discovery of clans or loosely altruistic families in ocellated antbirds opened a fascinating chapter in antbird biology. The very existence of antbird clans (or of any clans for that matter) suggests these birds possess some very special behavioral attributes, otherwise fighting would soon replace cooperation.

Clans develop when densities of ocellated antbirds increase to the point where one or several young male's offspring and their mates are superimposed upon the nesting territory of an older pair of birds. Obviously, such a density can occur only because the younger pairs show little or no aggression toward the preeminent pair.

For such complex clans to develop and remain stable, it is not surprising, then, that ocellated antbirds show a broad range of submissive behaviors and only a few relatively simple aggressive ones toward each other. In ocellated antbird society, one's success is likely to be greater by attempting to get along with one's relatives—in this case by a series of submissive and appeasing behaviors—rather than by confronting them with overt aggression.

The advantage of submissive behavior becomes critical when large numbers of birds are crowded together over an ant swarm. The dominant pair maintain a place at the front and center of the swarm, but well-developed submissive behaviors allow even low-ranking birds to join them at this coveted spot. Furthermore, reduced aggressive behavior toward other clan members by the dominant bird also enables subordinate birds to forage very close by. This contrasts with bicolored antbirds, which have a more complex array of aggressive behaviors and are likely to spend more time bickering among themselves while foraging.

At the other extreme, spotted antbirds, which have no submissive behaviors in their repertoire at all, try to drive away all other spotted antbirds that intrude. Consequently, spotteds are poorly adapted to the stress of life over ant swarms, where many birds are crowded closely together. Because of this and their small size, which does not let them compete with the larger antbirds, they forage away from ants or take the less stressful areas at the rear of the swarm where their aggression and territorial nature are more advantageous.

Curiously, one group that has not been particularly successful at following army ants is terrestrial birds. These species may be found within the ranks of many neotropical families—tinamous, cracids, rails, doves, cuckoos, furnariids, flycatchers, fringillids—as well as antbirds. But few are more than incidental at swarms, and none are obligate followers. If the general failure of terrestrial species to professionally take up ant following seems surprising, consider for a moment the frequent fate that befalls humans, another terrestrial species, around ant swarms. Those of us that carelessly blunder among army ants soon learn a painful lesson. Perhaps it is true for these birds as well.

On the other hand, some woodcreepers have been successful at exploiting army ant raids from above. Clinging to trunks and sallying for fleeing prey, they generally stay above the seething legions of ants. Some obtain half or more of their food at ant swarms, though none are truly obligate ant followers.

Antbirds remain one of the largest and most complex neotropical families. Nowhere has the family reached such diversity as in Amazonia, where fully half of them are found. Their remarkable radiation is well exemplified by the variety of names applied to them. By their appearance or behavior, they have reminded ornithologists of shrikes, wrens, thrushes, vireos and pittas—hence we find antshrikes, antwrens, antthrushes and so on. While some evolutionary lines within the family have been ranging higher into the mountains, the ant-following group has remained behind, mired in the steamy lowland forests favored by the ants they faithfully follow.

Some species less encumbered by specialization, such as the ubiquitous barred antshrike, have benefitted from the destructive activities of humans in the last century, but most species have not. The vast majority of the members of this family dwell in forested habitats within the limits of tropical latitudes, and their continued success—indeed the existence of many—is very much in the hands of humans who increasingly share these forests with them.

# *Who Is the Fairest?*

## Colorfulness in Tropical
## and Temperate Birds

WHEN I TELL some of my nonbirding friends that I'm just back from a birding trip in the Tropics, one of the first things they are likely to ask is, "Oh, did you see lots of beautiful birds like parrots and toucans?"

A menagerie of colorful birds peering down from the verdant exuberance of a rainforest—it's an image we all secretly harbor, even when we know better. The famous nineteenth-century naturalist Alfred Russell Wallace clearly knew better when he commented on colorfulness in tropical birds in his now classic *Malay Archipelago* writing, "Although the number of brilliantly colored birds in almost every part of the tropics is very great. . . they are by no means conspicuous, and as a rule they can hardly be said to add much to the general effect of the equatorial scenery."

Travel promotional paraphernalia featuring tropical lands invariably feature glorious sandy beaches, lovely bikini-clad girls and a colorful toucan or parrot grinning down from the corner of the brochure or poster. The audience to whom the message is aimed may never see a parrot or toucan on their tropical holiday, and the bird portrait itself is likely to be a colorful composite, dreamed up in the mind of someone who relied more on artistic license and scattered memories of childhood trips to the local zoo than on acquaintance with the bird. But in the stampede to the beach, no one much seems to mind.

Beyond such popular images, we might begin to wonder about the colorfulness of tropical birds. Are they really more colorful than their temperate-latitude counterparts? And if so why? These question aren't easy to answer objectively, but it is true that tropical latitudes are fertile evolutionary stages for showcasing unusual and exotic-looking plumages and bizarre adornments.

Asking why tropical birds are more colorful than temperate ones is the sort of question that makes some evolutionary biologists' hair stand on end. While it may be easy to dream up possible explanations for why some birds are colorful and others are not, it is very difficult to actually test such theories. Nevertheless, colorful birds and the plumages of any bird, for that matter, have not evolved solely for our enjoyment, and biologists are left searching for clues to their possible adaptive value.

Are colors and patterns adaptive? Most biologists would argue that they are, and for a scientific framework upon which to base their case, they would turn to Charles Darwin who has provided a way for biologists to ask questions about birds and animals. Fundamentally, the Darwinian hypothesis states that an organism's appearance, behavior and physiology must be adaptive to contribute to a greater overall level of reproductive success. The assumption is that, over generations, well-adapted individuals will leave more offspring than those less well adapted.

This doesn't necessarily mean that every bird or mammal represents a perfect solution to the environment in which it lives. All organisms, including humans, doubtless carry an unspecified load of nonadaptive genetic baggage from earlier times, and present anatomies and physiologies may not necessarily be the best ones. Nevertheless, most colors and color patterns in nature probably do have underlying adaptive value.

To appreciate the adaptive value of colors or patterns, we need look no further for an illustration than the streaked upperparts of many open-country birds. Streaked backs appear in both temperate-latitude and tropical-latitude birds in such diverse taxonomic lines as thick-knees, sandpipers, pipits, meadowlarks, longspurs, grass-finches and sparrows. Almost anyone who has walked across a prairie has had the experience of a pipit or a sparrow, completely disguised, suddenly flushing from underfoot. It is a persuasive example of the power of protective coloration, and illustrates why we don't usually find birds with brightly colored upperparts in open habitats.

The paradise tanager is one of the most colorful of all birds. Found in the foothills of the Andes and across much of the Amazon Basin, it joins other birds in search of fruit and insects in the rainforest canopy. Its velvety black upperparts are set off by an apple green head, red and yellow rump, purple throat, turquoise breast and black belly. The Spanish name *siete colores*, or "seven colors," alludes to the remarkable number of colors in its plumage. Although questioning how and why such a marriage of colors evolved may not lead to testable hypotheses, it is certainly worth pondering broader questions about color and pattern in nature.

Biologist Mary Willson and artist Robert von Neumann of the University of Illinois were the first to tackle the question of why tropical birds are more colorful than temperate birds. In their attempt to classify plumages, they swept all birds into two broad and arbitrary categories— birds that are colorful and those that are not colorful. Their tabulated results reveal a greater proportion of colorful birds in the Neotropics than either in North America or Europe. They went on to point out that colorfulness did not seem to be associated with particular habitats, rather they found about equal proportions of colorful birds living in open and forested areas.

In a more detailed analysis of latitudinal color gradients in birds, Stephen Bailey of the University of California at Berkeley arrived at a different set of conclusions from those of Willson and von Neumann. Bailey found scant evidence for the supposed greater colorfulness among the tropical songbirds he examined. He noted that there are more colorful birds in tropical latitudes but only because there are more species of birds. The proportion of colorful birds in each region, Bailey argued, is rather similar, and dull-colored birds predominate everywhere. Naturalists who have tried to identify *Empidonax* flycatchers and sparrows in North America or the hordes of furnariids, antbirds and flycatchers in the Neotropics would, no doubt, be inclined to agree that dull birds do seem to predominate.

Nevertheless, anyone who has followed mixed-species flocks in Andean cloud forests can hardly fail to be impressed by the colorfulness of the tanagers, flower-piercers and finches that make up most of these flocks. Lowland rainforests certainly contain their share of colorful birds, too, and this is where most visitors gain impressions of colorfulness in tropical birds. Some of the most colorful and conspicuous of all rainforest birds are to be found in nonpasserine families such as parrots, hummingbirds, trogons, toucans, barbets, jacamars and motmots. Yet curiously, Bailey did not include these families in his analysis although many of these birds are large and easily seen, which contributes to the perception that tropical birds are very colorful.

The forests of temperate and tropical latitudes are an excellent starting point for comparing the frequency with which certain colors and patterns appear in bird populations. Tropical rainforests are green year-round—the result of abundant moisture and warm temperatures—while temperate hardwood forests are bare and devoid of green foliage for nearly half the year. Not surprisingly, birds with green or yellow-green coloring are common in the Neotropics as well as in the tropical latitudes of Africa and Asia, although they are rare in temperate latitudes.

The increased frequency of green plumage in tropical-latitude birds suggests that it functions as a form of protective coloration. Almost every naturalist working in the rainforest has seen flocks of green parrots or parakeets fly into a tree and "disappear." The effectiveness of concealing colors is confirmed by any attempt to count the numbers of these birds once they are in a heavily foliaged rainforest tree.

When feeding, parrots and parakeets are quite methodical and slow-moving, making ample use of their bills as extra "hands" as they clamber around in search of ripe fruits. A flock of parrots, in fact, is often so quiet and stealthy when feeding that on a walk through the rainforest, one might never be aware of their presence except for their careless habit of dropping bits and pieces of fruit from the canopy. The cost of such sloppy dining habits, however, is surely balanced by their inconspicuous movements, concealing green color and highly social and vigilant behavior.

In temperate latitudes, there is a corresponding increase in the frequency of gray and brown color in birds. This seems to be a direct consequence of the greater amount of gray and brown color in temperate habitats, especially during the winter months. Tropical habitats have their share of gray and brown birds, too, but they are concentrated either in the lower strata of the rainforest where light levels are low or in tropical dry forests, grasslands and deserts.

Hermit hummingbirds are characteristic inhabitants of the rainforest understory, and unlike their canopy-inhabiting relatives who flaunt sparkling plumages in well-lighted treetops, hermits wear somber shades of gray, brown and dull green and lack reflective or iridescent colors. Although most have a long and flashing white tail spike, it is more apt to be taken for a flickering spot of sunlight dancing in the foliage than the embodiment of a bird, so hermits attract little attention to themselves.

The plumages of most understory rainforest birds are not unlike those of the hermits. Woodcreepers, antbirds, ovenbirds and wrens are mainly clothed in simple grays or browns or other dark colors that closely match the leaves and leaf litter on or near the forest floor.

Occasionally, we see a bright flash of color in the understory—a blaze of red or yellow, perhaps, of a male manakin darting past. But such brightness in the dim understory seems out of place. Bright color, especially in the forest understory, is usually not an adaptation for concealment, nor are the antics and noise associated with displaying groups of male manakins. The very function of these groups is to attract the attention of female manakins. Although bright colors also attract potential predators, small, fast-moving manakins are not easy targets, and the most colorful manakins are social birds that display in groups of two or three or up to several dozen birds. With so many individuals together, it is virtually assured that several pairs of eyes will intercept any incoming predator, thus offsetting the conspicuousness of their bright plumages.

But somehow these birds seem irrelevant in the understory. They are bits of colored splendor in a world of muted colors. The lower levels of the rainforest belong to the dull, the cryptic and the shy, such as antbirds and foliage-gleaners. Indeed, some antbirds are so confident of their powers of concealment in the dim forest light that they are known to sing from their nests. We may hear their haunting whistles and trills and know they are lurking nearby, but only occasionally do we glimpse these birds—furtive apparitions tantalizing us with disembodied sounds that emanate from the damp, dark vegetation.

Brightly colored eyes and colorful legs and feet adorn many tropical birds, especially those that live in the dark forest interior. Manakins and antbirds often have brilliantly colored eyes; rails and nightingale-thrushes, which rarely leave the concealment of dense vegetation, have colorful bills and legs and often sport bold red or yellow eye rings as well. Colored soft parts are found much more often on tropical species than on temperate species. Patches of brightly colored bare skin, like goggles, encircle the eyes of many antbirds, but such features are rarely found on birds north of Mexico. The reasons for the commonness of colorful eyes, bills and feet in the Neotropics are not clear, although they must somehow function as social signals that, close up, are easy to see in the perpetually dim light of the forest understory.

To see colorful tropical birds, you have to look up into the brightly lit branches of the rainforest canopy. There, strong sunlight fashions a high-contrast world of lights and darks that simultaneously dazzle and confuse. Bright birds move easily in a world where color catches the sun one moment and then fades in a shadow the next. Color is riotous and often flaunted with impunity in the rainforest canopy. It may also be adaptive.

Concealing color does not have to be dull and drab. Colorful birds, reptiles and insects may appear conspicuous when taken from their environment, but these colors often closely match the reflective properties of the vegetation where they live. Large patches of bright and dark colors mimic the harsh, high-contrast lighting of the forest canopy. The plumages of quetzals, trogons and jacamars, with dark green backs and bright yellow, red or rufous underparts, are evidence of the effectiveness of this coloration. It might seem difficult to believe that such colors would help conceal a bird, but anyone who has squinted into a sunlit rainforest canopy in search of a trogon or jacamar will appreciate how bright colors can disrupt a bird's shape.

The brilliant colors of a resplendent quetzal, considered by many to be one of the most beautiful birds in the world, may actually confuse a predator. In misty Central American cloud forest, a quetzal hurtles head-long through the trees, its brilliant emerald body and shrieking red underparts flashing through patches of sunlight. But in the next instant, it rests in the shadows of a high mossy branch, and it is difficult to pick out its form. Its emerald plumage no longer sparkles, and long green scapular feathers obscure its brilliant belly. Long filmy tail coverts that trailed like colorful green ribbons in flight are now wafted like gossamer by breezes we do not feel. They now resemble slender leaves in the near stillness of the forest. This remarkable creature, so vibrant and real a moment earlier, is now lost to human senses.

In such cases, our eyes do not react to the sudden change in light quickly enough to follow the movement. When the pupils of our eyes open to receive more light, we lose visual acuity, making the image of the quetzal even more difficult to follow. Additionally, our retinas do not immediately respond to the dramatic change in light intensity when we look from bright light into darkness, so for a moment, our retinas remain stimulated, even after the light has changed. These extreme variations in brightness that occur when birds dart from sun to shade and back again make it difficult for predators to accurately track their location.

Naturalists have long admired the amazing plumages of many neotropical hummingbirds. Their dazzling combinations of iridescence encompass virtually every color in the spectrum. Some, such as the intensely violet tails of the sylphs and the red, orange and green colors of the red-tailed comet, are among the most brilliant to be found in nature.

Though it is less well known, many neotropical birds besides hummingbirds, and some temperate-latitude birds as well, have iridescent plumages. Iridescence, which we see as reflected light because of structural features of the feather rather than pigment, is responsible for the deep bottle-green plumage of trogons, the glittery golds and coppers of jacamars and the straws, golds, greens, blues and violets of many tanagers. Watching a jacamar sitting in a shaft of sunlight in a rainforest clearing, the sun illuminating its shimmering, metallic-looking plumage as the bird rapidly whips its head from side to side, one is unlikely to be struck by the notion that such colors could be concealing. Yet just such a possibility has been suggested.

Iridescent colors reflect light only at very small angles. In other words, the observer must be close to the plane of the incoming light to receive the full benefit of the reflected colors. As a consequence of this property, highly iridescent birds often look black, and at any instant, only a small portion of a bird's plumage will appear brightly colored. Iridescence, then, misrepresents a bird's true appearance and may function as a disruptive color pattern. In display, iridescence should make possible a more highly directional signal than pigmented plumage colors.

Stephen Bailey argued that iridescence is well suited to the varying light conditions in tropical forests because shade and heavy foliage should reduce the chance of the display attracting the unwanted attention of predators. By contrast, many temperate habitats are more open, at least seasonally, and the likelihood that a flash of iridescence would be spotted by a predator from afar is greater. Furthermore, the low angle of the sun in temperate latitudes, especially in the winter, would often trigger the iridescence, making it highly visible. If Bailey's ideas are correct, tropical forests may indeed provide a safer environment for the use of highly iridescent colors because the combination of unobstructed views and low sun angles occur infrequently.

Iridescent plumages are found on birds that inhabit the upper levels of the rainforest but rarely on those that live in the forest understory. Iridescence almost completely disappears from the plumages of understory hummingbirds, and the only tanagers with iridescent plumages are those that inhabit the mid-levels or canopy of the rainforest.

Several jacamars live in the lower forest zones and might seem to be exceptions at first glance, but these birds habitually sit in small sunlit forest openings when foraging. The implication is that iridescence in birds is associated with species that are relatively immune to predation, as are hummingbirds, or with species that inhabit areas with a combination of bright light and shade. Iridescence may make it possible for birds in these environments to use very bright colors for sexual or social signaling while simultaneously looking black and relatively inconspicuous most of the time.

Many disappointed field naturalists quickly learn this lesson with tropical hummingbirds. Quite unlike the dazzling creatures portrayed in books, most hummingbirds usually appear dull and black in real life. Only occasionally, when a head is turned or a bird faces the viewer at a certain angle, do we catch a pulse-quickening glimpse of the fire in their plumages. A small number of temperate-latitude species, such as grackles, blackbirds and swallows, have iridescent plumages. These birds may compensate for their attention-getting properties of iridescence in open habitats where they live through their social habits and, in the case of swallows, highly maneuverable flight.

With the exception of a few social species like manakins and highly aerobatic and difficult-to-capture species like jacamars, colorful birds are packed largely into the upper layers of the rainforest. Some species, such as macaws and toucans, may afford the cost of bright coloration, in part because their large size limits the number of predators capable of attacking them. For the vast majority of birds, however, this is not true. I suspect that, in many cases, birds can get away with colorful plumages in the rainforest canopy because it is a relatively open place with good visibility, and birds that combine vigilant habits and low-risk foraging behavior may be relatively unthreatened despite their colorfulness.

Males and females of resident tropical birds, whether colorful or not, are more apt to be similar in appearance than temperate species or species that migrate between tropical and temperate latitudes. This is especially true when tropical-temperate migratory species are considered. Males are often brighter than females in temperate latitudes, and in some instances, males molt into a duller plumage prior to their return to the Tropics.

Through the process of sexual selection, males may develop colorful plumages or displays that enhance their ability to attract females as well as serve as warnings to rival males. If a male does not help the female with nesting duties or is involved in only part of the activities, his color-ful plumage or display may enhance his ability to attract more than one female and thus increase his reproductive success.

Bright plumage, which is also likely to be a good indication of vigor and physical health, is of particular importance to males, which must reestablish their dominance on a territory each breeding season and vie to attract a female. This helps explain why males of many migratory species are considerably brighter than females. Furthermore, bright col-ors may be less important to males of resident tropical and temperate species alike because they remain on or near their territories year-round and do not have to reestablish dominance each breeding season. However, females, which spend greater amounts of time engaged in nest-ing duties, are likely to have dull, concealing colors that reduce their conspicuousness in the nest.

Very bright males, of course, may pay a price for their beauty—their colorfulness makes them more visible and, therefore, more vulnerable to predators. The very plumage that serves them so well in establishing ter-ritories and attracting females is also bound to attract the attention of predators. This may be one reason why some bright males, such as goldfinches and longspurs, quickly molt into a dull femalelike plumage after the breeding season. Migratory bobolinks, scarlet tanagers and some wood-warblers also keep their bright plumages only during the brief breeding season. Even more importantly, molting into a dull plumage after breeding facilitates a shift from territorial to gregarious habits. Species that undergo this transformation may benefit by being less colorful and, hence, less threatening to competitors.

Color is an important social signal that has been experimentally shown to convey much information about a bird. Bright plumage espe-cially may signal a dominant social rank, good health and physical con-dition and breeding readiness. Dull plumage, on the other hand, because it elicits little aggression from a dominant competitor, may make it pos-sible for a migrant bird to fit in more easily with dominant tropical birds in mixed-species flocks, and it may make it easier for birds that form flocks of their own, whether migratory or not, to do so. For example, red-breasted blackbirds of lower Central America and northern South America molt into a femalelike plumage after breeding and gather in large flocks. As with bobolinks, they acquire a full breeding plumage only after several months of feather abrasion removes the brown feather tips and exposes a striking black and red breeding plumage beneath.

Young hummingbirds, which are duller than adults, often exploit the advantage of dull plumage. When nectar resources are scarce, inexperienced young hummingbirds may intrude onto the richer flower patches of territorial adults. Remarkably, they are able to do so more successfully than adult birds, despite their low social status. Biologists suspect that the immature birds are tolerated on adult territories because they lack a bright gorget or any other color that would identify them as adults and therefore as potential sexual or social competitors.

The pervasiveness of dull coloration among immature birds in general may be linked to social signaling. Eugene Morton of the National Zoo observed that dull, immature yellow warblers were frequently able to intrude upon the territories of adult males and feed without encountering strong aggression from the adults. The dull plumages of the immature warblers, a mark of low social rank, appears not to be regarded as threatening to adult males.

Female tropical birds are often as brightly colored as their mates, unlike most temperate-breeding species. Female parrots, toucans, motmots and puffbirds and the females of many tanagers and finches are the equal of their mates, the result, biologists believe, of a process called social selection rather than sexual selection. Female toucans, for example, are virtually identical to their mates. They even have the same brilliant colors around their eyes and the same markings on their bills.

Females that are as brightly colored as their mates usually live on permanent territories and remain mated for life. They actively assist their mates in territorial defense, and their bright colors are an indication of their competitive status. It is competition among females, biologists believe, that may lead to the evolution of their bright colors in much the same way that sexual selection has led to beautiful plumages in males. One does not have to travel to tropical latitudes to find evidence of this process at work. In temperate latitudes, the females of several common backyard birds, such as jays, chickadees and nuthatches, are as bright or boldly patterned as their male counterparts.

Temperate-tropical migrants are a complicating factor in a comparison of colorfulness. Many temperate-breeding birds spend more than half of each year in the Tropics. Historically, most of these birds are, in fact, tropical birds that make long-distance migrations, risking the hazards of long journeys for the chance to increase their breeding success during the brief exuberance of a temperate summer.

Anyone who rises at dawn on brisk spring mornings to witness the return of these tiny pilgrims knows that half of the excitement of their arrival is one's first glimpse of their bright, cheery colors. We enjoy the lilting phrases of a thrush, and we may admire its subtle brown plumage, but it is that dab of color on a male blackburnian's throat, aflame in the morning sun, or the sprightly black and orange zigzags of a redstart that really sends our blood racing.

Male orioles, tanagers, grosbeaks and wood-warblers are especially brilliant when they return in the spring, a consequence of their need to establish territorial dominance and attract a mate. But to what geographical latitude should we assign them in a discussion of color in temperate and tropical latitudes? They attain their brilliance in tropical latitudes, even before the long journey northward, yet their young are nurtured in temperate lands.

By almost any measure, the most colorful tropical birds are usually fruit-eating and nectar-feeding species. These are followed in a colorfulness ranking by partly fruit-eating birds, while the legions of dull-colored species are drawn mostly from the ranks of insect-eating birds. But why are fruit-eating and nectar-feeding birds so often colorful while their hard-working, insect-eating counterparts are so rarely dressed in finery? When biologists try to find causes for such patterns, it is difficult to move beyond the realm of speculation.

David Snow, a British ornithologist who spent several years in Trinidad's Arima Valley, worked both at and near the famous Asa Wright Nature Center. He was one of the first people to link the courtship dances, colorful plumages and unusual vocal powers of certain birds with the fruit-eating habit.

Many of Snow's ideas were popularized in his delightful book *The Web of Adaptation*, in which he argued that, because fruit is so easy to find compared to insects, females that eat fruit might not need the help of their males at nests. This provides an opportunity for males with extra time on their hands to spend it displaying. The males then become intense sexual rivals, each trying to outdo his neighbors to attract a female. According to Darwinian theory, females that select particularly colorful or ornately patterned males thus set the stage for the evolution of colorful plumages and ever more sophisticated dances.

The picture that Snow paints of fruit-eating males lazily spending their time gathered in permanent bachelor groups—displaying, resting and vying for the sexual favors of every passing female—is in sharp contrast to that of insect-eating birds, which must spend a large part of every day searching for their prey just to feed themselves. The greater amount of time and attention required to find insects also places insect-eating birds at greater risk of predation, compared to fruit eaters.

Bright colors further increase the risk, probably to unacceptable levels for insect eaters. It is this difference in foraging behavior between fruit-eating and insect-eating birds that seems to explain why bright colors evolve much less frequently on birds that are forced to search in places where their backs are turned and their vision is obscured—just the places where insects are likely to hide.

Our perception that there are more colorful tropical birds may be real or it may be an illusion. Perhaps we are misled by the mystique of the rainforest, or perhaps our perceptions are colored by encounters with a few truly brilliant or bizarre tropical birds. Who could deny that the bright orange flash of a cock-of-the-rock is more likely to remain forever burned into our memory than the sight, however close, of a drab little tyrannulet.

It is certainly true that the most colorful birds in the world are to be found in tropical latitudes, but they are not truly representative of the majority of tropical birds. A great many tropical birds, however much we may want to think otherwise, are ordinary in appearance. What is impressive in tropical regions is the tremendous diversity of birds, and it is perhaps the assortment of colorful species within this diversity that our subconscious mind wants to remember most.

We may not be able to resolve all the questions relating to colorfulness in temperate and tropical latitudes, but we do have the opportunity to think about many interesting aspects of color. And who can deny that a great deal of the pleasure that we derive from watching birds comes from the colors and patterns they show?

# Fruit of the Land

## Birds, Fruit and Seed Dispersal

THE CHANCES are good that if you've visited the rainforest, a bird that eats fruit turned out to be one of your favorites. Fruit-eating birds are generally easy to see and some are among the showiest in tropical latitudes. They're an important part of the birdlife in the New World Tropics—about one out of every three species eats some fruit. So why haven't brightly colored fruit-eating birds evolved in the same way in temperate latitudes? Where are the toucans and cotingas that could brighten up those cold, gray winter days in Buffalo or Cleveland?

In many respects, fruit-eating birds have evolved along similar lines in temperate latitudes because there is about the same proportion of fruit-eating birds in northern latitudes as there is in the Tropics. The big difference is the ability of tropical birds to specialize on fruit year-round. This has made possible life-style changes that would be unattainable in harsh temperate climates.

Only a few northern birds have attempted a year-round regime of fruit. Waxwings and phainopeplas come closest perhaps, but even these hardy birds feed insects to their young and often eat insects themselves. In just two families in the New World Tropics, the manakins and cotingas, there are more than 100 fruit specialists. In addition, there are trogons, flycatchers, tanagers, saltators and toucans—the quintessential standard-bearers of fruit eating—whose colorful, grinning faces, splashed on practically every travel brochure imaginable, beckon irresistibly to snowbound northern travelers.

In the Tropics, fruit-eating takes many forms, varying from a few

KEEL-BILLED TOUCANS FEED ON A
WIDE RANGE OF FRUITS.

species that are truly fruit specialists, such as oilbirds and bellbirds who even feed fruit to their young, to primarily insect-eating birds that occasionally eat fruit. The vast majority of fruit-eating birds fall somewhere between these extremes.

What are the consequences, if any, of a fruit diet? Do birds favor certain fruits over others? How do plants cope with or exploit the fickle and often discriminatory fruit preferences of birds? Ecologists are seeking answers to these and other questions. In the last two decades, they have taken a closer look at the long and sometimes bumpy relationship between plants that bear edible fruits and the birds that eat these fruits and, in the process, disperse or destroy the plant's seeds.

Fruit is simply a bribe. Trees bribe birds with various kinds of enticing fruits in return for their services as seed dispersers. A bird eats a fruit, which has one or more seeds hidden in it, and in return for the fruit, the tree's seeds are carried away unharmed to a distant location.

But in the real world, things are rarely that simple. If the seed is large, it may be dropped right on the spot because the bird or animal doesn't want to bother carrying around all that extra weight. This is logical behavior for the consumer, but it is of no value to the plant. Furthermore, as the seed is passed through the gut of a bird or animal, it may be scarred or partially digested so that its ability to germinate is hindered. And finally, if the seed is nutritious, and often it is more nutritious than the fruit, then there is the risk that the seed will be eaten and digested instead of the fruit.

Birds that eat seeds are blatant cheaters because such behavior short-circuits a tree's dispersal strategy. Some of the most incorrigible cheaters of all are the very birds that are likely to come to mind when fruit-eating birds are mentioned—parrots, parakeets and macaws. Whoever would think of them as predators? When we keep them as pets, they amuse us with wisecracks, clever tricks and crooked grins. But it is just these attributes—their intelligence, agility and enormously strong bills—that throughout their evolution have enabled parrots to crack the hardest seed coverings in nature, digest poisonous seeds and circumvent an array of vicious spines.

So plants must deal with the consequences of an array of fickle animal consumers that are often wasteful, selfish and self-serving. But plants fight back with a surprising arsenal of chemical and mechanical barriers.

Plants must somehow encourage appropriate animal or bird dispersers of their seeds while at the same time discouraging the inappropriate ones that mishandle or destroy their seeds. Poisonous seeds, large seeds, unusual positioning of fruit and fruit size are all devices that deter seed enemies and at the same time permit appropriate consumers to feed.

But the defenses are never perfect. Some bats, for example, thrive on heavy doses of strychnine and cyanide, which are embedded in seeds to deter rodents. Parrots and macaws also somehow overcome a veritable minefield of chemical and armored defenses of plants. Even the hardest seed coverings and strongest seeds fall prey to the enormous crushing power of their beaks, and they destroy most of the seeds they ingest. They may deal with particularly toxic chemicals in seeds and fruit by eating clay from riverbanks, thus emulsifying the poisons. Alternatively, they manage to avoid poisoning themselves by eating only small amounts of toxic seeds at any one time and combining these with larger amounts of harmless seeds, thereby diluting any deleterious effects from the poisons. Pigeons grind up small seeds in strong stomachs. Cute little tanagers often mash fruits and berries and squeeze the seeds out right on the spot before eating the pulp, thus making an end run around the plant's dispersal strategy.

Manakins, on the other hand, are quintessential "gulpers," that usually hover momentarily, pluck a berry and then, almost instantly, swallow it whole. Among manakins, there are no epicures; no time is lost savoring exotic tropical flavors. Their gulping behavior should make them good agents of seed dispersal, but males spend most of their time displaying at leks and are likely to void most seeds in the tiny area where the lek is located. The same is true of displaying male bellbirds, which regurgitate most seeds at the base of their calling perches, virtually guaranteeing that the seeds will fail because so many fall in the same place.

It is a struggle that no plant can win outright, and in the end, most seeds are destroyed, lost or wind up in the wrong place. The best that can happen, in most cases, is that a few lucky seeds will germinate in the right places. Nevertheless, plants can up the odds of success with fruits of appropriate color and size that are attractive to certain groups of birds that provide good seed dispersal.

That said, birds and bats are still the most useful seed dispersers in tropical forests. They are mobile and likely to carry seeds away from the parent tree and thus away from insect infestations and to favorable locations. It isn't surprising, then, that a majority of tropical trees have seized upon them as a means of dispersing their seeds. Nearly two-thirds of the canopy trees in eastern Costa Rica bear fruits that are dispersed by birds, bats and other animals. In some areas, the figure is higher. As many as 90 percent of the trees and shrubs in the rainforest understory rely upon bird and animal dispersal.

This is far higher than in eastern North America, where the majority of trees depend upon wind for seed dispersal. The reason for this difference isn't difficult to understand. Wind dispersal of seeds is a strategy that works well in the spring when trees are bare and there are no leaves to slow the breeze. In the dense foliage of the rainforest, breezes are likely to be felt only in the canopy; most rainforest trees are completely sheltered from the wind. Heavy rains also limit the effectiveness of wind dispersal because rains wash the feathery, wind-borne seeds onto the ground beneath the parent tree. Here, they compete with the parent tree for sunlight and suffer from its insect infestations as well. Consequently, only a few of the tallest rainforest trees and vines rely upon wind for seed dispersal, and these plants usually broadcast their seeds during the driest periods of the year.

A small number of plants use novel techniques to accomplish seed dispersal: they use mechanical devices that rely upon large changes in humidity to trigger seedpods that explode and expel seeds. These are effective in dry forests, but they don't work well in the uniformly high humidity of a rainforest.

With so many plants vying for the attention and services of birds and animals, it is not surprising that there is a wide range of different fruit-bearing tactics employed by plants to attract dispersers. One solution to this problem is exemplified by wild fig trees. These trees, of the genus *Ficus*, produce enormous quantities of small fruits that are filled with hundreds of gritty little seeds embedded in a juicy and easily digestible, if somewhat tasteless, fruit pulp. Because they are small and easy to digest, wild figs are attractive to a great variety of birds and animals that mostly pass the seeds through their guts quickly and without damage. The huge crops of wild figs, which bear scant resemblance to commercially grown domestic figs, are a keystone resource in the diets of many fruit-eating birds and animals in the rainforest.

The fig's strategy is one of the most successful seed-dispersal strategies in the rainforest, but there is a catch. Fig seeds are extremely small and they must germinate where there is an abundance of light because they have no stored energy reserves. This limits figs to natural openings in the forest, to the rainforest canopy, where many get their start as epiphytes, and to zones of early plant succession, such as along riverbanks. For this reason, someone traveling by river through the Amazon Basin might be inclined to think that the rainforest is composed mostly of figs. In fact, it isn't. It is only that figs are most numerous in the floodplain, and with their whitish bark, long, smooth, rather open limbs and shiny dark green leaves, they are one of the most easily identifiable trees. Figs bear enormous crops of fruit, often more than once a year, and among the millions of seeds that are rained down on the forest floor by bats and birds, a few seeds reach favorable spots where they can survive.

The fig's shotgun approach to seed dispersal—attempting to target as many different kinds of consumers as possible—also works well for other trees in such diverse families as the melastome, mulberry, pepper, coffee and nightshade. Their seeds are so tiny that they are swallowed whole and usually passed right through the bird's gut without harm. Their berries are often bright red, orange, yellow or blackish—colors that make them easy to see. The finger-shaped fruits of *Cecropia* and *Piper* trees, two other widespread genera, don't fall into this syndrome of colors, but the shapes of their fruits, called catkins, are unmistakable, and these fruits are easy to reach.

Most berries are quite sweet, and they are the bait that lures the crowd of bird consumers, many of which are only part-time or opportunistic fruit eaters. Sweet little berries, though, are a bit like the time-honored tradition of lowering the price on cheap but eye-catching products to lure customers into a store. The berries contain some sugar and organic acids, but little or no protein and fat, so they don't offer a balanced diet. The value of the berries lies in the rapidity with which their simple sugars can be assimilated to provide a boost of energy. It is like eating candy—providing a quick energy boost that doesn't last. To balance their diets, most birds turn to insects, which are far more difficult and time-consuming to find.

Trees and shrubs that produce large crops of sugary berries usually grow in forest openings and high-light edge habitats. There is an important connection between this strategy and the habitat because it takes sunlight to produce sugar, and figs and most other trees that produce an abundance of sweet berries can only thrive in the high-light environment of forest gaps and edges. Tree falls and abandoned clearings and pastures surrounded by forest are quickly blanketed with seeds scattered by birds, and in no time, the seeds dropped in sunny places germinate and hordes of seedlings appear.

Unlike the fig strategy, the majority of rainforest trees take a somewhat different approach to seed dispersal. Light in the rainforest is a precious commodity because many layers of foliage intercept the sunlight before it reaches the forest floor. Seedlings without energy reserves quickly wither and die, so seeds must carry their own energy supply—essentially a built-in survival kit—which helps them wait, years if necessary, in an arrested state of growth for a light gap to appear. This is why the seeds of many rainforest trees are large—they carry a large amount of energy that aids the young seedling during the difficult period of getting established.

The fruits of these trees have also evolved to attract certain types of fruit-eating birds and other animals. To attract dispersers that might otherwise pass up fruits with large, heavy seeds, trees often up the ante with fruit pulp that is highly nutritious but hard enough that it cannot be easily stolen off the seed. Wild avocados, close relatives of the ones we purchase in supermarkets, are good examples of this kind of fruit. Wild avocados may contain as much as 20 percent protein and 40 percent fat— enough nutrition to win the approval of a number of large fruit-eating birds and animals. Species like oilbirds, bellbirds and toucans, in turn, digest the rich, oily flesh of the fruit and regurgitate the seed unharmed and ready to sprout.

The fruit-eating activities of birds and other animals have an immense impact on the rainforest. Fruit-eating specialists like bellbirds and capuchinbirds rarely risk an alliance with just a few trees. Instead, most eat a wide variety of large, nutritious fruits as well as small berries, and thus are potential dispersal agents for many kinds of trees.

During several years of study in Trinidad, British ornithologists David and Barbara Snow found that bearded bellbirds fed on the fruits of at least 32 kinds of trees, and many of the fruits were large and highly nutritious ones belonging to trees of the laurel and incense family. In the same area, white-bearded manakins fed on the fruits of more than 105 kinds of trees.

Birds also adjust the variety of fruit they eat to the diversity that is available. Working for more than a year in the cloud forests of western Colombia, I recorded what tanagers ate and how they foraged, using them as a yardstick for the fruit-eating bird community as a whole. The study formed part of my doctoral dissertation, and along with finding that fruit is most abundant during the two rainiest periods of the year, I also discovered that these seasonal differences in the amount of fruit in the forest showed up in the foraging behavior of the tanagers. They expanded their diet from a low of 23 species of fruit during July to 46 during March through April and 41 in October. Not only were the tanagers tracking and making use of the resources available in their environment, they were replanting the forest all year long. From this one small corner of one valley in the Andes, I recorded birds eating more than 160 different kinds of fruits during the year, and the seeds were surely scattered far and wide.

Naturalists are still only beginning to fully appreciate the contribution that fruit-eating birds make to the dynamics of a rainforest.

Probably few people were more surprised at the impact that a fruit-eating bird can make on a forest than former graduate student Roberto Roca, a young Venezuelan scientist, who undertook an ambitious radio-tracking study of oilbirds at the famous Caripe Oilbird Cave in eastern Venezuela. Upon realizing just how valuable the oilbirds were to forest dynamics, Roca turned his discovery into a *cause célèbre* for conservation.

Although oilbirds are found from Trinidad to Bolivia, they remain in caves during the day, hidden from view and safe from predators. Consequently, few people are ever likely to see oilbirds unless they make a concerted effort to find them. Nevertheless, oilbirds are not safe from massive deforestation that robs them of the fruit trees they require for food.

At Caripe, where Roca worked, more than 10,000 oilbirds spent their days sleeping in the cave and their nights venturing forth in search of fruit. With a keen sense of smell and a head crammed with sophisticated radar, these remarkable birds navigated through miles of uncharted rainforest at night, seeking out the large, nutritious fruits of various laurel, incense and palm trees—and 10,000 oilbirds require an enormous amount of fruit.

Roca found that oilbirds ate the fruits of more than 40 species of canopy trees, and like most other fruit specialists, they regurgitated the heavy seeds unharmed. But earlier naturalists held the view that oilbirds weren't good seed dispersers because there were always tons of seeds inside the caves where the birds slept. Looking at the immense piles of seeds beneath some of their cave nests—one pile in the Caripe Cave was nearly 50 feet high—it seemed only natural to conclude that the oilbirds were indeed poor seed dispersers. How else would so many seeds from the fruits they eat wind up condemned to darkness and death in the caves where the oilbirds roosted and nested? Roberto Roca wasn't so sure.

Roca placed seed traps beneath the nests of many oilbirds and then, from atop an 8,000-foot-high mountain, he followed his radio-tagged birds on their nightly rounds. His traps and radios helped reveal a new chapter in the seed-dispersal story of the oilbirds. While seeds accumulated beneath nests with young, traps beneath empty nests and at roosts lay nearly empty. The enormous seed piles in the caves, as it turned out, were mostly from fruits fed to the young. The adults were broadcasting the seeds they ate as they flew—an average of about 1,500 seeds each month per bird. The colony of 10,000 birds at Caripe was regurgitating some 15 million seeds every month over an area as far as 60 miles away. Roca estimated that at least 60 percent of this total was sown directly in the forest. The impact of such a reforestation effort, which continues every night of the year, cannot be dismissed.

Fruit specialists often have behavioral and anatomical adaptations that allow them to quickly deal with the ballast of large, heavy seeds. Oilbirds and bellbirds have enormously wide bills and gapes that enable them to swallow fruits that are as large as the diameter of their heads, thanks to an elastic jaw articulation. Their thin stomachs are well adapted for stripping away fruit pulp, but not for grinding up the heavy seeds that are regurgitated after 15 to 20 minutes—usually when the bird has left the fruiting tree. Lacking a powerful crushing bill or a strong grinding stomach, such fruit specialists have little choice but to get rid of the heavy seed ballast as quickly as possible. Quick handling of the seed plays into the hand of the tree's strategy, as well, because the seeds are not likely to be harmed during their short stay in the gut.

Not all fruit specialists are big birds that eat large, nutritious rainforest fruits. Many are small birds, and they often possess an array of behavioral and morphological adaptations for eating fruit that are just as sophisticated as those of the large species. Some, such as tyrannulets, chlorophonias and euphonias, are well adapted for feeding on berries and other small fruits. Several drab little flycatchers as well as some brightly colored chlorophonias and euphonias are mistletoe specialists. Their digestive tracts are very thin and weak—just strong enough to strip away the outer flesh of each berry without damaging the seed.

There is a good reason for the soft handling of mistletoe seeds by these birds. A sticky layer of viscin surrounds each seed, and it is impregnated with toxic chemicals that offer some protection to the seed and at the same time help speed passage through the gut. In some cases, no more than seven or eight minutes is required for the seed to pass completely through the gut of these birds. As long as the viscin layer is un-damaged, the seeds remain viable and the bird is not poisoned.

Because of this glutinous covering, mistletoe seeds are very sticky. When they are defecated by birds, the seeds tend to stick together in long, stringy masses like pearly beads on a necklace. These strings usually have to be wiped across branches because they are so glutinous that they don't break apart easily. This improves the chances that the soft, rapidly germinating seeds will be deposited in suitable places because mistletoe seeds germinate best on twigs and branches. Nevertheless, surprisingly few seeds actually survive because each mistletoe will grow only on certain kinds of trees and sometimes only on branches of a certain size. With such remarkably exacting requirements, it is perhaps surprising that mistletoes survive at all.

Watching a little euphonia defecating a sticky chain of mistletoe seeds, one might not immediately make the mental leap to connect the bird's behavior with the mistletoe seed-dispersal strategy. The first time I saw an orange-bellied euphonia attempting to defecate mistletoe seeds by bobbing its rear end alternately up and down and back and forth in a series of contorted motions, I thought the bird was sick or injured. Then, after I saw what it deposited on the branch, I was more convinced than ever that this bird was sick—perhaps even near death. After this first incomprehensible experience with mistletoe seed dispersal, I watched other euphonias undergoing this same ordeal and began paying more attention to what euphonias were eating. Still, it wasn't until months later that I realized the significance of this sticky defecation process.

Mistletoes, of course, occur almost worldwide, and similar evolutionary solutions have been reinvented, so to speak, by a number of other unrelated birds on other continents. Like disarming a bomb, consuming mistletoe seeds is a delicate business best done by a specialist.

As is often the case in seed-dispersal systems, the best seed dispersers are not always the ones we might predict. In Costa Rica, postdoctoral student Priya Davidas found that the most effective dispersers of mistletoe seeds were not chlorophonias and euphonias but an unheralded flycatcher, the paultry tyrannulet. This bird was a more consistent consumer of mistletoe seeds than any other bird and just as likely to deposit chains of seeds on suitable branches.

Bellbirds, mistletoebirds, chlorophonias, euphonias and tyrannulets are all examples of birds specialized toward their food plants. Through behavioral, physiological and anatomical specialization, they are exceedingly well adapted for processing certain kinds of berries and fruits. In this regard, they are unusual among tropical or temperate birds because most fruit-eating birds don't show such highly evolved adaptations for eating fruit, and very few pairs of plants and birds anywhere are strongly dependent upon each other.

Birds are not concerned with seed dispersal, nor with the welfare of the plant's future generations; they are only concerned with obtaining food, and if the seeds cannot be digested, they are a waste of time and energy. Consequently, relationships between birds and their food plants are often rather one-sided, with one party benefitting more than the other. A bird, for example, may depend upon only one or a few keystone plants for the bulk of its diet, but the plant may benefit more from the dispersal services of another species. Likewise, the bulk of a plant's seeds may be dispersed by a bird for whom its fruits are a relatively minor part of its diet.

An example of this asymmetric kind of relationship is provided by two *Casearia corymbosa* trees that were observed by ecologist Henry Howe during their two-month-long fruiting season in Costa Rica. Seeing large numbers of birds feeding in fruiting trees like the *Casearia*, many naturalists had concluded that a lot of birds, especially small ones whose diets are varied, were not choosy about the kinds of fruits they ate and would opportunistically take whatever was available. It also seemed reasonable that many of these birds were good dispersers of the seeds they ate.

Howe set about to reexamine these ideas, which were then well established in scientific literature. He recorded 22 species of birds feeding at the trees, though surprisingly, only one of them—the masked tityra—was a regular visitor throughout the fruiting period. Two large toucans were common visitors early in the season, but they abandoned the tree when other fruits they liked better became ripe. Two small flycatchers ignored the trees for the first month, but then they began visiting the *Casearia* trees regularly after the dry season reduced the abundance of their insect prey.

Howe's observations are important because they show that, while many species may converge on a particular fruiting tree, one cannot automatically assume that it is a preferred fruit choice or that all of the birds feeding there will be equally effective at seed dispersal. For many species, the fruit may be an alternate choice, or even a choice of last resort.

Of all the species at the *Casearia*, only the masked tityra's behavior assured good seed dispersal. It took several fruits on each visit, regurgitated the seeds away from the tree and came throughout the fruiting season. On the other hand, the toucans and flycatchers fed for only a part of the fruiting season and often dropped many seeds directly under the tree where they had little chance of survival. Two *Amazona* parrots stripped the fleshy arils and then dropped the seeds—sometimes hundreds in a single morning. From the tree's perspective, the toucans, parrots and flycatchers are fruit thieves because they contribute little or nothing to seed dispersal.

Fruit is nature's fast-food industry—with all of the advantages and disadvantages of the human counterpart. An advantage is that it is easy to find and a bird can fill up on fruit in only a few minutes—far quicker than it could if it were searching for insects. David and Barbara Snow, who studied manakins for four and a half years, calculated that manakins, which feed almost entirely on fruits and berries as adults, need to spend only about 10 percent of each day foraging. Resplendent quetzals need only about six minutes to find and return to the nest with a fruit, according to Nathaniel Wheelwright, who studied these birds at Monteverde in Costa Rica. By contrast, the quetzals took, on average, about 24 minutes to find an insect. As a result of the difference in time required to find insects, most insect-eating birds must spend from 50 to 70 percent of each day foraging.

If fruit is so much easier to find than insects, one wonders why more birds haven't specialized on fruit. But, like most fast food, eating only fruit has its disadvantages. Fruit is low in protein and nestlings fed only on fruit grow slowly. Purple-throated fruitcrow fledglings need more than 30 days before they are ready to leave the nest, oilbirds more than 3 months, but a flycatcher that is stuffed with insects may leave the nest and be on its own in a mere 12 days. The difference is important because slow growth means more time in a nest and more exposure to predators. More than three-quarters of all nests in the Tropics fail, and the longer a fledgling remains helpless in the nest, the greater is the risk that it will not survive.

To protect against this disadvantage, fruit-eating birds have been forced to alter their nesting strategies. Oilbirds have moved inside caves, which are a relatively safe environment. Cocks-of-the-rock plaster their nests to rock ledges, which is another site that is relatively inaccessible to most predators. Bellbirds, manakins and fruitcrows employ yet another strategy—they build nests that are extremely small and cryptic and they visit them only a few times each day. Bellbirds, for example, build tiny nests that are little more than a few twigs placed far out on a high limb. With an insignificant nest and only a few very furtive trips to the nest each day, they strive to avoid detection.

Another disadvantage of depending upon fruit is that it is not always uniformly available in the Tropics. Wet and dry seasons are often well defined, and a lack of rain is an important arbitrator of a plant's ability to produce flowers and fruits and grow new leaves. There may also be corresponding seasonal gluts of fruit followed by periods of relative scarcity. Complicating matters even more, these periods of scarcity may vary in intensity from year to year, making it difficult for birds to subsist entirely on fruit.

Some fruit-eating birds ride out the hard times by switching to low-quality fruits when their preferred foods are unavailable. This may include eating unripe fruit, which is difficult to digest, or fruits of very low nutritional value. While this enables them to get through periods of scarcity, the stress of eating poor-quality foods may inhibit breeding activity and feather molt, thus introducing a distinct seasonality into some of the breeding activities of fruit eaters.

Birds that are efficient at obtaining and digesting fruit are best equipped to ride out the hard times when fruit is scarce. These species can afford the cost of eating low-quality or unripe fruit. Toucans, for example, are able to harvest fruit with relatively little expenditure of energy. By contrast, a quetzal feeds only by hovering, taking one fruit at a time. Hovering, even momentarily, requires a considerable expenditure of energy, thus making feeding costs high, and quetzals can ill afford to waste energy going after unripe or low-quality fruit. Seasonal shortages of fruit are likely to affect quetzals more than toucans, and this explains why quetzals, bellbirds and oilbirds, which have relatively high feeding costs, are often migratory.

Biologists today are likely to look upon most bird-plant dispersal interactions as rather loose and variable associations. Most birds rely on fruit for only part of their diet, and a much smaller number eat only fruit as adults, instead depending on insects to boost nestling growth rates. And only a handful of true specialists have embraced fruit as a dietary way of life.

Whether we find a close coevolutionary fit between bird and plant does not seem to matter much because more than enough seeds germinate to replace the rainforest. Nevertheless, we must not forget that much of the forest structure we see today is the result of what birds and animals did in these forests in the past. If one or two seed dispersers are lost, there are probably substitutes that can fill in. Likewise, the loss of a few species of trees may not be devastating to a population of fruit-eating birds. But it is difficult to imagine that a forest without its toucans, bellbirds and other fruit eaters would continue to remain healthy, nor would these birds long persist without the rich diversity of trees they use.

We may be able to observe changes in the populations of birds in a few years, but because trees live a century or more, it may be a long time before we see the impact of a lack of fruit-eating birds on the forest. In view of the rapid loss of rainforests today, we must ask ourselves if we can afford to wait.

# *Anatomy of a Fruit Eater*

## Foraging Tactics of Fruit-Eating Birds

THE PACIFIC SLOPE of Colombia's Andes is one of the wettest regions on earth. Narrow, steep-walled river valleys have etched innumerable lines into its wrinkled, rainforest-covered slopes. From where I stood, near the top of a long ridge, I saw flecks and shimmers of one of those rivers far below me. It rushed through an emerald canyon that offered tantalizing glimpses of ribbonlike waterfalls, then seductively wrapped itself in gossamer clouds. Westward, the river abruptly spilled onto the flat coastal plain. There, it undulated in sinuous brown curves toward the nearby Pacific Ocean.

The Pacific is the source of the rainfall that bathes this region in perpetual wetness, and waters cascading off Colombia's western slope and rushing seaward will soon return carried by the gray-white rain clouds that I could see tiptoeing up the valley. The birds sensed its arrival, too, for even before the first big, cold raindrops pelted my back, the two fruiting *Miconia* trees I was watching filled with small birds. As if choreographed, they arrived all at once—euphonias, tanagers, manakins and flycatchers—right on cue. I watched, fascinated, as gaily colored heads and tails popped up and disappeared like glittering ornaments among shiny, wet leaves.

I took refuge from the rain by hunkering beneath some palm fronds. The shelter was more symbolic than real, and after a few minutes, I began to doubt the wisdom of maintaining my watch over those two trees. The foliage was wiggling and fluttering from the patter of rain and the frantically foraging birds, which were on a last-minute foraging binge, bringing in supplies in anticipation of a rainy afternoon. Their behavior, in fact, reminded me of humans queuing up for food, gasoline or some other commodity—a panic buying spree—prior to an anticipated crisis. Generally tropical rains don't last long—maybe only an hour or two— but rains continuing for a day or more aren't unusual on Colombia's Pacific slope. Watching these birds in the *Miconia* trees, I couldn't help but wonder if they had already gotten the weather forecast.

*Miconia* are members of the melastome family, one of the largest plant families in the Neotropics. Melastome leaves—with parallel veins emerging at one end and joining at the tip—are so distinctive that even a novice can recognize most of them at a glance. But it is their small, sugary berries, not their leaves, that are of most interest to naturalists. Their berries are eaten by an amazing variety of birds that scatter their seeds far and wide through forests and clearings. The two *Miconia* trees I was watching were covered with tens of thousands of berries—tiny pale green ones, each a watery package of sugar and a few small seeds but not much else. Eating these berries is a little like snacking on sweets—there's a bit of quick carbohydrate energy from the sugar but virtually no fat or protein.

Eventually the rain sent me slogging back down the trail to the little tin-roofed house where I was staying. My Colombian hosts would probably be waiting with a hot cup of *agua panela* as they stared into the rainy landscape beyond the rough-hewn timbers of the porch.

As I returned, I wondered about the 32 species of birds and the capuchin monkey that I had just seen eating the *Miconia*'s berries. In one day, more than 10 percent of the bird species in the immediate area had eaten the berries of the two trees. There was a sickle-winged guan over two feet in length, a toucan with a bill five inches long and tiny chlorophonias with bills barely a quarter of an inch long. There were manakins and tityras, which eat almost nothing but fruit, and a family of rusty-margined flycatchers for which the berries were only incidental to their normal fare of flying insects. A blackburnian warbler also ate a few berries. Like many of its temperate-latitude breeding kin, it eats nothing but insects during the nesting season, but upon returning to the Tropics, it adopts a more catholic attitude toward food and occasionally includes berries in its diet.

The most numerically abundant consumers of the *Miconia* berries were the small, sprightly *Tangara* tanagers. There were eight different kinds, as colorful a cross-section of birds as could be imagined, and all of them traveled together in fast-moving, excitable flocks that streamed from one fruiting tree to the next.

Most temperate-latitude visitors are surprised by the number of different kinds of tropical birds that eat fruit. Flocks with 10 or 12 species of tanagers at a fruiting tree are not unusual. Fruit-eating birds have adapted to all levels in the rainforest from ground level to the treetops.

Tropical fruit-eating birds also span a wide range of sizes—much more so than in temperate latitudes—and they vary widely in such traits as wing and bill shape as well as leg length and leg musculature. Considering the wide range of birds that eat fruit, it isn't too surprising that it is difficult to pick out any particular physical adaptations that would set fruit-eating birds apart from other species. Even their bills, which you might expect to be similar because they are involved in harvesting fruit, vary from broad and flat to narrow and round.

However, there is a connection between bill shape and the method that a fruit-eating bird uses to pluck fruits. Species that capture fruits in flight have proportionally wider and flatter bills than those that pick fruit while perched.

Although birds with wide bill shapes are often specialized insect eaters or aerial-feeding species, proportionally the widest bills of all are those of fruit-eating species. If you have been fortunate enough to see a male bellbird calling from a display perch, you can appreciate just how far gape size can evolve among fruit-eating birds. A male bellbird's maw, at the height of his *bonk* call, is an awesome sight indeed for it opens like a gigantic black cavern and is far larger than would seem possible for the size of the bird.

The great width of a bellbird's gape is an advantage for sound production, but it is probably not essential for that purpose alone because

BAG-HEADED (LEFT), RUFOUS-THROATED (TOP)
AND GOLDEN-HOODED (RIGHT) TANAGERS
FORAGE FOR BERRIES IN A MICONIA TREE.

smaller birds, such as pihas, also have very loud voices. Screamers and red-throated caracaras have among the loudest of all voices in neotropical forests, and their bill gape is smaller in proportion to their size than that of a bellbird.

There seems little doubt that a broad bill and gape are advantageous for handling and swallowing large fruits. Among flycatchers that feed by sallying, those that eat some fruit, such as *Myiozetetes*, *Megarhynchus*, *Myiodynastes* and *Legatus*, have broader and flatter bills than is average for the family. This contrasts with the short, round bills of elaenias, tyrannulets and *Mionectes* flycatchers, which eat mostly small berries they can reach from a perch or by hovering.

Minor differences in the shapes of bills of closely related birds can result in important differences in the way birds handle and eat fruits. The resplendent quetzal and slaty-tailed trogon eat a wide variety of fruits. Both species obtain fruit by snatching it in flight. Both birds also are fond of big, oily laurel fruits, which are tough-skinned and hard and resemble small avocados.

The bills of the two differ only slightly. Overall, the trogon's bill is a little narrower, longer and thicker than that of the quetzal. Therefore, the trogon, although it is the smaller of the two birds, appears to be a bit heavier-billed. Minor as these differences may seem, it means the trogon has significantly more bill strength and biting power because it is capable of tearing out chunks of tough-skinned fruits and eating them piecemeal. The quetzal, which swallows its fruit whole, has not been observed eating fruits in a piecemeal fashion, and this may be because its bill is too weak to tear apart even relatively soft fruit. These kinds of observations reinforce the idea that a bird's bill shape, even when it differs only slightly from that of another species, can affect the efficiency with which a bird handles a fruit and perhaps ultimately the fruit that a bird chooses to eat.

Birds eat or capture fruit in basically one of two ways—in flight or from a perch. A bird's wing and body shape have a lot to do with which method is chosen and with the particular flight or perch maneuver it employs to capture the fruit. Just as certain human body shapes or sizes are more likely to lead to excellence in one kind of sport than another, the anatomical shape of each bird also facilitates or limits how it forages and eats.

In a search for relationships between form and function in fruit-eating birds, researchers Tim Moermond and Julie Denslow designed a series of experiments at the La Selva Biological Station in eastern Costa Rica. They offered several trogons, manakins and tanagers choices of fruits placed in different positions and at different distances from a perch in a cage.

The researchers hoped that the types and positions of the fruit— above the perch, below the perch, suspended in the air away from a perch—could be correlated with the normal method that each bird uses to take fruit in the wild. For example, trogons, manakins and some fly-catchers are adept at hovering (trogons actually stall momentarily), and they readily pluck fruits in this manner. But they have difficulty reaching for fruits, especially when the fruit is located below their perch, because their legs and feet are small and weak. On the other hand, toucans and most tanagers, which have short, strong legs and feet, easily reach in almost any direction for fruit. Many are so adept at reaching that they can grasp something that is nearly a full body length away.

In the experiments, the reaching and hovering species quickly demonstrated their different preferences of fruit placement. Tanagers responded to fruits placed anywhere within reaching distance above or below their perches. Birds that normally hover to pluck fruits and berries showed a clear preference for fruits above their perch and had great difficulty obtaining or ignored fruits that were below their perch. This suggested to the researchers that the position of fruits on a branch is like a selective filter, encouraging those species that can harvest it efficiently and discouraging those that cannot.

The *Miconia* trees illustrate this filtering effect. Their clusters of small juicy berries are grouped in panicles, or little sprays, at the tips of twigs and branches, so they are difficult for heavy birds to reach without considerable effort. Furthermore, the small size and low caloric reward of each berry better suits the needs of small birds. Not surprisingly, small tanagers accounted for more than 85 percent of the fruit-eating species observed in the *Miconia* trees in Colombia, and in most instances, the seeds were swallowed whole rather than discarded, so the tiny seeds were scattered widely.

The tanagers are good reachers and can easily scramble among the branch tips and locate berries without any trouble. On the other hand, an emerald toucanet and a black-mandibled toucan, hopping heavily and somewhat clumsily among the slender twigs, were able to reach only a few berries, even with the advantage of their long bills, and neither stayed more than a minute or two in the tree.

Biologists have only recently begun to appreciate the often subtle interactions between the body form of fruit-eating birds and the fruits that they choose to eat. Although fruit is meant to be eaten, not all birds and animals are equal in their ability to harvest it. Small birds, for example, cannot eat fruits with large seeds nor can they swallow them whole. Some birds may not be able to pluck fruits efficiently if they are hanging from the tips of branches. Small berries may simply not be worth the bother for large birds—the energy used to find or eat them may be greater than what the berries supply. Plants, then, by the size of their seeds and fruits and by their accessibility, can influence which species ultimately distribute their seeds.

The idea that birds may partition up the fruit resources in an environment, on the basis of the sizes and locations of various kinds of tropical fruit is relatively new. Biologists are used to categorizing insect-eating birds according to whether they glean prey from foliage, bark, curled-up dead leaves, the ground and so on, but less attention has been paid to fruit-eating birds. Biologists have tended to lump all fruit-eating birds together, regardless of how or where they forage for and eat fruit.

Following the experiments of Moermond and Denslow, two other researchers, Bette Loiselle and John Blake, began to look carefully at fruit-eating birds in eastern Costa Rica. They concluded that the decisions birds were making about which fruits to eat were determined by what each bird could do best. They began to see fruit-eating birds not as a single category, or guild, but as a more complex community composed of several guilds. Their ideas help explain why some birds are able to exploit a wider range of habitats better than others, and why some species seem to be confined to particular habitats.

Scarlet-rumped tanagers and buff-throated saltators are common birds in clearings and along forest edges in Central America. Both have short legs and good perching and reaching ability. This enables them to feed at almost any height and in many second-growth habitats. Furthermore, both show clear preferences for fruits that grow between branches (an axillary position) rather than at the tips of branches (a terminal position) because they can more easily reach the axillary fruits. Yet despite this, most forest-edge and light-gap shrubs in Costa Rica present their berries at the ends of branches where it is harder for these two important dispersers of the seeds to get at them. Why does this happen?

Loiselle speculated that most berries are positioned on the tips of branches not because birds prefer them there (they don't) but because they are safer from marauding rodents, which eat and destroy many seeds. In the tug-of-war between the destruction and distribution of seeds, selection has favored safer positioning at the expense of accessibility to the birds that distribute them. Pollinators may also exert an influence on the position of the flowers and ultimately the seeds.

The ability of the tanager and saltator to exploit the berries of so many light-gap shrubs contrasts with that of two forest-dwelling species: the red-throated ant-tanager and orange-billed sparrow, which occur in the interior of lowland rainforest. Neither bird is adept at reaching outward or downward from its perch for prey. The sparrow, in fact, has such long legs and is so incompetent at reaching down that it prefers to leave its perch, drop to the ground first and then jump up to grab a fruit. These two species, as might be expected, feed mostly on the more accessible axillary fruits, which are commoner inside the forest. Neither bird is able to efficiently pluck berries positioned at the ends of branches. Because fruit displayed in the terminal position on shrubs and treelets is by far the most common configuration in clearings and along forest edges, these birds are effectively excluded from these habitats.

Airplane designers have developed different wing shapes to suit the purposes of planes as diverse as gliders, jet fighters and stunt planes. The wings of birds are equally varied to suit different purposes. Each shape reflects an evolutionary compromise of the many behavioral and environmental factors that the bird encounters. The differences are particularly noticeable between birds of open areas and forest dwellers. For instance, aerial-feeding flycatchers and swallows have long, narrow wings for fast and efficient flight. Small forest birds tend to have shorter, more rounded wings than their open-country allies. This shape increases maneuverability and acceleration at the expense of speed and efficiency. Other differences can be traced to the way in which birds forage.

Tanagers and honeycreepers have short, strong legs that make them good reachers. They also have proportionally much longer and narrower wings than most forest flycatchers. With their longer wings, tanagers sacrifice maneuverability and acceleration but gain an advantage in their ability to sally for fruits located in hard-to-reach places. Long wings are also more efficient for long-distance flights, which reduce commuting costs between fruiting trees and enable the tanagers to travel in mixed-species flocks composed mostly of other similar-sized fruit-eating birds. These flocks often travel very rapidly through the forest canopy or between emergent rainforest trees.

Some tyrannulets that eat only fruit have short, rounded wings that serve them well for hovering but are inefficient for covering long distances. The golden-faced tyrannulet, which is found at lower elevations in the Andes from Venezuela to Peru, exemplifies this trade-off in wing anatomy. With its short wings, it is unable to keep up for long with the fast-moving flocks of fruit-eating tanagers and honeycreepers. Instead, it finds most of its food in a relatively small area of the rainforest canopy by visiting clusters of mistletoes and epiphytic plants and hovering to pluck their small berries.

Large birds that aren't able to hover efficiently may use other foraging techniques to reach fruit that is suspended in the open away from foliage. Three large fruit-eating birds that occur together in lower Central America—the purple-throated fruitcrow, slaty-tailed trogon and collared aracari—have very different wing shapes that illustrate the dramatically different techniques that may be used by birds to capture hard-to-reach fruits.

The fruitcrow, with the broadest wings of the three, swoops up and, with wings extended, grabs a fruit without stopping. The trogon banks up steeply, stalls with its wings outstretched and grabs a fruit while momentarily suspended in mid-air. Its small wings do not permit a slow gliding approach, like that of the fruitcrow, but deep slots between the flight feathers of the outstretched wing add extra lift as the bird angles steeply upward and begins to pause in front of a fruit.

The trogon's wing slotting works much like the slots on an airplane, which increase the lift at critically slow speeds. Slotted wings, for example, are often used on bush planes that have to operate from very short runways. The increased lift enables them to get airborne even at very slow speeds. The trogon also has an unusually large tail that it spreads wide at the moment of the stall. The tail helps the bird to slow down and to control the point at which the stall occurs.

The aracari, on the other hand, simply plucks fruit while it remains perched, using its long toucan bill as deftly as a surgeon uses forceps. With its heavy body and small wings, the aracari has to fly faster than the others to stay airborne, and it lands on a branch with a relatively high impact. Aracaris are usually seen in groups, and in flight they tend to go in a straight line—one after the other, from one tree to the next. Their high body weight in relation to wing surface results in a sacrifice of maneuverability, and aracaris are unable to take fruit in flight.

Common piping-guans illustrate yet another solution to the problem of reaching hard-to-get fruit. Widespread in Amazonian forests, these primitive-looking turkeylike birds are much too clumsy to take fruit in the air. Furthermore, they are too heavy to perch on the tips of branches, and their bills are short. But guans compensate for all of these shortcomings by having a long, flexible neck and great reaching ability. Once a suitable fruiting tree is located, guans tend to settle in and make themselves at home for hours or even days at a time. Their lack of mobility reduces foraging costs, but because of their sedentary ways, guans sacrifice diversity in their diet and have to put up with more unripe or low-quality fruits than other fruit-eating birds.

The experiments of Moermond and Denslow also reveal some hidden costs associated with each foraging method—costs that can affect the quality of fruit a bird chooses. The slaty-tailed trogon, which takes all of its fruit by stalling, eats only ripe fruit. The aracari, on the other hand, is not averse to occasionally eating unripe fruit. The difference between these two species is significant because it suggests that, for the trogon, there is a high expenditure of energy associated with each fruit that it eats, so every fruit should be of high quality. The aracari, by virtue of its long reach, expends little energy to pluck fruits. It has a low cost associated with each fruit it eats, but it pays a higher flight cost than other fruit eaters when flying from one tree to another. Therefore, the aracari can well afford to eat unripe fruits—indeed it may be obliged to do so—because, like reaching for another appetizer at a party, the food may be of low value but little effort is expended to obtain it once the aracari is in the tree.

We may not see much beauty in the twiggy legs of a bird. In fact, we rarely see much of their legs (what we see is the bare tarsus, which is technically a part of the foot), but legs, like wings and bills, influence the way in which fruits are procured. Ground birds usually have longer legs (tarsi) than do their close relatives that feed above-ground, but long, strong legs do not necessarily equip a bird for feeding efficiently on fruit.

Temperate-breeding *Catharus* thrushes, such as the Swainson's and gray-cheeked, have long legs that serve them well for hopping on the ground. Both species forage mostly on or near the ground inside the rainforest when they are on their wintering grounds. But prior to their northward migration, they turn heavily to fruit to fatten up for their long flight. Their long legs make reaching out or down for fruit difficult, so these thrushes must obtain most of the fruit by leaping up and snatching it or hovering and plucking it. Their jumping and fluttering in fruiting trees and their habit of concentrating in areas of superabundant fruit make them more conspicuous at this time of year and helps explain why these birds usually seem most common in northern South America just prior to their migration.

There is a reciprocity between leg structure and feeding ability that is worth considering. When thrushes and other similar long-legged birds attempt to take fruit, they are forced to adopt methods of obtaining it that are compromised by opposing forces which facilitate foraging for insects. When watching a Swainson's thrush pluck fruits from a melastome bush or attempt to snatch a piece of the fruiting catkin of a *Cecropia* while in flight, I am struck by the awkwardness of their movements compared with those of a resident tanager, which seems to harvest the same fruits with the grace and precision of a ballet dancer. The thrush, however, eats primarily fruits for only a few weeks each year, while the tanager is tested for its fruit-harvesting ability year-round. And despite the thrush's apparent inefficiency, it is able to nearly double its weight by feeding mostly on fruit in the few weeks prior to its migration.

The range of feeding options available to quetzals and trogons is also restricted by the anatomy of their legs but for reasons quite the opposite of those that restrict the long- and strong-legged *Catharus* thrushes. A mere 3 to 4 percent of the total body weight of quetzals and trogons is leg muscle—less than a quarter of that of some tanagers and toucans. Trogons are so weak-legged that they may even be unable to execute an about-face on a branch without the assistance of their wings. It isn't hard to guess, then, that trogons have virtually no reaching ability at all—a limitation that forces them to obtain their fruit on the wing and generally in places where they have an unobstructed flight approach to the fruit.

Could trogons and quetzals live in the dense lower vegetation of the rainforest? Probably not because the habitat where a bird lives influences the anatomical options available to it, and both species need more space to execute their foraging maneuvers than is available in the understory. A parallel can be found among some tanagers examined by Moermond and Denslow. Large canopy tanagers, like the palm tanager and blue-gray tanager, have longer wings and more flight muscle but less leg muscle than their counterparts in low vegetation. Biologists have barely begun to examine relationships such as this, so we can only speculate that strong legs must help a bird hop and reach in thick vegetation near the ground, but in the canopy, long wings, which increase sallying ability and lower the costs of flying between trees, are favored.

In pondering such questions, we are reminded that whenever we see a diverse and colorful association of birds feeding together at fruiting trees, the species are not necessarily equal in their ability to harvest the banquet of fruit before them. The presence of so many fruit-eating birds in a wide range of families indicates that there have been many opportunities for specialization. As we look at a manakin or a tanager, its plumage sleek and sparkling as it perches momentarily on a sun-kissed rainforest branch, we may marvel at its beauty and energy, but we should also find satisfaction in pondering the more intangible relationships between bodily form and ecological function.

# A Good Song and Dance
## Alternative Life-Styles of Manakins and Cotingas

MANAKINS AND COTINGAS are among the most colorful birds in the Neotropics. Even in a world where color is commonplace, their brilliant plumages and often bizarre courtship rituals have attracted the attention of scientists and laymen alike since the days of Darwin and Humboldt. Today, more than a century and a half later, they have become the focus of intense behavioral and ecological research, and as a group, they are among the most coveted by legions of birders and naturalists who come from all over the planet to glimpse their fiery colors and strange antics in the rainforest.

There are more than 50 kinds of manakins and 75 cotingas, all found from southern Mexico to Argentina. Manakins are composed of several distinct ancestral lineages, though all of them are made up of birds that are small and chunky with rounded heads and large eyes. They are related by various anatomical features (for example, they have the second and third toe partly joined), but despite their shared anatomical features and similarity of shape, they often look different from each other.

Many male manakins are extraordinarily colorful; they are often black with various amounts of glistening red, blue, yellow, gold or white on the head, rump and underparts. The most colorful species perform eye-catching, high-energy courtship dances accompanied by a variety of unusual mechanical and vocal sounds.

Cotingas are more heterogeneous in appearance than manakins. The smallest ones are tinier than sparrows, but the largest—hulking fruit-crows and umbrellabirds—are larger than crows. Their plumages are equally unusual: some are pure white, some jet black and others sport a royal blue, purple, red and deep wine coloring so intense they seem electrified. Glistening feathers are found on many species, and some species are further ornamented with crests, wattles and dangling feathered pendulums.

As a whole, there is little of the uniformity in body shape and size that characterizes manakins, and cotingas are something of a taxonomic nightmare—some species have no obviously close ancestors. If their origins remain fuzzy, their brilliant colors and bizarre adornments are clear enough and certain to quicken the pulse of the most jaded traveler, for it would be difficult indeed not to admire a family with so many spectacular and colorful species.

The colors and courtship displays of manakins and cotingas are a manifestation of sexual selection, a theory proposed by Charles Darwin to account for the striking differences between males and females in some birds. Sexual selection is the process whereby some individuals—usually males—gain the right to mate with the opposite sex while others lose it. When access to one sex is restricted or limited in some way, competition increases. In general, the less access there is to one sex, the more intense the sexual selection becomes. Sexual selection produces the striking differences between males and females in species ranging from ducks and pheasants to bellbirds and manakins.

Today, scientists know that much of the diversity of social and sexual behavior in birds has an ecological basis. However, many questions concerning the nature of the interactions between males and of those between males and females are yet to be answered. Why, for example, have differences between males and females in plumage, display and vocal powers been carried to such extraordinary lengths in some species but not in others? Are such attributes as the fiery orange colors of a male cock-of-the-rock or the powerful vocal *bonk* call of a bellbird a manifestation of dominance among males? And if so, how does a male establish himself in a dominant position? Or, on the other hand, are all of the male's extra bells and whistles merely a good advertisement of his physical condition and breeding readiness to females that choose among a field of splendid competitors?

Although there are few definitive answers to these questions, scientists have discovered enough pieces of the puzzle to lay the outline of a fascinating story. The story begins deep inside steamy Guianan rainforests. There, male Guianan cocks-of-the-rock gather at traditional locations, largely hidden from the eyes of the world, and perform breathtakingly beautiful displays for the benefit of drab and unassuming females.

Guianan cocks-of-the-rock are among the showiest birds in the world—the male's brilliant orange color, circular crest and springy, filamentous back plumes are without equal in the New World Tropics. Few observers who see this bird are disappointed. If their rather stiff, formal displays lack the cuteness and exuberant spontaneity of manakins, this shortcoming is more than offset by the visual impact of the bird itself. Male cocks-of-the-rock shock you with color—they are breathtaking flames of orange amid cool greenness in the rainforest. Those who encounter one are often awestruck and stand frozen, staring into the golden eyes of a creature whose beauty seems to transcend mere mortality.

But females share little of this beauty. Lacking the male's bright colors and wiry plumes and with a very small crest, they seem instead like dull, misshapen copies of their gaudy mates. Groups of males assemble at the same place each morning and divide their time during the day between bouts of rather ritualized display and periods of resting or loafing near their display courts. This cluster of displaying males, called a lek, serves one and only one purpose—it is a rendezvous site where the males and females meet for sex. Usually leks are located in the vicinity of rocky outcrops and cliffs and are thus close to where the females nest, though occasionally females might nest as much as a kilometer away.

One lek assemblage in Surinam was studied by graduate student

Pepper Trail from Cornell University. Trail counted 55 permanent display courts, each belonging to a different male. Every male "owns" a small court, which he cleans of leaves and debris, and there he faithfully carries out his displays. In the most densely clustered central part of the lek, courts may be so close they almost touch. The males call and occasionally display all through the day, leaving only for a few minutes at a time to fill up on fruit from nearby trees.

The level of female attention to their displays waxes and wanes during the course of the day, but a female's arrival jump-starts every male to a feverish pitch. She is met with a spectacular greeting display of raucous crowing calls, and all of the males rush to their arenas and immediately begin a wing-fanning display. This is followed by a ritualistic posture display, in which the birds may remain frozen for a minute or more. Courts are often positioned so as to take advantage of stray beams of sunshine that reach the dark forest floor, and each male, when suitably illuminated in his court, is indeed an object of rare and extraordinary beauty.

Females perch well above the rigidly posturing males and observe their performances. Eventually, a female may join a male on his court, and if she is suitably impressed, she may stay a minute or two as the male continues his performance. Throughout his display, the male endeavors to keep his back turned to the female presumably to show off his colorful plumage and long filamentous feathers to best advantage.

Prior to copulation, the female may touch the male on the rump, perhaps signaling mating readiness. If the pair is not interrupted by rivals or by the bumbling arrival of an inept yearling male, copulation may ensue. Females often return one or more times, usually to the same male, before an egg is laid a day or two later. Thus ends the romantic involvement of the two sexes. Males are interested only in mating and take no part in nesting duties. As soon as a female leaves the lek, males turn their attention to other females.

Consider how different the courtship display of the cock-of-the-rock is from that of the white bellbird. Both species live in the same hilly lowland forests of the Guianan plateau—a vast region of rainforests, rocky outcrops and flat-topped tepui mountains that extend in a broad belt from the Guianas to eastern Colombia. Instead of tight clusters of birds on the forest floor, male white bellbirds gather in loose associations called exploded leks, where the birds may be separated by hundreds of yards, even half a mile. Bellbirds call from bare branches overlooking the canopy or from perches inside the forest. Although the white plumage and black nose-wattle of the bellbird are striking, bellbirds rely upon the power of their remarkable voices to advertise themselves. With their cavernous mouths held wide open, they utter a flat, clanging, two-noted call that is somewhat bell-like and loud enough to be heard up to a mile away. Males call persistently, even through the heat of the day, for months on end in an effort to attract mates.

The mating system of the saffron-crowned tyrant-manakin provides even greater contrast. These manakins live in the understory of the same Guianan forests as the cock-of-the-rock and the bellbird, but they have neither bright colors nor powerful voices. The dull olive-colored males have pale eyes and a small yellow crest that is usually concealed; little else distinguishes them. Males are well scattered in the middle story of the forest, though usually two or three birds call within earshot of each other. Their unremarkable display—a short upward jump accompanied by a twangy call—does little to enhance the overall performance of these drab and easily overlooked birds.

Why are the displays so different? Cocks-of-the-rock are extraordinarily beautiful birds, and their displays and calls are so conspicuous that they attract the attention of predators, no doubt at a far higher rate than do the calls and display of the drab little tyrant-manakin. Indeed, Pepper Trail, who spent hundreds of hours over a five-year period observing the Guianan cocks-of-the-rock, found that when the males were on leks, they spooked very easily. Trail witnessed ambushes by six species of bird-eating hawks at cock-of-the-rock leks, and at least four other raptors in the Surinam rainforest are capable of attacking displaying cocks-of-the-rock. Interestingly, he found predator attacks were somewhat more successful at small leks than at a very large one.

This suggested to Trail that increased safety is one possible explanation why species like cocks-of-the-rock prefer to cluster together in large leks. Because cocks-of-the-rock are most vulnerable when engaged in a display, there is an advantage to having many eyes available to watch for incoming predators.

The same argument may explain why noisy and conspicuous manakin displays are performed by males that cluster tightly together. Like the Guianan cocks-of-the-rock, these manakins display on or very close to the ground—a much riskier location for a colorful and noisy bird than the canopy. Bellbirds are conspicuous and noisy, too, but they apparently do not need to gather in dense groups because their displays are carried out mostly high in the canopy where their chances of being successfully attacked are much fewer than if they were low inside the forest.

The most basic mating strategy among birds is monogamy, in which a bird has only one mate during the breeding season. Two others— polygyny, in which a male mates with multiple females, and polyandry, where a female mates with several males—account for the remainder. Polygyny is especially common in manakins and cotingas; monogamy is much less common. A review of plumages and mating strategies sheds some light on the social organization of species in these families.

In about 15 species of manakins and a small number of cotingas, the males and females are nearly identical—they are quite dull and nondescript. In some species, the males are so similar to females that, unless they are calling or displaying, they are indistinguishable from females. These species often lack elaborate displays and form monogamous pair-bonds in which both sexes share in nesting duties.

Sometimes intense sexual selection is evident not by bright colors and plumage finery but by sheer vocal power. Hardly a visitor leaves the Amazon rainforest without an encounter with one of its most famous voices, the screaming piha's. These pihas are gray and thrush-sized with nothing extraordinary about their outward appearance. But their "plain Jane" appearance belies a remarkable voice. After a few low-pitched, throaty whistles, their heads jerk back violently once, then a second time as the bird belts out an ear-splitting, three-syllabled *we WEEEE-u*!

The forest is filled with screaming pihas—or so it seems from the center of the lek. But these extraordinary vocal powers are merely the tools of passion for the piha. Males impress females not with brilliant colors or dazzling displays but with their awesome sound production. Pound for pound, pihas may have among the most potent vocal machinery of any bird in the world. When a female piha visits the lek, decibel levels approach the threshold of pain, and most biologists would prefer to retire to a quieter corner of the rainforest. Yet we are reminded that a piha performance is the vocal equivalent of the finest manakin dance or the most spectacular cock-of-the-rock display. It doesn't matter if males and females look alike. Their universe is one in which sound production is everything and brilliant colors mean nothing.

The majority of manakins and cotingas are strikingly dimorphic—males are colorful or boldly patterned while females are drab and cryptically colored. In this group, polygyny is the predominant breeding system. But in a few species like pihas, it is voice, not color or display, that has evolved as the chief means of attracting females. In these species, polygyny is also the predominant breeding system. Pihas are not the exceptions they might seem to be. Rather, they are part of the general link between polygyny and bright colors, elaborate displays or a powerful voice that is well illustrated in manakins and cotingas.

About 88 percent of all manakins and nearly half of the cotingas have polygynous mating strategies—percentages that are much higher than the approximately 10 percent found in birds worldwide. Why is polygyny so much more common in these families? And why are some species monogamous and others polygynous? The answer has at least two parts. The first part has to do with the different "investments" the two sexes bring to the fertilization process. The second part has to do with the diet and foraging behavior of the species.

With regard to the investment that males and females make to fertilization, sperm are energetically cheap to produce, eggs are not. Thus a female may gain reproductive success through a conservative monogamous strategy that emphasizes protection of her eggs. On the other hand, a male may gain more through the polygynous spreading of his genes as widely as possible. Thus, every mating, at least potentially, brings these two opposing evolutionary forces into play.

Where monogamy predominates, competition between males for mates is not as strong as in polygynous breeding systems because a permanent pair-bond is formed, and there is little further opportunity for other males to compete for the female. In monogamous populations, there is little opportunity for either sex to monopolize several members of the opposite sex. Sexual selection for bright colors and elaborate displays is not strong, and in the majority of monogamous species, the sexes are relatively similar.

Contrast this with polygynous species, where promiscuous males fight and display intensely throughout each breeding season to win as many matings as possible. Competition is high, and any advantage, such as brighter colors, a more attractive display, a louder voice or larger body size, will result in more matings if it gives a male an edge over his competitors. In polygynous breeding systems, there is a real possibility that a few members of one sex (usually males) can limit the access of their competitors to mates. Consequently, in polygynous species, males are very often larger or more brightly colored than females or have some other attribute that helps their sexual success.

The contribution that a bird's diet brings to the evolution of monogamous or polygynous mating systems leads to the second part of the answer. Monogamous pairs predominate whenever food resources are widely scattered and hard to find, making it necessary for both parents to contribute to the care and feeding of their young. Most seabirds as well as raptors and insect-eating birds invest a substantial amount of their time simply searching for food. One parent is usually unable to locate enough food to feed both itself and the young.

The first evidence that polygyny might be related to a bird's diet was uncovered by David and Barbara Snow of the British Museum. Working in Trinidad in the 1960s, they became curious as to why polygynous mating systems were so prevalent in manakins and cotingas. Their discovery of a link between fruit-eating and nectar-eating birds and a polygynous life-style was instrumental in focusing attention on the foraging ecology of these and other tropical birds.

Tropical birds that eat mostly insects, as it turns out, are almost always monogamous. The reason is due to time budgets—fruit and nectar are easy to find and easy to harvest, and a bird subsisting on these items can find enough to eat in a very short period of time. Male manakins spend only about 10 percent of their time foraging for berries and small fruits each day; the rest is spent at their display courts.

Insects, on the other hand, are usually cryptic and difficult to find. They hide in all kinds of places, and hunting them is time-consuming. Simply put, fruits are designed to be eaten, insects attempt to avoid being eaten. Searching for insects occupies so much of a bird's time and energy that there is little free time left for displays. Tropical birds that eat insects spend an average of 60 to 70 percent of each day just finding enough insects to feed themselves. When there are nestlings to feed, the efforts of both sexes are needed.

The Snows argued that, because of these differences, only females from predominately fruit-eating or nectar-eating species can feed their young alone. Males may then become unessential to the nesting process, perhaps even liabilities if they are too brightly colored or use too much of the female's food resources. Thus emancipated from nesting duties, males may become sexual rivals, turning to promiscuous behavior and spending nearly all of their time engaging in displays to attract females.

Emancipation of males from nesting duties may depend upon more than simply a switch in diet to fruit or nectar. Some hole-nesting species, such as quetzals and toucans, are largely fruit-eating, yet polygyny has not evolved in any of these species. The reason may have to do with the choice of nest sites. Cavities are generally safe nest sites, but both parents may be needed to defend hole-nests against predators or would-be usurpers. Likewise, large forest pigeons are almost wholly fruit-eating but remain steeped in monogamy. Pigeons, however, are unique among birds in secreting crop milk to their young—a behavior that may require the contribution of both parents for the young to receive adequate nourishment.

The ability of females to carry large amounts of food to nestlings, a factor often overlooked by biologists, may also play a role in male emancipation. Female manakins and cotingas, as well as fruit-eating *Pipromorpha* flycatchers, carry fruit in their throat and stomach, as well as in their bill, and regurgitate the mashed fruit to their young. Because of the large quantities they can carry, these females need only infrequently visit the nest. This, in turn, draws less attention to the nest site, which helps to protect the young from predators.

The details of manakin and cotinga mating displays vary considerably. In a few species, males display alone or are only vaguely clumped in certain areas where they give simple calls from somewhere inside the forest. In a larger number of cases, males are loosely aggregated. Although the males are still relatively dispersed, such exploded leks function as a single display and mating unit, offering females the opportunity to choose from among the various suitors.

Much better known to scientists and laymen alike are the leks in which many performing male birds are gathered close together. These leks are attended by manakins of the genus *Manacus*, and they are the species that usually come to mind when the word manakin is mentioned. They make up, however, only a minority of all manakins.

At several popular destinations in Costa Rica and Trinidad, thousands of visitors annually are treated to the spectacular vocal and visual antics of white-bearded and white-collared manakins, both members of the genus *Manacus*. A few hours spent watching a lek of these charming little performers at the peak of their display is an unforgettable experience. A lek may contain up to 70 males, though usually there are far fewer. Each male owns a circular little display court on the forest floor where he clears away the leaves and performs his displays and dances. In the prized center positions, the courts may be so close together that they nearly touch, and the intensity of activity is almost overwhelming at times. The arrival of a female always sets off a frantic barrage of display, accompanied by buzzing and snapping sounds. It sounds to a passerby as if several packages of small firecrackers were just tossed into the thicket.

Most often manakins perform in small groups located well above the ground or even in the forest subcanopy. Golden-headed manakins are common in lowland tropical forests in South America, and they have a

GROUPS OF MALE WHITE-BEARDED MANAKINS
GATHER AT LEKS AND PUT ON DISPLAYS TO
ATTRACT FEMALES.

fascinating variety of displays. A long swooping flight may begin 50 yards away from their perch, but typically, the first indication that a display flight is in progress is when an observer hears the accelerating stream of buzzy notes emitted as the bird swoops back to its main perch. A complex array of side-stepping, hops, flips and wing raises are performed on favorite high perches, and these, too, can be difficult to observe.

The most complex and evoluntionarily advanced displays are performed by four species of *Chiroxiphia* manakins. The males—velvety black with sky blue backs and crimson caps—differ mainly in the length or shape of their central tail feathers. *Chiroxiphia* males form permanent male-male attachments and cooperate to attract females—a highly unusual arrangement because males are usually intense rivals rather than cooperating partners. Two, sometimes three, males participate in coordinated dances at a small court near the ground. In a common variation, they rapidly leap backward over each other—performing what looks much like a spinning cartwheel.

Apart from their fascinating dances, naturalists are interested in these birds because only the dominant male mates. Why would a subordinate male cooperate if he has little chance of copulation? Mercedes Foster, who studied one of these species, the long-tailed manakin, in Costa Rica, believes the subdominant males aren't as altruistic as they might seem. There are chances for stolen copulations, and eventually they may replace the dominant male. This long period of cooperation is, therefore, more beneficial than performing alone, when there is probably no chance of attracting a female.

Cotingas include species that display alone and others that gather in groups. A few large cotingas—umbrellabirds and the red-ruffed fruit-crows—gather in spectacular lek assemblages in canopy trees. When displaying, they bob and bow and utter low-pitched, hollow calls that sound like someone blowing across the top of an open soft-drink bottle. Several species in the genus *Cotinga* are brilliantly colored but perform their displays alone and with almost no vocal or mechanical sounds. The displays consist of primarily long, circular flights, occasionally accompanied by a few faint mechanical sounds produced by the wings.

That leks have evolved at all might seem remarkable when we consider that in most leks, only one or two dominant males, usually those that occupy a central position within the lek cluster, do most of the mating. Lower-ranking males only infrequently get the opportunity to mate, and some may never mate at all. At the Guianan cock-of-the-rock lek studied by Pepper Trail, for example, he found that a single male obtained 30 percent of all copulations in one season; fully 57 percent of males passed the entire breeding season with no copulations at all. Even more highly skewed mating relationships have been reported in white-bearded manakins by the Snows.

Why do males cluster if competition for mates is so intense? Why not display away from the group? The answers to these questions also relate, at least in part, to diet and the way that the birds forage.

Jack Bradbury of the University of California at San Diego suggests that the evolution of lek behavior can be traced to the availability of females, which is, in turn, related to what the birds eat and how they forage. He argues that leks form when females forage widely for food and overlap extensively with each other. This occurs among fruit-eating birds when they travel to a distant fruiting tree. Males that gather to display in certain areas, known as hotspots, thus have the opportunity to catch the attention of many of the wide-ranging females. Hotspots may develop because a particularly rich distribution of fruiting trees is in an area or because nesting sites are readily available. Bradbury's hypothesis emphasizes that it is the location of the lek that is important, and that it is the females that choose the males.

Bruce Beeler and Mercedes Foster, who have studied birds-of-paradise and manakins in the field, believe that Bradbury's hypothesis falls short because it does not take into account the ability of dominant males to control their own destiny by controlling the behavior of other males. They argue that some males, which they dub hotshots, are more successful than other males, and the success of a few dominant birds also attracts less successful males to the area where they bide their time waiting for the chance to move up in the hierarchy. Hotshots, through both physical and psychological means, control subordinate males. This hypothesis places emphasis upon interactions between males and suggests that females, by default, simply select the most dominant male.

If dominant males effectively control the female's choice, what does a female get out of the bargain? In his studies of the Guianan cock-of-the-rock, Pepper Trail found that when females visit a lek to mate, they show distinct preferences for males with central courts. Because females visit a number of courts but prefer to mate only with the dominant males in the center, Trail believed that the females do actively discriminate.

What the females get, then, is a good song and dance and, presumably, the best mate available. By relying upon the males to jockey for positions of dominance and sort things out among themselves, the females need only choose from a small pool of males that have already proved themselves. A young or low-ranking male may also benefit by joining a hotshot male, even if its chances of mating are low. Over time, a low-ranking apprentice bird may gain experience and move up through the hierarchy. And by virtue of his association with a high-ranking male in a high-traffic area, he may obtain more copulations and thus be better off than if he were displaying alone.

A dominance hierarchy also plays a functional role in maintaining order within a lek. Top males, by virtue of their ability to bully subordinates, usually without actually resorting to physical violence, provide a stabilizing influence in leks. In small leks, where linear relationships are quickly established, each male soon becomes familiar with his neighbors, and the level of disruption and overt aggression is low. As the number of participants at a lek increases, the potential exists for more disruption as competing males jockey for position.

Exploded leks may represent a logical conclusion to the chaos of excessive disruptions. If law and order breaks down within a tight lek, or if it is never achieved, males may adjust their spacing more widely to avoid constant harassment and disruption of their displays and mating attempts. Remaining clumped within a general area of the forest but keeping a safe distance from competitors—the equivalent of an exploded lek—appears to be the modus operandi for the majority of tropical lek-forming species, including manakins, cotingas and a number of flycatchers. Mating success is probably less skewed in favor of one or two dominant males in exploded leks than at tight leks, where one or two males consistently control most matings.

Why don't males help females rather than gathering in lekking groups and casting their genetic fates to single unassisted females? This may, in part, be because they are not critical to the nesting effort and because they are unable to control something in the environment that is important to females. Nest sites and food are crucial to nesting success, but males may be unable to monopolize these resources and force females to stay on a territory. Fruit, because of its unpredictable distribution in the rainforest, is a resource that is almost impossible for a male to hoard. Thus a male may have little to offer a female except his genetic contribution, and leks, rather than monogamous pairings, probably offer females the best opportunity to mate with a successful male.

If males are unnecessary to the nesting effort, then females must be able to successfully rear the young alone. Small clutch sizes reduce the need for male help at the nest, but this isn't sufficient by itself. Nesting success in lowland tropical rainforests is generally low because of the large number of nest-robbing predators. Snakes, monkeys, opossums, squirrels and coatimundis as well as caracaras, hawks and toucans find and rob the nests of most tropical birds. Small clutches appear to be largely a response to high predation rates, for a female that loses one or two eggs can replace them at far less cost than a female that loses four or five. In view of such high nest losses, males may not help because their presence only increases the chance of predators finding the nest.

About a third of all cotingas are found not in hot lowland rainforests but in the cold upper-elevation cloud forests of the Andes. While male parental care is unnecessary, perhaps even a liability in the lowlands, a dramatic turn of events occurs in the Andes. There, monogamy prevails and the clutch size increases to three eggs. The pairs build substantial, well-insulated nests, and males no longer display in leks but instead form permanent pair-bonds and help their mates with nesting activities.

This remarkable turnaround in behavior is linked to some important environmental changes. There are fewer predators at higher elevations, so females can produce a larger clutch without so much risk of losing it, and there may be less dependence strictly upon fruit. Furthermore, the increased thermal demands of nestlings at high elevations may necessitate a warmer nest. Although well-insulated nests require more effort to build, this cost is perhaps justified by a higher probability of nesting success. These differences appear to have tipped the balance in favor of a monogamous breeding strategy for cotingas in the Andes.

Studying the evolution of social and sexual behavior in manakins and cotingas has led modern biologists down a serpentine path of discovery that involves complex interrelationships between plumages, displays, diets and behaviors. More secrets await discovery, and more riddles will be untangled before all the pieces of the puzzle fall into place. But whenever we watch manakins dance or listen to pihas scream, we should be reminded of what a remarkable opportunity it is to attend such a first-class song-and-dance routine at one of nature's most fascinating theaters of evolution.

# *Territories or Traplines?*
## Hummingbird Foraging Strategies

SOONER OR LATER, almost everyone who visits the American Tropics will see a flowering tree buzzing with hummingbirds. At the height of flowering, a large tree may attract up to a dozen species of hummingbirds and scores of individuals—each an argumentative fleck of color proclaiming its rights to flowers and constantly chasing its neighbors. But what happens to this mad blur of activity when the flowers fade and the nectar disappears? Wondering about the intertwined fates of these energetic players in the rainforest drama and the flowers they so hotly contest has led naturalists into a fascinating, if miniature, world of mobile life-styles and high metabolisms.

Two ecologists, Gary Stiles and Larry Wolf, observed a flowering tree in northwestern Costa Rica a number of years ago and began wondering about the costs and benefits of such extreme territorial behavior among hummingbirds. Their observations were made during the long dry season when there were very few other flowers available, and they soon found that individual hummingbirds divided the tree into a series of mini-territories. Each bird generally held sway over a portion of the tree, and by constant vigilance, it was able to enjoy more or less exclusive use of the flowers growing there.

Whether male or female, each individual had to constantly fight off intruders, but the advantage of defending such a valuable food resource seemed clear. There weren't many other flowers around, and faced with a shortage of nectar, the birds had few alternatives—stay and fight, switch to insects or emigrate to another area.

The ones that Stiles and Wolf watched were the fighters, or territorialists as hummingbird biologists call them—those willing to risk a scuffle in order to have a few flowers all to themselves. Where were the others? Why didn't they visit these flowers? How do they cope with the varying abundance of flowers through the year? Such questions, which examine how tropical hummingbird communities are organized, are the theme of this chapter.

Nectar-feeding birds are found worldwide in tropical and some subtropical regions, though none rival the behavioral or physiological specializations of hummingbirds, nor have they evolved such close co-dependence with flowers. Their counterparts in Africa and Asia are the sunbirds, but only a few are closely associated with particular flowers. The Australian honeyeaters show even wider variation in their dependency on nectar; some are specialized, others rarely visit flowers. The majority of Australian flowers are of the brush type—a flat flower with a mass of protruding stamens easily pollinated by many kinds of birds, mammals, insects and bats. The lack of specificity in so many Australian flowers is unusual, but it may be a result of the dry, unpredictable climate. Where flower pollinators are nomadic and often unreliable, plants probably favor a flower that is accessible to as many kinds of pollinators as possible.

Neotropical bird-flower communities have developed differently from those in Australia, Asia and Africa. Hummingbirds are an important reason for the difference because they do not occur outside of the western hemisphere and they are most numerous and diverse in the neotropical region. Several other groups, among them honeycreepers, flower-piercers, bananaquits, some tanagers and icterids are locally important nectar feeders, but none is so numerically dominant from the lowland rainforest to Andean tree line as hummingbirds.

Some flower-piercers feed almost entirely on nectar but they are usually nectar thieves, hence parasites of hummingbird-flower systems. With sharp-pointed bills and inverted, U-shaped tongues, they poke tiny holes into the base of tubular flower corollas and drink the nectar without aiding the plants in pollination. The ubiquitous bananaquit, on the other hand, is a nectar-eating jack-of-all-trades that is a legitimate pollinator of some plants, such as those with brushlike stamens, but also a notorious nectar thief of some others.

Oropendolas, caciques and orioles often feed on nectar, but they also eat many other kinds of food. Biologists call them opportunists because they take advantage of brief bursts of flowering, especially at large trees, but quickly switch to other foods when nectar runs low.

On a scale of evolutionary time, oropendolas, caciques and orioles are relative newcomers in their associations with plant-pollinator systems. Biologists support this claim by pointing to the bird's ranges, which usually don't correspond very well with those of the plants whose nectar they drink. Their geographical distributions tend to be different from those of hummingbirds too—an indication that they complement hummingbird pollination systems rather than that they evolved with them. Orioles, for example, are most effective as pollinators in dry tropical regions where hummingbirds are scarce. In humid areas, caciques and oropendolas often concentrate in river-edge woodland, especially where there are *Erythrina* trees.

The behavior of these birds resembles that of Old World nectar-eating species in that they tend to concentrate in groups at certain large flowering trees. Caciques and oropendolas can exhaust the nectar resources of a large tree quickly, and then they go elsewhere. By moving among successive trees, these large tropical blackbirds are better cross-pollinators of large trees than hummingbirds, who tend to divide up the tree into numerous little territories. Consequently, by remaining there until flowering ceases, hummingbirds may contribute little to the pollination of some large flowering trees.

Hummingbirds are highly specialized for nectar feeding but they vary tremendously in their behavior and dependence upon nectar and in their degree of specialization upon flowers. You can get an idea of just how diverse the family is by examining a few pictures in a modern guide to the birds of a country such as Colombia or Venezuela. One could hardly fail to be amazed by the range of body sizes, bill lengths and tail shapes among hummingbirds. There are coquettes no bigger than the end of your thumb and hulking sapphirewings as big as sparrows. While many hummingbirds prove to be excellent, if unwitting, pollinators for plants, others have adapted more unsavory tactics in their insatiable thirst for nectar, turning to petty thievery without transferring any pollen for the plant.

The purple-crowned fairy and its nearly identical Amazonian cousin, the black-eared fairy, are co-conspirators in this nefarious business of stealing nectar. Dressed in sparkling green and immaculate white and delightfully impish, they dart from flower to flower, stabbing the base of each corolla from the outside with their sharp-pointed bills. In doing this, they are able to sip nectar through the tiny hole they make without disturbing or brushing against the pollen-bearing stamens inside. In the Andes, the wedge-billed hummingbird, another nectar bandit armed with a sharp-pointed bill, steals nectar from cloud-forest flowers in the same way.

But why bother to steal in the first place when many flowers can be probed directly? Pollination is, after all, only an incidental by-product of a hummingbird's activities, and it requires no extra energy output. The answer is analogous to a burglar who learns to pick locks on doors. He now has more places available to burglarize. Hummingbirds that learn to steal nectar have a greater range of flowers at their disposal. The nectar produced by flowers with very long or curved corollas can only be reached by hummingbirds whose bills fit these flowers. These birds are almost invariably the legitimate pollinators of these flowers and, other hummers, because of improper bill shape or length, are denied access to the nectar within. The only other way to reach the nectar is to steal it by poking a hole in the flower from the outside.

Nectar thievery takes many forms, and it isn't always the flower that is victimized. Hummingbirds regularly burglarize each other's nectar supplies using a variety of sly tactics. I once watched an enormous concentration of hummingbirds in a flowering *Inga* tree in central Colombia. *Ingas* are often planted for shade trees on Colombia's famous coffee plantations, and their brushlike flowers produce great quantities of nectar that is attractive to hummingbirds. This particular tree was being contested by perhaps 50 individuals of 11 species of hummingbirds, each bird an ill-humored blur of pugnacity. The dazzling little indigo-capped hummingbird was one of the commonest ones that morning. While dozens of these birds carved up the tree into a series of hotly contested little fiefdoms, bickered constantly over the sizes and shapes of their miniature territories and readjusted their holdings almost hourly as nectar supplies ebbed and flowed, a tiny coquette sneaked in and began to feed. It resembled a bee more than a bird, and its slow weaving flight made it look as if it were suspended by a string—a behavior that only added to the bee illusion. For a moment, it fed unnoticed. Then, the owner of the territory in which it was feeding spotted the coquette and attacked immediately.

Coquettes are too small to win battles in a contest for nectar, but their peculiar, floating flight makes them agile fliers and elusive targets. They are adept at sidestepping a confrontation—a tactic that often wins extra feeding time. When the harassment becomes unbearable, they simply leave. The coquette's strategy, then—dubbed territorial parasitism—is one of thievery, too, though it steals not from flowers but from other hummingbirds. With a body too small to do battle and a bill too short and straight to be closely adapted to specific flowers, this little imp survives by maintaining a low profile and filching nectar wherever it finds flowers unguarded.

Taxonomists divide hummingbirds into two broad subfamilies: hermits and typical hummingbirds. The division is unequal because typical hummingbirds comprise nearly 90 percent of all hummingbirds. Nevertheless, it draws attention to two very different ways in which hummingbird communities are organized.

The hermits and their barbthroat and sicklebill relatives are, on the whole, birds of the understory in humid tropical forests—the kind of forest we usually think of as tropical rainforest. Their numbers diminish rapidly at higher elevations, and none are found much higher than about 6,000 feet in the Andes. They don't occur at all in dry areas except within tall humid forest along creeks and rivers. Their northern and southern distribution extends only to the limits of humid tropical forest—about as far north as southern Veracruz, Mexico, and as far south as

LONG-TAILED HERMITS ARE FREQUENT
VISITORS TO PASSION FLOWER VINES IN THE
RAINFOREST UNDERSTORY.

southern Amazonia and southeastern Brazil.

If you walk through a tropical forest, one of the first hummingbirds you are likely to meet is the long-tailed hermit or one of its close relatives. Especially if you wear something red, you are certain to be accosted by a curious hermit, who, mistaking you for a flower, will dash up and hover momentarily in your face as it takes a good close look. Soon recognizing its error, it will dash off just as quickly with a squeak and a wiggle of its long, white tail. That is the last you are likely to see of it on your walk because hermits, unlike many typical hummingbirds, are not territorial. They visit scattered flowers in the forest understory, much as a trapper might run his traps in the north woods. These hummingbirds are here one moment and then gone in a twinkling the next to feed at some distant flower or to glean insects from beneath a leaf that has momentarily attracted their attention.

Traplining nectar was first studied in large tropical bees. Later, it was discovered that hermit hummingbirds employ a similar strategy when visiting flowers. Now, biologists have identified two kinds of traplining behavior in hummingbirds—high-reward and low-reward. As the names imply, high-reward trapliners seek flowers with high volumes of nectar and high sugar concentrations, while low-reward species visit insect-pollinated flowers or those with small amounts of nectar.

Of all hummingbirds, hermits are the quintessential high-reward trapliners. They fly long distances to visit flowers with enough nectar to make their trips worthwhile. For their efforts, they are compensated by a large nectar reward at each stop. Hermit-visited flowers are usually not guarded because they are scattered over an area much too large to defend. Sometimes flowers are hundreds of meters apart, and a single feeding route may take a hermit through more than a kilometer of tropical forest. A premium is placed on the ability to locate widely scattered flowers as they come into bloom, and at this hermits excel for they are fast-flying and very curious. This explains a hermit's almost obsessive preoccupation with investigating every new flower along its route. And traplining also explains why, on our tropical walk, the first hummingbird we are likely to encounter is a hermit. Their wide-ranging movements and insatiable curiosity make it all the more likely that they will find us in the rainforest—perhaps mistaking us for a huge flower—than will a sedentary hummingbird defending a small territory.

Hermits are the exclusive pollinators of many understory herbs and vines, but they never visit canopy flowers and they only infrequently visit forest edges. To appreciate why hummingbird traplining behavior is confined mostly to understory plants, it is necessary to look at the environment where these plants grow.

In the rainforest, understory plants are insulated from daily and seasonal changes in temperature and desiccation that occur in the canopy, but the amount of light reaching the understory is very small. This makes it difficult for understory plants to store enough energy to produce large numbers of flowers. What understory plants do best is produce just a few flowers at a time, often spread throughout the year. This perfectly suits the nonmigratory hermits and other trapliners that reap the benefits of a reliable and long-term nectar supply.

At very high elevations in the Andes, a number of hummingbirds, including the sword-billed hummingbird and several starthroats and Incas, often behave much like hermits in lowland forests. At these elevations, traplining isn't necessarily confined to vines and herbaceous understory plants because the forests are usually short and grow on very steep slopes, where distinctions between canopy and understory zones become blurred. Here plants find growing conditions difficult—in this case due more to cold temperatures than low light—and very low but sustained flower production is a better bet for keeping hummingbird pollinators around than an occasional, massive burst of flowering.

The flowers of understory plants usually have long, curved tubular corollas that perfectly fit the long, curved bills of the hermits that visit them. Because these kinds of flowers are difficult to use by typical hummingbirds with straight bills, hermits suffer little competition. Among hermits themselves, one typically finds only two to four species coexisting, though in western Amazonia, five or six species may occur together. When so many species coexist, differences in body and bill size and in choice of microhabitat help them avoid direct competition.

One of the most extreme examples of specialization is found in sickle-bill hummingbirds. Sporting bills that are curved downward a full 90 degrees, these bizarre-looking relatives of hermits are able to extract nectar from certain *Heliconia* (wild plantain) flowers that are so curved in shape that their nectar cannot be extracted by any other bird.

The result of a long period of co-ocurrence between hermits and their food plants is that flowers pollinated by these birds have often evolved delicate adjustments in floral shape and in the position of reproductive parts to minimize pollination mistakes. Ecologist Gary Stiles observed that among nine species of hermit-pollinated *Heliconia* in the lowlands of eastern Costa Rica, each flower and its reproductive parts are shaped in such a way that when a hummingbird visits the flower, the pollen grains are dusted onto only one part of the bird. One plant deposits pollen on the forehead, another one on the crown, a third on the throat or bill and so on. In each case, such precise placement of pollen helps ensure that pollination is successful when the bird visits another flower of the same species. In one unusual species of *Heliconia,* a bird must rotate its head at an angle of more than 90 degrees, or nearly upside down, in order to insert its bill. In doing so, pollen is placed on the chin and base of the bill, thereby reducing the possibility that its pollen will be deposited later on the wrong kind of flower.

Hummingbirds familiar to North Americans belong to the subfamily known collectively as typical hummingbirds, or Trochilinae. They also comprise most of the species at such tropical hotspots as Monteverde in Costa Rica, the Asa Wright Nature Center in Trinidad, and the Itatiaia National Park in southeastern Brazil, and practically all of the species in the Andes. In contrast to hermits, typical hummingbirds are most diverse in the tropical highlands, especially between about 2,000 and 6,000 feet elevation. Remarkably, many thrive in the cold high Andes, even at tree line or above. The buffy hummingbird and a few others prosper in tropical deserts, and goldenthroats live in very seasonal tropical grasslands. All of these are habitats where hermits hardly occur at all. In rainforests, this group of hummingbirds is most numerous in the canopy rather than in the understory, where hermits predominate.

Why typical hummingbirds have radiated into so many habitats while hermits remain almost exclusively birds of humid forest is a question best explored by examining the flowers that each group pollinates. Hermits are usually associated with large terrestrial herbs such as *Heliconias* and gingers. These plants are commonest in lowland rainforests, but hardly any grow at high elevations on tropical mountains, nor do they occur to any extent in dry habitats. Their chief pollinators, the hermits, show a strikingly similar range distribution. Only a couple of hermits even reach subtropical elevations in the Andes, and they do so only in cloud-forest habitats where broad-leaved vines and terrestrial herbs persist.

In Central America and northern South America, there is only a single widespread *Heliconia* that occurs in dry or open areas. As might be expected, it is not pollinated by hermits. On the other hand, typical hummingbirds are most often associated with various dicot families such as shrubs in the Rubiaceae family and epiphytes in the Ericaceae and Onagraceae families. Plants in these and other families contain many species adapted for pollination by typical straight-billed hummingbirds, and these plant families are especially common in cooler mountain regions. The distribution of the two hummingbird subfamilies, then, is somewhat determined by the plant groups with which they have become most closely associated.

To naturalists familiar only with hummingbirds in North America, the diversity of hummingbird sizes and shapes in the Tropics might come as a surprise. Even the similar-looking hermits come in many sizes, and the heaviest hummingbirds are more than ten times the weight of the lightest ones. Bill variation is also amazing. There are hummingbirds with very long bills, some with very short bills and many with bills that are straight, curved down, sickle-shaped or, occasionally, curved up. In one, the rare tooth-billed hummingbird, its bill has dozens of tiny serrations that resemble miniature teeth.

All of this is exciting to scientists who look at bill and body shapes—the morphology of a bird—as an indication of possible feeding specializations. This incredible variety of sizes and shapes, many of which seem positively bizarre to humans, enable hummingbirds to drink nectar from a universe of flower varieties that is almost beyond comprehension.

While conducting studies on hummingbirds in Costa Rica and Trinidad, ecologists Peter Feinsinger and Robert Colwell noticed that, among the different hummingbird communities they were studying, foraging behaviors and body and bill shapes tended to recur in each community. This suggested to them that hummingbird communities might be organized along certain basic principles.

Among the roles Feinsinger and Colwell identified were species that behaved as high-reward trapliners, low-reward trapliners, territorialists, generalists and territory parasites. Bill and body shape generally guide each species toward one or another of these roles. But hummingbirds often switch from one role to another as nectar availability changes or as the hummingbird community changes.

The most well-known practitioners of high-reward traplining are the hermits, though they are not the only hummers to forage in this manner. The territorialists are usually easy to spot, too, because they zealously guard their flowers against all comers. Anyone who has stood on the porch of the Asa Wright Nature Center in Trinidad and watched the hummingbird show can tell you that the white-chested emerald and copper-rumped hummingbird are preeminent territorialists for they spend most of their days arguing with other hummingbirds and attempting to oust them from the shrubs and feeders that surround the house. Both species belong to the genus *Amazilia*—a large, "working class" group of tropical hummingbirds of average proportions. Almost all of them behave as territorialists in their respective communities.

Low-reward trapliners are harder to pick out. These small, mostly short-billed hummers are unable to win fights with the larger territorial species, and they lack the long and often decurved bills needed to be high-reward trapliners. Consequently, they rarely have access to the rich patches of flowers defended by territorial species.

This group, which includes the *Chlorostilbon* emeralds and many small, middle-elevation hummers, concentrates on scattered flowers that are normally insect-pollinated and hence have only small amounts of nectar. It may seem like members of this group are walking an energetic tightrope because of the low quality and scattered nature of their flowers, but their small size and low energy requirements make it possible for them to operate quite well in an environment where nectar rewards are low. Further, most of these birds can change roles easily, becoming generalists or even territory parasites when the need arises, and all of them capture small insects as well.

Hummingbirds that behave as generalists are usually medium to small species that sporadically visit scattered flowers or clumps of undefended nectar-rich flowers. Opportunistically, they steal from patches of flowers belonging to territorial species, so their rather loosely defined role lets them take advantage of many situations.

Generalist hummingbirds often show up at large flowering trees, along with territorialists and territory-parasites. But few large canopy trees are specifically adapted for pollination by hummingbirds. At these trees, hummingbirds are usually freeloaders, staying for only a few days until the nectar runs out. They are either ineffective pollinators compared to bees and other insects because once they find a tree they tend to remain there, or else they are outright thieves of the nectar of these trees. In either case, the tree's pollination strategy is largely circumvented.

Small hummingbirds such as woodstars, coquettes and thornbills may behave as territory parasites, but they readily switch to the role of generalists or low-reward trapliners too. Some large species also behave as territory parasites, but rather than sneaking in to filch nectar in an unguarded corner of a territory as a coquette might try to do, they boldly crash a territorial species' flower patch, often doing so with impunity because of their large size.

White-necked jacobins, mangos and scaly-breasted hummingbirds all practice this marauding technique. Because of their large size, these big hummingbird bullyboys are able to ignore the efforts of smaller territorialists to drive them away, and they generally go pretty much where they please. All of these marauders also spend a good deal of time catching flying insects, so they play a dual role in the community. The insect-catching technique of mangos and jacobins is so characteristic that the behavior has been nicknamed helicoptering—a reference to their habit of hovering for long periods of time high in the air in large open areas or above trees as they catch small flying insects.

But consider some of the problems of being a big hummingbird. At best, most flowers have only a drop or two of nectar, and because large hummingbirds need lots of nectar, they must seek out especially nectar-rich patches of flowers and feed only at plants that produce the most nectar. Usually they can't afford to feed at flowers with small amounts of nectar because they can't extract enough from each flower to cover the cost of hovering. This explains why large hummers often tolerate small species feeding within their territories even though they could easily drive them out. In the mountains of Costa Rica, the magnificent hummingbird feeds at a few kinds of nectar-rich flowers, which it defends against others of its kind. At the same time, it allows small species, such as the volcano hummingbird, to enter its territory and feast with impunity on a variety of flowers that it can't use.

Because nectar abundance is so variable, hummingbird communities can change quickly. Bird checklists for middle elevations in the Andes may contain 30 species of hummingbirds; even arid regions may show 12 to 15 species. From various habitats around Monteverde, a well-studied cloud forest in Costa Rica, the list runs to more than 30 species. Yet on a short visit, you might do well to find even half of them.

The truth is, the dynamics of hummingbird communities rarely permit every species to be present at the same time. A core group is resident year-round, with secondary species present for part of each year. As Feinsinger and Colwell discovered in the hummingbird communities they studied, this core group almost invariably begins with a territorial species and a low-reward trapliner or generalist. When conditions permit, the next role to be filled is that of a high-reward trapliner. Beyond this, various secondary species are added, some of which may migrate in for only a few days or weeks of each year. The migrations may be vertical—consisting of flights up and down mountains—or they may take place between dry and wet regions or between flowering trees that are a few hundred yards or a few kilometers apart.

From year to year, hummingbird migrations are fairly predictable—
at least they are as predictable and cyclical as the flower crops upon
which they depend—but because hummingbird migrations typically involve only a small portion of the bird population, they are often overlooked. One such example was recently uncovered in Henry Pittier
National Park in the coastal mountains of Venezuela by ornithologist
Miguel Lentino.

Lentino strung nearly invisible mist nets across a cloud forest pass
and documented the almost overnight exodus of an entire population of
golden-tailed sapphires from the dry coastal zone at the end of the rainy
season. Net captures zoomed from none to more than 100 a day, and
practically the entire population of these birds funneled through the
mountain pass in a mass migration that was over in a matter of days.

Superimposed upon major intratropical migrations, like the one uncovered by Lentino, are numerous minor adjustments that occur constantly within hummingbird communities. Areas where vegetation is in a
regrowth stage often have extremely dynamic hummingbird communities in which territories are frequently relocated and behavioral roles are
changed.

In disturbed habitats in the mountains around Monteverde, Costa
Rica, Peter Feinsinger found a large variation in the density of flowers
over the course of a year. When flowers were scarce, competition for nectar enabled only a few species to coexist, and these birds were obliged to
forage in very different ways. When flowers were abundant, additional
species immigrated from both nearby and distant areas, but these birds
remained only as long as nectar was abundant. The picture that emerged
was one of very dynamic interactions in which split-second decisions to
fight or flee are routine, and where almost all of the players were characterized by unstable, high-energy life-styles that were forever consigned to
the task of fine-tuning their densities and distributions to a finite and
constantly changing supply of nectar.

The next time you look at a long list of hummingbirds from an al-
luring tropical destination and perhaps wonder how so many could possibly occur there, recall that the list is a composite of species present at

various times during the year. Almost certainly you won't see all the species on the list on your vacation, but at least you'll feel better knowing why you didn't. And you may be able to see for yourself some of the behavioral interactions of the various species. That alone should add a great deal of pleasure to your hummingbird-watching outings.

# *Cold Reality*
## Highland Hummingbirds

I F YOU'RE ONE of those people whose thoughts turn to pristine rainforests or immaculate sandy beaches and swaying palm trees whenever the word Tropics is mentioned, your reaction is similar to mine. But these are stereotypes pushed upon us by a travel industry that sells images. These images ignore the great diversity of habitats and climates that exist within the realm of the Tropics—from deserts and grasslands to snow-capped mountains. More than half of the Andes lies within the Tropics, and the bleak, windswept altiplano is hardly the place to inspire thoughts of balmy weather, nor are the cold, wet elfin forests that cling, with a tenacity out of proportion to their miniature stature, to ridges and tree-line mountainsides.

Living in tropical latitudes does not necessarily mean warm environments and a life of languid abundance. High tropical mountains present a range of environmental conditions that are not unlike those that birds and animals face in the Arctic—but there is a difference. Arctic seasons differ markedly in temperature—winters are bitterly cold and summers are warm. On tropical mountains, it is the daily extremes much more than the seasonal differences that are important. There is only a small difference, for example, between temperatures in the rainy and dry season, but there is a much larger difference between daytime and nighttime temperatures. Biologist Marshton Bates, writing in *The Forest and the Sea,* was aware of this when he remarked, "In high latitudes winter comes once a year, but on the tops of high tropical mountains it comes every night."

Even on the equator, nighttime temperatures can be very cold at elevations above 10,000 feet, and the mercury frequently plunges below freezing. Ice forms along stream banks at night and thaws again each day. Plants grow with excruciating slowness and are often sculpted into strange, elfin shapes by constant wind and the burden of moss and other epiphytes that accumulate on them. Above tree line, an array of hardy grasses, cushionlike plants and mosses survive the extremes of temperature and moisture. High-Andean environments, where plants and animals face winterlike conditions every night, contrast sharply with the luxuriance and warmth of a lowland rainforest, and they call for different solutions to the problems of survival.

As one travels from the bottom to the top of a tropical mountain, the diversity of plants and animals declines. This is similar to traveling northward from, say, Mexico to the Arctic Circle, although in going up tropical mountains, distances are compressed from hundreds of miles to hundreds of feet. Whether one travels up tropical mountains or to higher latitudes, the decline in diversity of life is apparent. Yet hummingbirds, which are for their size some of the most energy-extravagant creatures on earth, prosper right up to tree line and even higher in tropical latitudes. Several thrive in the Andean puna and páramo habitats above tree line.

One of the birds likely to be found higher than almost any other in the Andes is the lovely Chimborazo hillstar, a hummingbird that has chosen some of Ecuador's highest volcanoes as its home. I was surprised once to see one of these remarkable birds at about 14,000 feet in elevation on the slopes of Cotopaxi Volcano.

It was a cold, damp morning and the sun's first rays were turning frosty meadows into fields of sparkling diamonds. Tiny rivulets were frozen solid, and flowers stood immobile in little jackets of frost. Suddenly a hillstar appeared, flew straight down to the frozen ground and began to probe a patch of flowers so short I hadn't noticed them. The flowers did not reach an inch in height—they were so low that the hillstar did not hover but sat directly on the ground to feed. It seemed curious that this bird, whose very existence depends heavily upon nectar, could live at an elevation where freezing temperature and snow can occur almost any day of the year. And hillstars live much higher too. Hikers

THE CHIMBORAZO HUMMINGBIRD SURVIVES AT
SNOWLINE ON ECUADOR'S HIGHEST VOLCANOES.

encounter them even near the permanent snowline at above 16,500 feet.

The abundance of hummingbirds at high elevations is even more remarkable when one considers that about 20 percent of the species in high-Andean bird communities are hummingbirds. This contrasts with only 5 to 8 percent in the Amazon lowlands. Those of us living in the north get only a glimpse of this marvelous hummingbird diversity, and then only for a few months of each year. All of eastern North America has only a single species—the ruby-throated hummingbird. Arizona has more: it is famous among birders for its hummingbirds, and thousands of people each year visit mountain canyons in the southern part of the state where it is possible to see eight or ten different kinds of hummingbirds.

Yet this pales in comparison with Colombia, which boasts over 140 species of hummingbirds that occur in every habitat from rainforest to páramo. Tiny Ecuador next door has nearly as many. At least 13 genera of hummingbirds are found above 10,000 feet in the Andes, and they bear a delightful roster of names that hint at some of their attributes—hillstars, sunbeams, velvetbreasts, sapphirewings, sun-angels, trainbearers, thornbills and metaltails.

Why are hummingbirds common at high elevations? The answer has less to do with hummingbirds themselves than with the flowers that provide them with food. Because plants are rooted in one spot, they face special problems in finding a way to transport their genes from one place to another. To overcome this difficulty, plants make use of mechanisms such as wind and water to disseminate their pollen, or they employ the services of unwitting pollen bearers, such as insects, birds and mammals. For their services, bearers are bribed with small rewards of nectar.

Wind pollination is a favorite mechanism among temperate-latitude plants—as is evidenced by the large number of people that suffer from hayfever allergies in temperate regions. Mountainous regions are often windy, and high tropical mountains are no exception to this, yet wind pollination is rare in the Tropics, even at high elevations. Plants that gamble their pollen to the wind are most successful when there are many other individuals of their species around to up the odds that the pollen will land in the right spot. This obviously works well for ragweeds and pine trees and many high-latitude plants, but precisely the opposite is true in the Tropics where there are many species, but most of them are rare.

Insects are faithful pollinators of plants in lowland tropical regions, but they become increasingly unreliable at high elevations on tropical mountains. At tree line, insect activity can be brought to a halt by days of prolonged cold weather. Nectar-feeding bats are important pollinators of flowers in the lowlands, but for various reasons they, too, are uncommon at high elevations.

For many high-elevation tropical plants, then, the solution to their pollination dilemma rests with hummingbirds. It is a bargain struck between plant and bird—food traded for sex. Hummingbirds, with their great mobility and frequent need to refuel, regardless of the weather, have become the pollinators of choice for many kinds of high-elevation plants. Hummingbirds constantly brush against cleverly placed pollen-bearing stamens while probing flowers for nectar. With their pollen-dusted bills and faces, these supercharged intermediaries in the sex life of plants ceaselessly transfer pollen from one plant to another during endless feeding bouts.

With such interdependence between Andean hummingbirds and their food plants, it is no surprise that bill and flower shapes are often in perfect accord. Starfrontlets, Incas and sword-billed hummingbirds have very long, straight bills adapted for probing flowers with unusually long corollas. The five-inch-long bill of the sword-billed hummingbird matches the tubular corolla of pink passion flowers in a perfect coupling of bird and plant. The bills of starfrontlets and Incas, though falling short of the sword-billed's magnificent rapierlike lance, are also well suited for drinking from the deep nectar wells of many highland flowers. With dabs and patches of glowing color and long bills probing upward to sip nectar, these darkly attired birds seem to be suspended beneath flowers in a kind of dance that embodies the mysterious, miniature world they inhabit.

Form meets function in many ways in these highland forests. In some hummers, such as the lovely velvetbreast, the gentle curve of its long bill can easily be reconciled with the curved shape of *Castilleja* and *Siphocampylus* flowers that it commonly visits. And such relationships are often more complex than they appear at first glance. Differences in bill length between male and female velvetbreasts lead to different behavioral roles even between the sexes. Longer-billed females are more sedentary than their shorter-billed mates.

While the extremely long bills of some hummingbirds seem to have been pushed evolutionarily to the limit of practicality, those of another group of high-Andean hummers have evolved along quite opposite lines. The bearded helmetcrest, which lives in the páramos of Venezuela and northeastern Colombia, and two genera of thornbills, the *Chalcostigma* and *Ramphomicron,* have extremely short bills. *Ramphomicron* thornbills have the shortest bills of any hummingbird, averaging just over one-quarter inch.

In the páramos of the northern Andes, most of these birds are found around one of the most characteristic páramo plants: a member of the sunflower family known as *frailejón.* These soft plants, with fuzzy leaves arranged in rosettes on thick stalks, are, more than anything else, responsible for the distinctive appearance of the páramo. Their bright yellow sunflowers produce no nectar. *Frailejóns* are pollinated mainly by bumble bees, which visit them for pollen, but helmetcrests and thornbills spend much of their time at *frailejón* flowers, too, even establishing territories in the páramo where there are dense concentrations of these plants. The attraction is not nectar or pollen, but small insects that heavily infest the flower heads.

David Snow, a British ornithologist who studied high-elevation hummingbird communities in the eastern Andes of Colombia, points out that nectar is apparently less important in the diet of these birds than insects, and at times these versatile birds feed heavily on insects. The short, sharp bills of these hummers are efficient at picking and probing for insects in the insect-infested flower heads of *frailejón.* Their bills also fit many small nectar-bearing flowers of páramo plants, and when flowers are not available, helmetcrests and thornbills readily switch to hawking small flying insects.

Both helmetcrests and the *Chalcostigma* thornbills are unusual among hummingbirds for their relatively long legs and large, strong feet, and they sometimes feed on insects they capture by walking or fluttering in densely matted grass or on the ground. Their ability to switch readily between various insect-feeding modes and nectar has apparently helped these uniquely equipped hummingbirds solve the riddle of obtaining food in an environment of temperature extremes and unforgiving weather.

Birds and other animals face the same physiological problems that you and I do at high elevations—a lack of oxygen and having to cope with cold temperatures. Even after months of acclimatization, strenuous exercise at very high elevations quickly pushes our body's oxygen processing ability to its limit. Lungs burn, muscles scream and heads throb and ache. How do hummingbirds, which seem perennially perched on an energetic knife-edge barely sufficient to sustain them through long, cold Andean nights, manage so well in an environment where so many others cannot? Contrary to what you might expect, hummingbirds, and most other birds for that matter, don't have a lot of special adaptations for living at high elevations.

Hummingbirds already come equipped with one of the most efficient respiratory systems in the world. It is practically made-to-order for dealing with the rarefied air of high elevations. When humans live at high elevations for long periods of time, they may develop large lung capacities and higher red blood cell volumes to cope with the reduced oxygen in the air. These changes don't seem to occur in hummingbirds or other birds, probably because they aren't necessary. The oxygen and ventilation demands of normal flight metabolism so greatly exceed those caused by changes in elevation—even a change from sea level to tree line—that a bird's respiratory system requires no additional adaptation for high-altitude life.

The thin air of high elevations affects a bird's ability to fly efficiently, just as it does that of an airplane or a helicopter. Air is less dense at increasingly higher elevations, and the lift generated by a wing is correspondingly less. This means a bird has to work harder to fly or hover at higher altitudes—expending more energy to stay airborne. Yet physiologists studying hummingbirds in the Peruvian Andes found that high-elevation hummingbirds burned no more calories when hovering than their lowland counterparts of approximately the same body weight. How could this be?

The solution to this enigma seems to lie in the length of the wings. For their body weight, highland hummingbirds are proportionately longer-winged than lowland ones. The longer wings seem to compensate for the reduction in lift at high elevations.

The relationship between a hummingbird's wing length and its body weight has several implications that aren't obvious at first glance. Hummingbirds with short wings relative to their body weight require more energy when they hover or fly than their long-winged counterparts, but they are very agile and are able to turn and accelerate quickly. Hummingbirds with this kind of a wing-to-body-weight ratio—airplane designers would call this high wing loading—make good territorialists. They are very maneuverable and good at defending their patches of flowers but are inefficient long-distance fliers.

Conversely, long-winged hummers use less energy on long flights and are better trapliners, but they fare poorly in territorial battles against speedier, more maneuverable, shorter-winged rivals. Long-distance migrants like ruby-throated and rufous hummingbirds, which reach northern North America, and green-backed firecrowns, which travel to the far southern end of Chile and Tierra del Fuego, lie at the long-winged end of the spectrum. Intermediates are likely to be the generalists—the low-reward trapliners and the ones whose behavior may vary with the amount of nectar around and with the behavior of other hummingbirds in the community. Most communities of tropical hummingbirds contain only one or two species at each extreme of the wing-length spectrum, while the rest fall somewhere in the middle.

The concept of wing loading also helps to illustrate the delicate energy balance that underlies the structure of all hummingbird communities. Because of their extraordinarily high energy needs, hummingbirds are forever teetering on an energy tightrope. Too few flowers, or too few of the right kind or too many competitors can quickly upset the delicate energy balancing act that each of these birds maintains throughout its life. When this happens, and it happens often and rapidly, hummingbirds may abandon an area or switch to a different feeding-behavior role.

An intriguing aspect of hummingbird migrations up or down mountains is that the change in air density may force a bird to adopt a different behavior role when foraging. At low elevations, short-winged hummers usually behave as territorialists because they are very agile and good at defending patches of flowers, but they may hover so inefficiently at high elevations, where the air is thin, that they cannot obtain enough food to keep up with the increased cost of flight. Consequently, the migratory movements of short-winged hummers are confined to relatively small changes in elevation.

For the same reasons, a hummingbird that occupies an intermediate foraging role at a low elevation may find itself forced into the role of a territorialist when it moves to a higher elevation. This happens because it finds itself competing in a community of higher-elevation hummingbirds, most of which have, on average, longer wings relative to their body weight and are less agile.

In Costa Rica, hummingbird biologist Peter Feinsinger and several co-workers noticed that the green violetear did not act aggressive or territorial at low elevations, but at high elevations it did. At low elevations, it coexisted with birds such as the steely-vented hummingbird, a typically aggressive territorial species, and the fork-tailed emerald, a nonterritorial traplining species. The violetear's behavior fell rather neatly into an intermediate position between these extremes and so did its hovering costs, calculated from its wing length and body weight. It rarely acted territorial; instead, it foraged at scattered flowers. High on Cerro de la Muerte, though, at more than twice the elevation, there are no hummingbirds with proportionately shorter wings than the violetear, and there it defended territories.

The explanation for this behavioral change seems to lie in the change in air density. Feinsinger and his co-workers calculated that at the higher elevation, the violetear's hovering cost was as high as that of the territorial steely-vented hummingbird. It could exist at high elevations by defending a patch of rich flowers, which did not require much flying, but it no longer had the luxury of being able to switch to other foraging methods that would require longer flights.

On the other hand, the steely-vented, which pays a high hovering cost at low elevations, does not occur on Cerro de la Muerte. Indeed, it cannot. Its wing-length-to-body-weight ratio is so high that it is impossible for this species to live much higher that it already does. The steely-vented is, in a sense, a victim of its own anatomy, for it is unable to sip nectar fast enough to fuel the tremendous energy it would need to hover at high elevations.

Because of their small body size, hummingbirds have a unique set of physiological problems not faced by larger birds and animals. Recalling that a small object has more surface area for its volume than a larger one, it is easy to see that hummingbirds have more body surface area for their size than do larger birds. This, in turn, means that hummingbirds are prone to losing body heat very rapidly, and metabolic rates must be elevated accordingly. Rapid heat loss may be advantageous in warm climates, but during cold nights in the tropical highlands, more energy may be needed to maintain a normal body temperature than can be stored in their small bodies.

Cold temperatures increase the rate at which body heat is lost, and this, in turn, means that hummingbirds have to eat more food to maintain body heat. Furthermore, cold temperatures slow down insect activity and nectar production—two essential food items for hummingbirds—and high elevations on the equator can be both cold and windy. Windy weather carries a double threat because it hinders birds from foraging and birds have to expend more energy to obtain food. A prolonged period of cold, rainy weather that prevents hummingbirds from feeding or an unusually cold night can be life-threatening.

Like humans, virtually all birds and mammals maintain a nearly constant high body temperature, even when the outside air temperature is much lower. In birds, this normal temperature is several degrees warmer than that of humans, and in hummingbirds, it may be as much as ten degrees warmer, making them truly hot little bodies.

What hummingbirds do to forestall an energy crisis is something that few other warm-blooded creatures are capable of doing: they voluntarily decrease their body temperature during long cold nights. While the loss of normal body temperature is fatal for most organisms, hummingbirds are able to survive large reductions in body temperature with no harmful effects. By temporarily reducing their body temperature, their metabolic activity slows down and they become torpid—a state in which body temperature and physiological function is maintained at a level so minimal it is barely above death itself. This condition greatly reduces the amount of energy hummingbirds need to expend.

Torpor is essentially a voluntary hypothermia, and the depth of torpor is under strict physiological control. The amount of reduction in body temperature is generally in the range of 30 to 50 degrees Fahrenheit. High-Andean hummingbirds allow their body temperature to drop much lower than that of their lowland counterparts, yet their temperature is always maintained a few degrees above the prevailing air temperature, down to a minimum of a few degrees above freezing.

Torpor can be thought of as a way for hummingbirds to overcome their problem of being small and therefore having only a limited capacity to store extra energy. Like shifting into overdrive to save fuel when we drive our automobiles, hummingbirds shift into torpor, drastically slowing down their motors and conserving precious energy.

This adaptation is not restricted to high-elevation hummingbirds. Scientists believe it can occur in all hummingbirds, although it is most often observed in highland hummingbirds because cold temperatures and frequent inhospitable weather often push energy reserves to critically low levels. But entering torpor is a gamble, too, because a hummer lowering its temperature is betting that there will be sufficient energy left to restart its motor at the end of the night. If there isn't, the hummer never regains consciousness.

When Lynn Carpenter, a hummingbird specialist, examined body temperatures of roosting Andean hillstars in the Peruvian Andes, she found that during the rainy season, only about 10 percent of the birds were torpid. She returned during the July and August dry season and found clear skies, colder nights and fewer flowers in bloom. When Carpenter reexamined this same population of hummingbirds during these months, about 60 percent of the sleeping birds were torpid—evidence that, when times get tough, these remarkable little birds frequently have to pull this ace out of their sleeve to survive the night.

I once spent several days at the tiny tree-line headquarters of Puracé National Park in Colombia. The park encompasses some of the highest mountain forests and páramos in the Central Cordillera of the Colombian Andes, and from this location I could reach a wide variety of habitats by foot. The skies were leaden and foreboding, spitting rain or sleet the whole time I was there. Worse still, the nights were damp and freezing cold. Each day, I slogged through miles of sodden, water-logged páramo, and each night, I spent my evenings huddled around a warm fire drying out my boots and clothes.

This is fairly typical of the conditions that one can expect in the wet season in the páramo zone, and Puracé Park is no exception. It is hard to come to peaceful terms with this cold, unforgiving region because one is rarely comfortable there. Yet, the fairyland of strange rosette plants and other floral novelties that thrive in the páramo, and the shadowy birds that prowled the dense elfin woodlands and hedgerows near the park buildings where I stayed, left a strong and lasting impression.

I was especially surprised by the hummingbirds. Almost all of them were larger than their lowland allies, some of them startlingly large. The great sapphirewing, rainbow-bearded thornbill, golden-breasted puffleg and shining sunbeam were four that I saw daily, and they are so large and hover with such slow wingbeats that they resemble bats as much as hummingbirds. Indeed, the two largest hummingbirds of all, the giant hummingbird and great sapphirewing, are chiefly birds of tree line or higher.

Other nectar-feeding birds show a similar tendency toward having large races or species at high elevation. In Colombia, the masked and black flower-piercers, which both inhabit tree-line elevations, are much larger than their low-elevation counterparts. So, also, are the high-

Andean mountain-tanagers which are larger than their middle-elevation and low-elevation allies.

There are advantages to large body size in a cold environment. Large bodies lose heat more slowly than small ones, and the ability to store enough energy for a long cold night or to wait out a day of bad weather is important in high-Andean environments. In this capacity, large hummingbirds have the advantage.

Physiologists studying relationships between body mass and metabolic rate point out that a large hummingbird can theoretically survive longer while fasting, at any temperature, than a smaller one can. The result is that large hummingbirds are able to fast longer than their small cousins. They still need more food than small hummingbirds, but for their size, they consume proportionally less. Furthermore, their imposing size lets them dominate and drive away competing hummers at a good flower patch.

At very high elevations, the number of hummingbirds that are present all year long is small. The communities in a park such as Puracé in Colombia or Las Cajas in Ecuador usually contain several hummers that are present there for only part of the year. Some breed in the wet season because of the presence of favorite flowers, others may favor the dry season and others may simply be visitors for varying periods of time. Within each community, however, those species that more or less permanently occupy the highest elevations are large-bodied. In Costa Rica and Panama, it is the fiery-throated hummingbird. In the Andes, from Venezuela southward, there is a succession of species that replace each other geographically at the highest elevations—bearded helmetcrest in Venezuela, bronze-tailed thornbill in Colombia, Chimborazo hillstar in Ecuador and Andean hillstar and bearded mountaineer in Peru.

Everyone knows that hummingbirds hover; it is the one attribute that sets them apart from all other birds. Yet anyone who watches high-Andean hummingbirds is sure to notice that large-bodied highland species are often reluctant to do so. Instead, these birds cling with their feet to the edges of flowers when feeding. Bounding from one flower to another, they hang or cling for a few moments at each one. There are practical reasons for this. Clinging saves energy and it also suggests that large hummingbirds hover less efficiently than smaller species. Although clinging to flowers when feeding is almost habitual in large highland species (and also in some small highland species), their large-bodied lowland counterparts rarely do so. If the advantage is purely in saving energy, one wonders why large-bodied species everywhere don't do it.

Hummingbirds are renowned for their exquisitely fashioned nests—they are well insulated with soft, downy materials. Newly hatched hummingbirds, naked and no larger than a bean, require a good deal of nest insulation to stay warm, even in the tropical lowlands. To survive the rigors of cold damp nights and doses of very intense solar heating during sunny days, hummingbird nestlings must be well protected.

Scientists working with high-elevation hummingbirds have pointed out that the nests of these birds are thicker and better insulated than those of their lowland counterparts. Helmetcrests and hillstars use woolly downlike material from various páramo and puna plants to construct a thick nest that insulates the eggs and nestlings very efficiently. Such nests also help reduce heat loss from incubating or brooding females—a critical factor during cold nights when they are obliged to maintain relatively high body temperatures to protect their eggs or nestlings.

Helmetcrests, hillstars and mountaineers regularly place their nests in caves, under earth banks, on rocky outcrops or in sheltered places. Sometimes even buildings are used. Several hillstars may nest close together in clusters on available rocky overhangs or cave entrances. When this occurs, each female defends a territory of only about a meter and a half in the vicinity of her nest but goes off to feed in different areas on nearby mountain slopes. Such reduced aggression permits high amounts of trespassing across feeding territories.

Hummingbirds, because of their very small bodies and high metabolism, would at first glance seem unlikely candidates for a success story in cold highland regions, yet, as a group, they are among the most successful of all birds in the high Andes. Despite a few minor behavioral or morphological variations, what they use most is a set of adaptations generally characteristic of all hummingbirds. They are already, in a sense, preadapted for survival in the high Andes. Nevertheless, the ability of hummingbirds to thrive there is the result of a delicate balance between the flowering plants they need and the particular combination of nectar-feeding competitors that are present. Their success is an especially fascinating one, and they assuredly have much more to show us about themselves, but we must watch carefully.

# *Sallying Forth*
## A Flycatcher Baedeker

NOT MANY BIRDERS would choose a flycatcher as their favorite bird. Perhaps this is because many flycatchers are ordinary looking and seem to do ordinary things, or perhaps it is because we are unfamiliar with them as so few occur in temperate latitudes. Many birders also ignore flycatchers because many species are difficult to identify. This is especially true in the Neotropics, where about one out of every ten species is a flycatcher and where merely mentioning the word is likely to elicit disparaging mumbles about "little brown-jobs." Unlike such popular and colorful icons as parrots, toucans, hummingbirds and quetzals, one seldom sees flycatchers adorning T-shirts, coffee cups and other memorabilia. For a different viewpoint, we need to visit the Neotropics.

Flycatchers did not burst upon the scene recently. In Amazon forests, the ancestors of flycatchers were pecking, probing and sallying forth in pursuit of prey even in pre-Pleistocene times. Flycatcher ancestors blossomed into part of a broad category of modern birds that ornithologists call suboscines or sometimes just nonoscines. This means the syrinx, or voice box, of flycatchers and other suboscines contains only one pair of vocal cords, rather than the two pairs that are found in oscines or modern songbirds. This may seem like a picky detail, of interest only to an anatomist perhaps, but you certainly notice the difference right away when you listen to them. The oscines include nearly all of our familiar backyard birds—wrens, thrushes, vireos, warblers, tanagers, grosbeaks and all of the little finches and buntings that please us with their sweet songs, as well as some that don't, such as crows and jays.

Flycatchers' songs usually amount to little more than simple notes or phrases that are sometimes whistled or trilled. None have songs that could be described as beautiful. Despite their lack of accomplishment as singers, virtually all flycatchers have a distinctive dawn song, which is only heard during a brief, predawn wake-up period. The dawn song is repeated over and over, virtually nonstop, as if it was the most urgent activity of the morning. Indeed it may be, for while the functional significance of dawn songs is still debated, it is hard to escape the impression that the territory owner is proclaiming his fitness to hold deed to his property, even while hunger pangs speak otherwise.

Have suboscine ancestors, like so many evolutionarily old lineages, become as obsolete as the extinct ground sloths that once shared the forests with them? If you poke around in bird family trees in North America, you would be inclined to agree that their heyday is over. Although there are few suboscines in North America, we need only take a trip to South America—the ancestral homeland of these birds— for a different perspective. Not only are suboscines still around, but they comprise some of the continent's most successful bird families.

The old suboscine lineage split into two independent pathways long ago. One line led to woodcreepers, tapaculos, antbirds and furnariids— neotropical families that occupy a wide range of habitats. The other ancestral lineage led to manakins, cotingas and tyrant flycatchers. These make up some of the largest bird families in South America today, and they are far more dominant in tropical forests than the newer singing birds.

Tyrant flycatchers spread into practically every habitat in South America, becoming the most successful of all the families that descended from the early suboscines. Today, they are the largest family in the western hemisphere—there are more than 390 species ranging from Alaska to Tierra del Fuego.

While some flycatchers stayed at home in tropical forests and woodlands, others were busy venturing out into the scrublands and grasslands of southern South America. Long-legged species became adept walkers and runners; others, with long, narrow wings that could slice through

Patagonian winds, found the latitudes of the "roaring forties" to their liking. Eventually, some of these long-legged and long-winged species of ground-tyrants and bush-tyrants colonized the high windswept slopes above tree line in the Andes. Flycatchers pushed northward and southward, ultimately nesting as far away as southernmost Argentina and the boreal forests of Canada.

Only about 33 species of flycatchers reach the latitude of the United States, and many of these barely get across the Mexican border into southern Arizona or Texas. Even this number is but a glimpse of the diversity in the American Tropics. Furthermore, with the exception of the phoebes, which retreat mostly to the southern part of the United States, and the odd flycatcher individual that occasionally attempts to overwinter, nearly all will retrace their routes southward toward tropical homelands even before the autumn leaves fall and the prairies turn brown. So for half the year or more, most of North America has no flycatchers at all.

In the upper end of a small cloud-forest valley in the Western Andes of Colombia, I once recorded over 50 species of flycatchers. Practically every one of them could be found within a few hundred yards of the house where I lived, and all but two, a pewee and the Acadian flycatcher, were permanent residents.

The list of flycatchers at Cocha Cashu, a biological station in southeastern Peru, has topped 60 species. In eastern Ecuador, the list of flycatchers at a tourist lodge popular with birders also stands at about 60 species. At Hato Pinero, a large cattle ranch and biological reserve in the grasslands of central Venezuela, about 45 species of flycatchers have been found—nearly all of them permanent residents. These numbers are typical of flycatchers in forested or partially wooded areas of tropical South America, and they are indicative of how successful flycatchers have been in exploiting a variety of habitats.

There is no simple answer to the question of why flycatchers are so successful, although scientists believe that part of their success lies buried in the family's long history and part of it lies in their ability to use many habitats. The success of flycatchers, along with several other large suboscine families in South America like antbirds and furnariids, is probably linked to their very long period of isolation from competing birds on other continents.

South America drifted for millions of years as an island continent. Few pioneer species from other continents reached its shores, so South American birds evolved without the foreign competitors they might have faced had South America been linked to other continents. Flycatchers and other suboscine groups eventually occupied nearly every South American habitat, effectively locking up many of the insect-eater niches. Only after Panama rose from the sea over two million years ago, forming first a series of mountaintop islands and eventually a land bridge, did an onslaught of modern songbirds push southward into South America. The most successful of these northerners were seed-eating finches and the tanagers, many of which incorporate a rather catholic mix of fruit and insects into their diets.

Modern insect-eating birds such as thrushes, wrens and vireos were less successful in their efforts to compete with hordes of specialized and already well-entrenched insect-eating species in suboscine families. In rainforests, the lack of success of these newcomers is quickly apparent. At the end of a day's birding in the lowland rainforest, one's list will be top-heavy with foliage-gleaners and their spine-tailed allies, legions of antbirds and a veritable army of sallying flycatchers, but there will be far fewer wrens, thrushes and tanagers.

John Fitzpatrick and Melvin Traylor, two ornithologists who have spent years studying flycatchers, think that the success of these birds is due to more than just South America's long period of isolation. They point out that flycatchers are unique among all bird families in the Neotropics in their ability to utilize every stratum of the vegetation, from the forest floor to the aerial zone above the canopy. This permitted flycatchers to establish successful lineages outside the forest—an important starting point for colonizations of distant lands.

Considering their radiation into practically every habitat on the South American continent, flycatchers don't show many unusual foraging techniques. But their many different sallying methods give them access to almost every part of the forest. For those of us with a North American bias, this might seem odd because field guides to this region typically describe flycatching behavior as sallying from an exposed perch after flying insects and often returning to the same spot. Called aerial hawking, this is the way most northern migratory flycatchers behave. But what an eye-opener a trip to the Tropics can be. Suddenly, there are species chasing leafhoppers, hovering beneath leaves, gleaning in thickets like warblers, eating fruit and walking on the ground.

Many of the foraging techniques used by tropical flycatchers are variations on the aerial hawking maneuver. Compared to North American migrants, however, the difference is that many tropical flycatchers capture prey from a surface such as a leaf or twig, rather than in the air. This is known as a sally-glean, and it gives flycatchers the ability to successfully exploit a tremendous variety of habitats, particularly high-light regions around forest edges and in open woodlands. These are areas where many of the scratching, probing and climbing techniques of other suboscine species can't be easily employed. And this is why, when we go for tropical birding walks, which are more often along the edges of forests than in them, we tend to see a disproportionate number of flycatchers. Flycatchers prosper along forest edges, in the very places where antbirds, foliage-gleaners and other creeping and climbing species are least successful. Inside the forest, flycatchers are much less dominant and certainly less conspicuous.

The sally-glean takes many forms—flying upward, outward or downward—and it may end with a brief hover, allowing the bird to pause momentarily in order to home in precisely on its intended victim. Yellow-olive flycatchers sally up and hover beneath the underside of a leaf. Attilas and mourners sally outward and hover beside or above a leaf. Bush-tyrants sally down toward the ground; marsh-tyrants sally to the surface of water. Each variation of the sally-glean opens up new foraging locations and new food possibilities. Some flycatchers eat fruit, and several subsist almost entirely on it, yet the shift of diet to fruit does not require any substantial change in foraging techniques.

Sallying is so widespread among flycatchers that to biologists, it's almost synonymous with the family itself. But it is not the sole foraging technique used by family members. Rather than sally, some flycatchers reach for insects while remaining perched. Dubbed perch-gleaners by ornithologists, this group includes elaenias and many small flycatchers of lighter woodland and open areas. These birds are fairly active and they can be found in a wide range of South American habitats. Doraditos, for example, perch-glean in tall marsh grass, beardless-tyrannulets perch-glean in dry scrub or humid forest edge and slender-billed tyrannulets forage among acacias in northern South American deserts. Lesser wagtail-tyrants perch-glean mostly from willowlike *Tessaria* shrubs that colonize sandbars in the Amazon river and its tributaries.

Another group of flycatchers exploits the vast, open terrain of southern South America. They are perfectly at home on the ground or in the low bushes of windswept Patagonia, but most of them use the same foraging techniques that their arboreal cousins use. One of the commonest variations seen among the bush-tyrants and chat-tyrants, which inhabit the open plains of southern South America and the treeless zones in the high Andes, is to drop to the ground from a low perch much like a bluebird does. Other species like pipits and thrushes run rapidly and obtain most of their food in the open on the ground.

Two species in the genus *Corythopis* are unusual because they are the only terrestrial forest-dwelling flycatchers—that is, if they really are flycatchers. At home in the shady rainforests of Amazonia and southern Brazil, these two shy little birds look so much like antbirds that they were once called antcatchers, and after that, gnateaters—even though they don't eat either. Despite the questionable taxonomic progress that science has made with these two birds, they remain interesting behavioral subjects. Although both walk on the floor of the rainforest, they don't search or scratch among the leaf litter as you might expect. Instead, they look up at the undersides of leaves and, when prey is spotted, leap upward and catch it with a loud snap of their bill.

Several large flycatchers, like the boat-billed, streaked and sulphur-bellied, are notable for the variety of foods they consume—fruit, large insects and flying prey—but none matches the versatility of the great kiskadee. A consummate generalist, the kiskadee stands in a class all its own. Kiskadees eat whatever food is most readily at hand, and populations sometimes develop peculiar short-term foraging specialties that enable them to capitalize on almost anything edible. A list of kiskadee cuisine may include fish, lizards, frogs, tadpoles and baby birds, as well as fruit, beetles, carrion and garbage. They wade in water, follow army ants and occasionally pirate food from other birds.

It is a small wonder that the kiskadee is capable of occupying habitats ranging from deserts and rainforests to the boulevards of large Latin American cities. A few even range far enough north to cross the Rio Grande into southern Texas; others summer along river valleys as far south as central Patagonia.

Many species of flycatchers forage in ways that differ relatively little from each other, and it is easy to fall into the mistaken notion that their diets are similar. One of the fundamental tenets of ecological theory, however, maintains that no two species can occupy the same habitat and feed on the same foods. Thomas Sherry, while a graduate student working in Costa Rica, wondered how the foraging behavior of a bird might affect its diet. His study was one of the first of its kind to examine this problem in flycatchers. He uncovered some surprising specializations.

The flycatchers in Sherry's community included three aerial hawking species and several that sally to foliage or strike upward at leaves. The aerial hawking species rely heavily upon flying bees, wasps and ants. They are so dependent upon these particular flying resources that Sherry doubted they could exist without them.

The long-tailed tyrant is one of these aerial hawkers, a beautiful little chocolate-colored bird with a white cap and long tail streamers that is always eagerly sought by visiting birders. Pairs can usually be found sitting near dead tree trunks or old rotten stubs. The stubs provide nest holes and excellent visibility for aerial sorties. But, as Sherry discovered, these little tyrants chose stubs for more than the nesting holes and visibility they provide. Old stubs and trunks are favorite nesting sites of small stingless *Trigona* bees, too, and long-tailed tyrants eat great quantities of these bees—a feeding specialization that provides them with a reliable year-round food source.

Small flycatchers that forage in dense vegetation usually capture prey by darting up to the underside of leaves, snapping up prey and continuing on to a new perch. This happens so quickly that the human eye cannot follow the details of the prey capture that, instead, appears as one continuous motion. It's a maneuver that ornithologists call upward striking, and it's the modus operandi among many little flycatchers that allows them to capture insects from places that are virtually inaccessible to other birds. Among its practitioners are pygmy-tyrants, tody-tyrants, tody-flycatchers, spadebills and flatbills—a group of mostly tiny little birds whose names reflect their diminutive stature as well as the unusual bill shapes of several of them. These birds dart up quickly with wide bills that function like little shovels, literally scooping prey off leaves and twigs with scarcely a pause in flight. Most of them are also amply adorned with stiff whiskers that seem to help trap errant prey. The royal flycatcher, though best known for its remarkable crest, has the longest whiskers of all, with some as long as its bill.

Sherry discovered that several small flycatchers with wide, flat bills feed mainly on leafhoppers. Such extreme specialization on just one taxon of insects is unusual, especially among foliage-gleaning birds whose prey is usually too widely scattered or in such low density that specialization is impractical.

The white-throated spadebill is a leafhopper specialist that relies on a sudden burst of speed to strike up and capture these insects before they can flee. It is, of course, just this behavior, combined with their small size and habit of sitting quite still in shady places when scanning foliage, that makes spadebills so difficult for humans to see. Another leafhopper specialist, the tiny ruddy-tailed flycatcher, employs a different hunting tactic. In a flush-and-chase strategy, it pursues fleeing leafhoppers with astonishing skill in short, aerobatic chases. Leafhoppers are quick to jump and difficult to follow and catch on the wing, and the flycatcher's maneuvers appear designed to flush them from hiding so they can then be chased.

Once the dietary specialization of the ruddy-tailed flycatcher was known, its curious, often flitty behavior began to make sense. So, too, did the remarkable suite of physical attributes that it used to counter the evasive tactics of leafhoppers. The flycatcher's extraordinarily large eyes adjust instantly to rapidly changing light levels, and its rounded wings provide lift and acceleration. A long tail adds braking and steering ability, and stiff whiskers enclose the bill like a basket. Together, these attributes are a marvelous set of built-in adaptations that have turned an insignificant-looking little bird into an extremely potent predator.

The sulphur-rumped flycatcher has elevated the flush-and-chase strategy almost to an art form. Its habitual wing- and tail-spreading behavior, while acrobatically darting from branches to the sides of trunks and back again, is bound to remind northern observers of an American redstart. Exposing its chrome-yellow rump in what seems like an invitation to predators, the catch-me-if-you-can behavior of these impish birds has a functional role in foraging. Their chronic posturing flushes a wide array of insect prey that they can capture on the wing. And there may be even more to their bravado behavior.

Sulphur-rumpeds are persistent followers of small mixed-bird flocks, especially those containing understory antwrens. Sherry believes that sulphur-rumped flycatchers use the antwrens as beaters, darting about and waiting for them to flush prey as they inspect foliage and curled dead leaves. Because they are much quicker than the antwrens, the flycatchers then aerobatically chase down and capture the fleeing prey.

The similar and rather inflexible foraging behavior shown by many small flycatchers can lead to considerable overlap in their diets. When this happens, the species are often separated from each other by habitat. Tody-flycatchers of the genus *Todirostrum* all forage by striking upward at leaves in a very similar manner, but they usually do not occur together in the same habitat. Most birders, even first-time visitors to the Tropics, make the acquaintance of one or more of these droll little birds with long flat bills and wiggling tails that are sometimes cocked over their backs. Their snappy black and yellow plumages and white or golden eyes set them apart from hordes of drab-colored relatives.

The three species that Sherry studied are found in different habitats.

One lives in dense thickets, another in sunlit bushy areas and a third in the open, sunny canopy along forest edges. They all hop lightly among foliage and stare intently upward at nearby leaves. Drawing a bead on fast-moving flies and tiny parasitic wasps that like to rest under leaves, they leap up with short, lightning-quick attacks that are almost always successful.

There is one final chapter in the flycatcher success story and it involves their invasion of North America. The number of flycatchers in North America is small, so the invasion may not seem very remarkable until we consider that of all the suboscine families that developed in South America, flycatchers are the only ones that have come north. As a group, they were much more successful than any other family in colonizing northward after the Panama land bridge was established.

The reasons for their success are probably the same reasons they were successful in their South American homeland. Flycatchers can thrive in almost any habitat, and various lineages within the family were able to establish themselves successfully outside of tropical forests. Furthermore, there were probably no sallying insect eaters in North America, so few ecological competitors stood in their way.

Some lineages that were well equipped to take advantage of the new route northward were sallying insect eaters like *Empidonax* and *Contopus* and others that eat a mixed diet like *Myiarchus* and *Tyrannus*. All are genera familiar to North American birders. The habitats these birds encountered while expanding their ranges northward, and where they ultimately evolved, were mostly lighter woodland, forest edges and open country, which differed little from their ancestral habitats.

Those flycatchers going farthest north were, of necessity, migratory. The success of migratory flycatchers stands in sharp contrast to that of other suboscine families. There are no migratory antbirds or tapaculos, for example, and there are very few furnariids that migrate. Biologists do not know why so few members of these families are migratory, but strong-winged sallying flycatchers certainly have the anatomical machinery necessary to undertake migrations. As a result of the tyrannids' success as migrants, both north-temperate-latitude and south-temperate-latitude observers are treated each year to a little sample of one of the world's most diverse families.

From a north-temperate perspective, it is easy to view bird migration primarily as something that occurs each spring and fall between North America and someplace else to the south. That kind of perspective is perhaps understandable because we spend most of our lives viewing only one end of this annual miracle called migration.

But most passerine migrants trace their ancestral lineage to tropical rather than temperate latitudes. And just as we see only a glimpse of the flycatcher family from our northern vantage point, so, too, do we see only a glimpse of the complexity of migration. There are, for example, approximately as many migratory species of flycatchers in Argentina as there are in the United States and Canada. Although southern South America is far smaller in land area than North America, its southern latitudes offer the same opportunities for increased breeding success during the brief austral summer as our northern summers do. And the southern temperate regions of South America have been directly accessible to tropical flycatchers far longer than our northern lands.

There may be as many flycatchers whose migrations occur entirely within the Tropics as there are those that migrate to points outside the Tropics. Some species, like the piratic flycatcher, have remarkably complex migrations. These birds are migratory in Central America and Mexico and in the southern Amazonian portion of its range, but they are resident in northern South America. These birds migrate northward into Central America in January or February. Their breeding activity peaks during the latter part of the dry and early wet season, when small fruits and berries are most abundant. At this time, piratic flycatchers feed entirely on fruit and spend most of their time sitting above cacique and oropendola colonies, where they call constantly and occasionally fly off to fruit trees to fill up quickly only to return again to their perches. Rather than build a nest of their own, they pirate the hanging nests of the much larger caciques and oropendolas through continual harassment. By September, with the abundance of their favorite fruits declining, they return to northern South America, rejoining a small resident population that remained behind to breed there. In the southern portion of their range, there is a similar seasonal movement southward that begins at about the time the northern birds are returning.

Flycatcher migrations in southern South America are, by and large, mirror images of those in northern latitudes. Those that breed in North America generally return to wintering areas that are north of the equator; relatively few individuals make the longer and more hazardous journey farther south. In the same manner, spectacled tyrants, chocolate-vented tyrants, monjitas and others that breed in the pampas and Patagonia withdraw into grasslands and open zones along the southern fringes of Amazonia during the austral winter, but relatively few undertake long trans-Amazonian migrations to wintering grounds in northern South America.

The eastern kingbird's extremely long migration route, which takes it to the southwestern corner of the Amazon Basin, is a notable exception to the tendency of most long-distance migrants to return only to the edges of tropical latitudes. When I was growing up on a farm in western Missouri, I always looked forward to seeing eastern kingbirds return each April. They usually built their nests in a big mulberry tree near one of our barns and spent the greater part of their summer chasing and hurling insults at all passersby, including other birds, our cats and my pet crow. Neighbors called them bee martins, perhaps in reference to their habit of sometimes eating bees. The kingbirds were a part of my life for five months or so of each year, but I never thought much about where they went or what they did during the other half of the year. It seemed enough to be secure in the knowledge that they would return.

The eastern kingbird is highly territorial and pugnacious and feeds only on insects during the months when it breeds in North America. But during the other half of the year, it does a behavioral about-face that would do justice to Jekyll and Hyde. Its pugnacity is traded for docile subordination to virtually all of its tropical relatives, and its territoriality is traded for a period of nomadic wandering. Gathering in large, nervously acting waxwing-like flocks that wheel and turn on a dime and plunge into giant fruiting trees, eastern kingbirds roam the floodplain and river-edge rainforests of southwestern Amazonia in search of ripening fruit.

Why do eastern kingbirds have split personalities? If the eastern kingbird's off-breeding-season behavior of gathering in flocks seems peculiar, consider that in western Amazonia, where most of them spend the northern winter, there are at least eight other species of large-bodied flycatchers—all of them potential competitors—that also consume fruit. They include great kiskadees, social and gray-capped flycatchers and tropical kingbirds, which have well-deserved reputations for pugnacity.

Archbold Biological Station scientist John Fitzpatrick, who studied flycatchers in Peru, noted that these species persistently chase eastern kingbirds as well as other birds in fruiting trees, but the kingbirds overwhelm them by their sheer numbers. When a flock of eastern kingbirds descends on a fruit tree, they may outnumber the resident species ten to one. A few kingbirds are forced to flee the attacks of dominant resident flycatchers, but these individuals return as soon as their attackers turn their attention to other individuals. In this way, each kingbird, playing a game of averages, is likely to be harassed only occasionally by resident flycatchers, and flock members as a whole are able to feed.

Eastern kingbirds, by muscling in on resources used by large, pugnacious resident species, may have been forced to gather in flocks in order to compete. Other northern migrant tyrannids may not have adopted a similar strategy because most of those that winter in South America tend to fill peripheral areas within the much larger resident tyrannid community, where they simply avoid direct confrontation with dominant resident species.

Scientists, of course, should attempt to explain behavior in terms of survivorship, fitness and natural selection, but the unusually long migration of the eastern kingbird and its somewhat unusual off-breeding-season behavior seem difficult to justify even by comparison to the complex migrations of some of its tropical kin. The eastern kingbird, however, is not alone in its penchant for the unusual and bizarre with regard to flycatcher migrations, dietary switches and behavioral schizophrenias. Many of its tropical relatives may eventually prove to lead equally complicated lives once we get to know them better. And perhaps as biologists continue to unravel little pieces of migratory puzzles and behavioral riddles, we will better understand the reasons for the successful radiation of species within this remarkable family.

# *Finding a Needle in the Haystack*

## A Vulture's View of Paradise

I N 1968, I spent two weeks in the little banana port of Almirante, in northwestern Panama. Each morning, I left at dawn and walked westward along the railroad tracks, which led toward the Costa Rican border. Along the way, the tracks ran through miles of lovely lowland rainforest where a companion and I were capturing birds in mist nets.

Our work was part of a program aimed to identify diseases carried by migratory birds wintering in Central America. Any results we obtained from that study are little more than footnotes on pages yellowing with age and neglect now, doubtless lost amidst untold acquisitions gathering dust in some basement archive. What does remain are memories, as clear as yesterday, of that little town—its sounds, its smells and the intoxicating vibrancy of life in the coolness of dawn.

Since then, I have been in dozens of tropical towns, sometimes for a night, sometimes for much longer. In each one, dawn is perhaps the only time when there is a feeling of briskness and energy. People are chattering and singing and beginning their daily routines, vendors are already out hawking food and cigarettes, roosters are crowing and there is a mingling of children's voices, radios and dogs barking. Trucks and buses rumble by, and the smell of diesel, carried on gentle currents of humid tropical air, mixes with sweet and rancid odors of unfamiliar foods, damp earth and garbage in neglected muddy streets. At dawn, bird activity is at a peak, too, but the urgency of their song is as ephemeral as the caress of cool breezes at sunrise. In a few short hours, they will fall silent.

I didn't have to rush, but I did because I knew that withering mid-day heat was but a few steps behind. Hurrying down an alley in Almirante, I made detours around huge mud holes and piles of garbage that were cast aside by the town's inhabitants. Rows of black vultures sat stolidly on palm fronds at the end of the alley. Like hunched old men in black trench coats, they stared blankly, scarcely taking notice as I passed. The fronds on which they hunkered seemed tattered and droopy, and they were all splashed with white from poorly aimed vulture excrement.

These were thoroughly urban vultures, warily secure of their right to participate in the benefits and occasional costs of city life. They were the sanitation department—uninvited, largely unappreciated and usually ignored. Unlike their country cousins, they would not wait for the sun to warm the cool morning air and whip up rising thermals on which to glide effortlessly. They would be off even before sunrise, flapping rapidly to keep aloft, as they set off on their moribund task of sifting through yesterday's rotting food, fruit and filth.

Black vultures have aligned themselves with humans in an uneasy urban partnership that is mutually beneficial—a partnership forged of careless human habits and indifference that provides the vultures with food and humans with a sanitation service that is much needed, although little recognized. It is a serendipitous arrangement, for black vultures are the only New World vultures that regularly eat fruit, and they are naturally birds of open areas, riverbanks and forest edges. Both of these traits preadapt them to life on the easy streets of civilization.

In most areas of the humid Neotropics, black vultures will be one of the first birds visitors see. And unless they are misidentified as distant soaring hawks—which they sometimes are—they are seldom given a second look. But black vultures, along with other vultures and their majestic cousins, the condors, are worth a second look. There are seven species of vultures and condors in the New World and even more in southern Europe, Africa and Asia. Both New World and Old World vultures get virtually all of their food by scavenging dead animals rather than by killing prey.

BLACK VULTURES OFTEN ROOST IN PALMS.

The two groups look remarkably similar, yet they are quite unrelated. Taxonomists classify the Old World species with birds of prey, as members of the Accipitridae. New World vultures also have traditionally been placed near birds of prey because of their superficial resemblance to them, but the resemblance is just that—superficial. Their closest ancestors are storks, not birds of prey. Anatomists have said for years that vultures, on the inside, were very much like storks, and more recently, studies of the similarity of DNA sequences between the two groups has proved these anatomists correct.

The lack of a shared ancestry between New World and Old World vultures, then, is strong evidence that these two groups have independently evolved along the same lines, a situation that biologists refer to as convergent evolution. Though unrelated, both New World and Old World vultures have been shaped by similar environmental pressures, and the resemblance of the two groups to each other is stunning. They share such features as a similar type of soaring flight, a similar diversity of species and various plumage characteristics. All vultures have a naked, featherless head, and if one thinks for a moment about where vultures sometimes put their bald pates when feeding, what their heads sacrifice in beauty is more than offset by their utilitarian value for personal hygiene. Their bald heads, or at least bare faces, are the result of a selection pressure that seems to operate on all carrion feeders, vultures and caracaras, no matter what their ancestral background.

Old World vultures inhabit grasslands, deserts and open country across southern Europe, Africa and Asia. Yet despite the existence of large tropical forested regions in Africa, there are no vultures in Africa's forests. Vultures are also conspicuously absent from the Indo-Malay region and from New Guinea—areas that are predominantly forest-covered. Scavenging in tropical forests of the Old World is left to a few opportunistic birds, especially kites, as well as animals and hosts of insects and microorganisms.

New World vultures, on the other hand, thrive in both forested and nonforested habitats. Condors and lesser yellow-headed vultures occupy chiefly grassland habitats, while at the other end of the spectrum, greater yellow-headed vultures are found only over the lowland forests of Amazonia. The remaining three vulture species inhabit a combination of open terrain and forested regions: the black vulture occurs in forested regions mainly along rivers and lakeshores, the turkey vulture is almost equally numerous in all areas and the king vulture ranges predominantly over forested or partially forested habitats.

It is easy to marvel at the ability of vultures to find anything edible at all as they tilt and teeter on midday thermals over the rainforest. Yet they must eat well for they are among the most frequently seen soaring birds anywhere in lowland neotropical forests. For hours on end, vultures ply their trade from a lofty vantage point above forests and grasslands, and their silhouettes are so commonly seen that even first-time visitors to the Neotropics soon become familiar with them. Vultures search tirelessly for the carcasses of creatures large and small. Forest mammals would seem to be particularly difficult to locate because they are not especially numerous in life and because they often die in places where they are hidden from view. Searching for carcasses in a rainforest would be much like searching for the proverbial needle in a haystack.

British ecologist David Houston, who has studied vultures in both the Old World and New World, wondered why it is that New World vultures can find enough carrions to eat in rainforests but Old World vultures seem not to be able to do so. Noting that no Old World vultures hunt regularly over forest, he set about examining this problem by first estimating the amount of animal carcass biomass available to vultures in tropical African and American forests.

While we need not concern ourselves with the calculations, the results offer some interesting insights as to why vultures can make a living in American forests but not in those of Africa. If Houston's estimates are correct, the amount of animal carcass biomass at any given time in the Neotropics varies from about the same as that in African forests to more than three times as much. But the weight of the carcasses is only part of the story. As Houston emphasized, differences in the rates at which animals die and the lengths of time they remain available to be found after they are dead are also important. And in both of these cases, it is the

New World tropical forests that offer more opportunities for scavengers.

Neotropical forests have higher densities of small mammals than African forests. Among groups represented on both continents, some mammals, such as primates, have more small species in the New World. Sloths and opossums, which are common in neotropical forests, do not occur in Africa and seem to have no ecological counterparts there.

Generally, small species have shorter life-spans than large mammals, resulting in a faster turnover of the small animals. For scavengers, the rapid turnover does not necessarily imply that more meat is available, but it probably results in a steadier, more reliable supply and reduces the chances of scarcity. This distinction between the two mammal faunas may seem minor, but from the viewpoint of a scavenger, it could mean the difference between having a meal—even a small one—and not having one.

Surprisingly, the biomass of carcasses available to vultures in neotropical forests compares favorably with that available to vultures on the Serengeti Plains of eastern Africa. The Serengeti is widely acknowledged as supporting the greatest mammalian biomass in the world, and any sample of photos from eastern Africa is sure to contain one or two showing hordes of vultures ravaging the carcass of some hapless zebra or gazelle. At first, it seems astonishing that the flow of carcasses issuing from New World rainforests is comparable to that of the Serengeti.

But African vultures are forced to share their spoils with a wide array of efficient mammalian scavengers that roam the veld by day and by night. Consequently, although the amount of carcass biomass on the Serengeti is more than twice that of a comparable area in Amazonia, half or more is taken by mammalian carnivores before the vultures can get to it, so the amount of meat available to the two vulture communities turns out to be similar.

In neotropical forests, vultures compete with several mammalian scavengers, too, and a host of invertebrates and microorganisms. The mammalian scavengers are all opportunists, feeding on carcasses when they are encountered as well as on many other things. Coatimundis and opossums are the commonest scavengers in neotropical forests, but neither is very efficient at finding carcasses, and their impact on what is available to vultures is small. On the other hand, vultures can search very large areas of forest by soaring, which is extremely energy-efficient. This has given them the opportunity to become scavengers exclusively—a relatively secure if unenviable specialty.

Flies and various invertebrate carrion feeders are another matter for vultures. The speed with which they can consume carrion is startling, and they can directly affect what is available to vultures. Blowfly larvae can transform small animals into pools of unrecognizable goo in a few days. A seething mass of maggots engaged in the business of riddling a carcass is a gruesome sight to humans and one difficult to appreciate objectively, but there is no doubting its efficiency. Once a carcass is present, one need not wait long for the various participants in this grizzly business to begin work.

Curiously, the chain of events by which decomposition proceeds seems to be somewhat different in African forests than in American tropical forests. In simple African carrion communities, blowfly larvae are the chief consumers of forest mammals, and they usually complete the task, unmolested, within two or three days. Speed is essential for them because there are many kinds of flies, each competing for a piece of the action.

In the Neotropics, a more complex array of carrion insects may prolong the process. Here, ants are usually the first to arrive on the scene, but they feed mostly on blood and bits of soft tissue. Several kinds of carrion flies arrive soon after, and at that point, the pulse of activity quickens. Within minutes or hours, flies begin to lay eggs. Over the next two days or so, they may infuse a carcass with literally tens of thousands of eggs.

Amidst this seething mass of newly emerging life, staphylinid and histerid beetles make an appearance, along with several more kinds of ants. These new recruits have come not to enjoy the spoils of the carcass but to prey upon carrion fly eggs and maggots. Larger ants, such as *Camponotus* and *Ectatomma*, eagerly haul away eggs and maggots, and some even capture the adult flies and carry them off. The impact of the marauding ants at the carcass, coupled with that of the beetles, is considerable, for by preying heavily upon fly eggs and larvae, they may extend the life of the carcass from three or four days to as much as two and a half weeks.

For a vulture, this extension of carcass life is as good as food on the table, because even an extra day or two is significant, giving New World vultures that much longer to locate carcasses before they are destroyed by insects. Vultures seem untroubled by meat that is several days old. While flesh roasting in the tropical heat for a day or more would spell trouble for most birds and mammals (and certainly for you and me), vultures have a Herculean resistance to many bacterial toxins and have made a specialty of feeding on microbe-infested carcasses. Their ability to feed on such meat without ill effects is testimony to their incredible gut chemistry, which as yet has not been well studied. But there is a limit even to the tolerance of vultures, and meat that remains more than a week is often so putrefied that even vultures shun it.

The observational powers of vultures are legendary. All species in the Old World and New World alike have exceptional eyesight and are extraordinarily good at spotting carcasses in open terrain. But the chances of finding dead animals in the rainforest by eyesight alone are extremely small, yet New World species routinely locate carcasses in the rainforest.

Turkey vultures have large olfactory organs, and experiments indicate they have a keen sense of smell and can easily find hidden carcasses simply by the odor. Besides the turkey vulture, other Cathartid vultures—a taxonomic group that also includes the greater yellow-headed and lesser yellow-headed vulture—also probably have a good sense of smell. But what about king vultures and black vultures? Both are believed to have a very poor sense of smell, yet despite this apparent handicap, king vultures are occasionally found at carcasses even inside the rainforest. Black vultures, on the other hand, don't venture inside forests and seem to find all their prey by using their keen eyesight.

The ability of king vultures to locate carcasses inside rainforests remained puzzling until scientists began carefully observing them in flight. While turkey and greater yellow-headed vultures soar comparatively low, king vultures usually rise to great heights—normally to about 1,000 feet and occasionally to more than 3,000 feet above the ground. It seems inconceivable that they could be following chemical trails, which at such heights would be extraordinarily faint and thoroughly confused by breezes and rising thermals. Furthermore, soaring so high seems to be disadvantageous if they are relying upon visual cues to find food—unless they are watching other vultures, which is what they appear to do much of the time. Bait experiments show that, in most cases, smaller Cathartid vultures are the first to find the carcass, and the larger king vultures then follow them to share the spoils.

The parasitic behavior of king vultures on their smaller cousin's food may have an occasional redeeming aspect. Watching a gluttonous mob of vultures working over the bloated carcass of a horse is a sight so revolting to the sensitivities of humans that few might be able to conceive of any partitioning of resources among the various participants. But in both African and American vulture communities, there is a segregation of vultures by size that sometimes results in each species feeding in different ways and at different times. The skin of large reptiles and mammals is tough and difficult to rip open. King vultures, with superior size and strength, can tear through thick skin and open carcasses that the smaller species cannot open. In doing so, they make the booty available to weaker species such as turkey vultures, which find it first, but are denied the first feeding opportunity.

Biologist William Lemon, who studied vultures in southern Costa Rica, was aware that a size-related hierarchy existed at carcasses when vultures were feeding. He noted that, no matter when the larger king vultures arrived, they almost immediately elbowed their way to the front while the smaller blacks and turkeys had to wait. But he discovered that there was also a time-dependent hierarchy as well. Turkey vultures like their carrion relatively fresh. They were often the first to arrive at a new carcass but among the first to leave as well. King vultures often fed on older carrion but they, too, often left while carrion was still present. Lemon found that black vultures, the consummate generalists, not only ate almost anything but also remained to feed for up to two days after the other species had left. Their ability or willingness to consume older, more rotten meat than other vultures has allowed them to move into a dangerous and unenviable feeding niche contested mainly by microbes.

Black vultures are the most social American vultures and often amass in numbers at large conspicuous carcasses in open areas and on sandbars and along riverbanks. The carcasses they find—all easily seen from the air—perhaps reflect their poor sense of smell compared with other vultures; black vultures seem completely unable to find hidden items. With weaker bills than other vultures, they prefer soft tissue, which can be easily torn, and once a large carcass has been opened, they will climb inside, if necessary, to obtain soft tissue rather than feeding on the more accessible but tougher pieces clinging to bones. They associate with neighbors at large roosts, which serve as information-sharing centers, and successful foragers are followed to carcasses the next morning. This enables black vultures to quickly gather in very large numbers and take full advantage of a big carcass once one is found.

In comparison, the less social turkey and yellow-headed species pick small bits from bone and other hard-to-reach places and seem better able to make do at small carcasses. Both of the latter are more often found alone or in groups of only a few individuals at small carcasses.

Black vultures are unique among New World vultures in their habit of occasionally eating fruit. Palm fruits, in particular, are relished, and a wide variety of fruit scraps are scrounged from piles of garbage at sanitary landfills or around villages and homes. Fruit-eating behavior and their tendency to feed on carcasses that can be found by eyesight alone suggest that black vultures, unlike most other vultures, make limited use of smell when finding their food.

The genealogy of Old World and New World vultures reaches far back in time, perhaps as far as that of any modern birds. Yet they have remained in the evolutionary slow lane compared with many birds, for they do not differ greatly from their ancient ancestors. During the Pleistocene epoch, when there were mammoths, mastodons and many other big mammals in the Americas, large scavenging vultures and teratorns—a Pleistocene-sized supervulture—patrolled the plains and steppes of South America. But when the big mammals disappeared, so did the scavengers that picked their bones.

We are left today, in the New World, mostly with smaller, more efficient ancestors of the early scavengers. Only the ponderous condors remain—Pleistocene anachronisms that have survived in remote mountain strongholds into modern times.

Both species of condors have now crashed head-on with a rapidly changing twentieth-century world in which they are ill-equipped to operate. While their smaller cousins survive and, in the case of black vultures, prosper in the wake of human-altered environments, the condor is only hastened toward oblivion. Condors emerged onto the Pleistocene landscape superbly equipped to scavenge among those ancient wildlife communities, but they have now become dust collectors—obsolete curiosities that hang on by the merest thread in remote regions that have somehow escaped the double whammy of climatic upheaval and the environmental upheavals brought on by the activities of modern man. They are, nevertheless, contemporary reminders of the long, fascinating history that scavengers bring to our present-day landscape.

Watching a magnificent condor soar with its great broad wings held almost ruler-flat and with only the long wing-tip feathers bending up under the bird's weight, one might wonder why there are such pronounced differences in the soaring flight between vultures and condors. The authors of most field guides will tell you that turkey vultures hold their wings up in a distinctive V shape when soaring and that this dihedral is a good field mark. The dihedral is so strongly associated with the turkey vulture's flight profile that some have suggested the zone-tailed hawk, whose wing shape and habit of soaring are similar to the turkey vulture's, may be a vulture mimic. By mimicking the harmless vulture, the hawk, it is reasoned, may gain an advantage of surprise over unsuspecting prey. But is the similarity due to mimicry or merely the principles of aerodynamics in operation?

Zoologist Helmut Mueller has argued that the hawk's mimicry of the vulture is at least partly coincidental. Both birds often soar relatively low, and the best aerodynamic shape for a bird that soars low is long, narrow wings held up in a dihedral. The aerodynamic reasons for the dihedral have to do with frequent and unpredictable changes in wind currents close to the ground. Gusty breezes, thermals and other unstable air movements often cause each wing to generate different amounts of lift, and this causes a bird (or plane) to slip-slide if the wings are perfectly flat. Thus, such birds must make almost constant wing adjustments if they fly where there are many rapidly changing air currents. By contrast, the V shape adds an automatic stabilizing component to the lift on the wing—as the lift on the upper wing decreases, that on the lower wing increases.

As Mueller points out, birds that soar at high altitudes, like condors and king vultures, probably do not encounter such frequent fluctuations in wind currents, and because they can hold their wings flat, they obtain the greatest soaring efficiency, using essentially their entire wing surface for lift. If a bird holds its wings in a high dihedral, an additional component opposing wing lift tends to push the bird to the side, effectively canceling a small part of the lift. For birds that soar low, this loss of lift is more than offset by an increase in stability, so the birds don't need to make wing adjustments as frequently to maintain their flight control.

The lesser yellow-headed vulture habitually flies only a few feet above the ground—far below that of other vultures. It holds its wing up in the most pronounced dihedral of all, and even with the increased stability this presumably affords, it tips and teeters more in flight than its relatives that soar at higher altitudes. Keen observers of this vulture also know that it spends much more of its time soaring over marshes and damp fields, where the air is more stable, than over hot, dry terrain.

Whether vultures and condors soar on flat wings or dihedral wings, we must acknowledge, perhaps even envy, their almost unrivaled mastery of the air. But still, they must rank among the most unloved of birds, no doubt because of their appearance and their foraging specialty. At best, they are tolerated; at worst, they are ignored or vilified for habits that most humans perceive as filthy and disgusting. Whether we laugh as we watch them contest morsels with starving dogs in the dirty streets of a sweltering tropical town or are repulsed as we watch them engorge stinking meat with obvious relish, we cannot fail to be impressed with the adaptations that permit them to find the smallest morsels hidden deep within rainforests or to eat with impunity some of the most toxic compounds produced by microbes anywhere on earth.

I do not share the vulture's view of paradise nor do I admire vultures because their scavenging is essential to the completion of a food chain— it isn't. (Left alone, microorganisms and other scavengers would ultimately do what vultures do.) But I must marvel at their ability to venture gastronomically where others dare not follow.

# The Costs and Benefits of Growing Old

## Life and Love Among the Caciques

I N AN OXBOW LAKE in Peru's Manu National Park, a large black caiman cruised toward the opposite shore—its eyes and nose were the only parts of its swarthy head that broke the water's surface. Silent ripples slid away in long lines, creating a wide V-shaped wake, but little else betrayed its steady progress across the dark lake waters. Scott Robinson and I watched with interest from the shore because these great reptiles rarely exert any unnecessary effort, and almost certainly, something had attracted its attention.

A *Cecropia* tree on the opposite bank leaned far out over the old lake. It hosted a small colony of yellow-rumped caciques that had built nests among its wide-spaced limbs. Scott noticed an unusual amount of commotion at the colony. He had spent parts of the last six years studying yellow-rumped caciques in the Manu River Basin. Much of this work had been for his graduate studies at Princeton University, and little about the caciques escaped his attention.

In this instance, a female cacique was obviously in great distress. She was tangled in material from her own nest or in material she was trying to filch from a neighbor's nest. Caught in a long, tough fiber, she was dangling by a leg beneath her unfinished nest. I was astonished when Scott explained that, in her predicament, she would probably be the target of attempted rape by satellite males lurking near the colony. The dominant male, which would have probably prevented rape attempts by interlopers, was absent from the colony.

As we watched, two male caciques harassed the entangled female. One had been displaying from a nearby tree—a sure sign of his low social status—and he would almost certainly not have been permitted to enter the colony tree if any higher-ranking males were present. Neither male was successful in its attempt to copulate with the entangled female, but their commotion, and that of the hapless female, was attracting unwelcome attention even from across the lake. Unless the female could extricate herself quickly, she would soon die of fright and exhaustion, and the caiman would be waiting below. Time was on his side.

Almost every visitor to the American Tropics has seen nesting colonies of caciques and oropendolas. Their long, hanging nests suspended near the tips of slender branches are a characteristic sight in most humid lowland regions. Although nest colonies of caciques and oropendolas are superficially similar, they can be distinguished easily, even if no birds are present. Cacique nests are smaller and have a short neck suspending the baglike pouch. Because of the small size of the nests, cacique colonies are not as conspicuous from a distance as those of oropendolas. Even more importantly, cacique nests are often placed quite close together, and in almost every colony, there are clusters that are either touching each other or woven together.

During the lengthy nesting season, there is usually much coming and going around colonies as females build or repair nests and carry food to nestlings. Males, constantly in attendance, display with strange, gurgling and liquid calls and much wing-flapping commotion. Sometimes a pair of piratic flycatchers or troupials can be seen hanging around the colony. Both species are nest parasites and usually try to steal a newly completed nest for their own use. From time to time, giant cowbirds put in a furtive appearance, hoping to spot an unguarded nest in which to deposit an egg.

As a defensive measure, some colonies are built around large wasp nests. Monkeys may try to raid the colony, even braving the stings of attacking wasps for a handful of eggs and young, and so will toucans, great black-hawks and snakes. If the colony tree is suspended over water, a caiman or an occasional anaconda may lie in wait below for fledging young that fall. With so much activity, cacique colonies are exciting places to while away a few warm tropical afternoon hours. And if no predator attack seems imminent, the vocal antics of the males, which mimic everything from motorboats to the squeals of giant otters, will provide fine amusement.

Bird colonies everywhere are fascinating places—whether they are made up of thousands of seabirds crowded on rocky sea cliff ledges, a shimmering pink blush of nesting flamingos on a distant alkaline lake or martins chattering around their man-made apartment. Naturalists, however, see more than merely the excitement, the noise and the beauty of the birds in these colonies. Bird colonies are natural experiments in over-crowding, with all of the disadvantages that go along with such high-density living.

Life for humans in a big-city environment is an experiment in over-crowding, too, and one not unlike that in a bird colony. Our decision to live in a large, crowded city, or alone in the country, is an exercise in weighing the advantages and disadvantages of each. Naturalists use the same kind of judgmental process when they study bird colonies. Birds should live in colonies only when they have greater reproductive success than if they lived alone—in other words, when the advantages are greater than the disadvantages. The naturalist, then, searches among the commotion, the noise and the filth in a bird colony for clues that will help determine the costs and benefits for colony members.

The reasons for living in colonies, of course, are not the same for all species. For some, such as seabirds, the advantage may lie in obtaining information on the location of prime feeding areas by following successful birds out to sea. The same may be true for cliff swallows, which follow neighbors to swarms of midges. Bees may directly share information about the discovery of nectar-rich flowers with other members in a hive. In the case of the caciques, with so many predators lurking around, the advantage could lie with some kind of predator protection.

Scott Robinson thinks so, arguing that defense against a host of predators has played an important part in the evolution of coloniality in caciques. Robinson's research was conducted at the Cocha Cashu

Biological Station in the heart of Peru's world-renowned Manu National Park. It is an ideal place for naturalists to study complex relationships between birds and animals and their environment because the park's enormous size and the absence of hunting, except for occasional forays by indigenous Indian tribes, assures that the environment is natural. All of the top predators are present, as well as their prey—something that is all too often not true in research areas.

Robinson initially set out to study the foraging behavior of the caciques, but switched to nesting strategies, because, as he puts it, "From my first predator attack [on caciques], I was hooked." From then on, Robinson roamed the perimeter of Cocha Cashu—*cocha* is a Quechua Indian word for an oxbow lake—and neighboring lagoons in native dugout canoes, keeping track of the comings and goings of hundreds of caciques and observing how they defended their nests against would-be predators.

We never knew if the young female we watched with her foot entangled lived to complete her nest and raise her young. If she did survive, surely she would have realized some advantages of nesting together with others of her kind.

But cacique colonies are practically an advertisement to predators because they are so conspicuous. Nests are clumped together in trees at forest edges or in isolated trees, and displaying males at colonies are noisy and easy to see. Caciques themselves are hardly inconspicuous—they are large and black with an ivory-colored bill, calculating, icy blue eyes and bold yellow patches on their wings, rump and tail.

So why nest in a big noisy colony that seems to invite predators? As any real estate agent will tell you, location is the key to any successful property and it seems to be true for cacique colonies. Several things work to the colony's advantage if it is located in the right place.

The most successful colonies are built in trees away from the forest, either in clearings or on tiny islands in lagoons—safely out of reach of monkeys. Of the 13 kinds of primates in the rainforest around Cocha Cashu, three of them—the squirrel monkey, brown capuchin and white-fronted capuchin—are relentless plunderers of cacique colonies, and an improperly chosen site has little chance of success. But these predators can be thwarted by nests placed in an isolated tree in a clearing. To reach such a tree, the monkeys have to leave the safety of the forest—something wild primates are loath to do because they then become vulnerable themselves.

A tree standing apart in an oxbow lake is even better. With caimans patrolling the murky water around the base of the tree, such places are virtual fortresses, safe from all marauding mammals as well as snakes. Colonies are established close to paper wasp nests whenever possible, and this provides a measure of protection, too, because the wasps attack would-be mammal invaders. In Panama, researcher Neal Smith believed that wasps also discouraged the presence of botflies, which lay their eggs on oropendola and cacique young.

No colony location offers any protection from avian predators, and the noise and activity frequently attracts opportunistic Cuvier's toucans, black caracaras and great black-hawks, all of which eat a wide variety of food items and are not above robbing nests. Yet the colony is not defenseless against such petty marauders. The cacique's nest construction and placement provide at least two lines of defense. Cacique nests are beautifully woven, suspended bags with long narrow openings at the top, and like other New World orioles, their nests are difficult to enter and very time-consuming to tear apart. Toucans and caracaras risk mobbing and pecking attacks if they take the time to pull cacique nests apart. Furthermore, when several nests are interwoven in clusters, each female is assured of having many neighbors that will join the attack. Group defense becomes an important advantage in cacique colonies because if enough caciques dive and peck at the backsides of toucans and caracaras, these invaders will usually give up and leave the colony.

The other defense relies on the mathematics of probability. Robinson observed that when great black-hawks raided a colony, the caciques left rather than risk mobbing the invaders. This may be just as well because black-hawks probably represent a real threat to caciques, and they aren't easily intimidated by the caciques' mobbing tactics. With the black-hawks free to pilfer nests unopposed, the colony would seem to be hopelessly vulnerable, yet the hawks are poor mathematicians and are easily confounded by unfinished nests and old nests from the previous year that are scattered throughout the colony. If a hawk checks two or three nests by shaking them and finds nothing inside, it is likely to become discouraged and leave.

Robinson believes that the cacique's best defense against black-hawks is to have a few active nests hidden amidst a ghost town of empty ones. Even if an occupied nest or two is found, it is more likely to be one of the outer nests belonging to a young female than a centrally placed nest belonging to an established bird. Once, however, Robinson observed this strategy fail the caciques. A black-hawk raided a colony in which most of the nests contained eggs or young. Striking pay dirt on its first three nests, this hawk returned seven more times in the next three days, eventually dining on the contents of twelve nests. Only a few nests well hidden among abandoned ones escaped detection.

The cacique's various nesting strategies enable them to take this rogue's gallery of petty thieves and felons in stride, but caciques have no well-developed defense against pirate birds stealing nests. Piratic flycatchers and troupials take over the nests of caciques by persistently badgering the owners. Piratic flycatchers are usually content with occupying a single nest on the perimeter of the colony, and once the nest is in their possession, they vigorously defend it against all would-be predators. Troupials, dressed in beautiful black and orange colors are more like wolves in sheep's clothing because they can be systematic in their destructive activities. Though smaller than the caciques, a pair working together can easily oust a female cacique and destroy or throw out the contents of her nest.

Troupials employ the cacique's own ghost-town strategy and may continue to destroy many cacique nests until their own is surrounded by many empty cacique nests. Robinson once watched a pair of troupials evict 12 female caciques in a single afternoon. Damaging as their activities may seem, both piratic flycatchers and troupials are rare in rainforest habitats compared to the number of caciques, and their depredations have little overall effect on a cacique's eternal quest for the perfect, safe nest site. The problem with safe nesting sites is that they are rare. Under natural conditions in the rainforest, trees only occasionally become isolated around lakes, along rivers or in clearings opened up by tree falls. Even wasp nests, unless they are on high, isolated branches, may provide only partial protection. But caciques, unlike many rainforest birds, are sometimes able to take advantage of the incursions of humans into rainforests and undoubtedly they profit from it.

Whenever a lone tree is left standing in a clearing, even if it is immediately beside a house full of noisy children or in the midst of a small village with people coming and going all day long, it may be taken over by a bustling colony of caciques that seem almost completely oblivious to the human occupants with whom they share the space.

One of the largest cacique colonies I've seen was a group of scarlet-rumped caciques at Iguazú Falls in Argentina. This colony of nearly a hundred nesting pairs took over a tree right beside a restaurant that served hundreds if not thousands of tourists that were bussed to the falls each day. It was not by coincidence that the caciques chose to locate their nesting colony amidst dozens of enormous diesel buses belching smoke, noisy camera-toting tourists and hawkers of cigarettes, chewing gum and soft drinks. Few predators would risk such a close encounter with humans.

All female caciques aspire to one of the secure nesting positions in the midst of a safe colony. But good sites are at a premium, and females compete fiercely for the best spots.

Females are heaviest during their first year or two of breeding and thereafter gradually lose weight; by their fifth season, they may have lost 10 percent or more of their original weight—a significant loss for a bird. Yet it is the older females that tend to control most of the favorable nesting positions, and young and inexperienced females have a difficult time establishing themselves in a colony despite the fact they are heavier and presumably stronger than older females.

Although the heaviest young birds are usually successful in gaining a good nest site, many young females are forced into vulnerable locations on the outside of the colony or are driven out entirely. The nests of these young unsuccessful females and abandoned nests from previous years often form a buffer zone around the birds that have established themselves in the center of the colony.

Newcomers must also withstand attacks from established females that steal material from their nests either by direct confrontation or covertly when the newcomers temporarily leave their nests. Some new females are badgered so persistently that they never successfully complete their nests.

But securing a nest site is not entirely accomplished by fighting. As females grow older and have nested together with others for a few years, they gradually form alliances with neighbors, begin to weave their nests together and combine forces to obtain access to nest sites. These old-gal coalitions are as successful in securing the safest nest locations within the center of the colony as the heaviest young females, and they are the most successful in establishing colonies near new wasp nests.

Whenever females are clustered together at nesting colonies, there is an opportunity for a dominant male to monopolize the breeding within a colony. Social dominance also enables males to keep other males away. This has happened with the caciques. First-year males are seldom seen around the colony, but by their third year, male caciques are sexually mature and begin displaying and following females. They fight to establish their position in the dominance hierarchy at the colony, and it is a contest in which the heaviest bird usually wins.

Robinson's data leave no doubt about the advantage of weight. Males in the top quartile of their weight class consorted with an average of ten females during a breeding season; males in the bottom half averaged fewer than one female per season.

The dominant male isn't difficult to spot at a busy colony. From his prominent position within the colony, he sings, flutters his wings in display and keeps a close watch on the females and any suspicious activities of rival, subordinate males. If a new male arrives at the colony, a series of quarrels with established males ensues. Quarrels may escalate into fights so intense that grappling birds tumble from the trees. Fights typically result in clear winners and losers, and a roughly linear dominance hierarchy, based on weight, is established.

Dominant males choose females that are most likely to nest successfully, and because it is the older females that are the ones most likely to
nest in well-defended dense clumps in the colonies, dominant young
males usually consort with old females. Low-ranking males are forced to
consort with perimeter-nesting young females. Dominant males, according to Robinson, also choose to consort with females nesting on islands
or near wasp nests. This preference is so marked that some females that
attempt to nest in very vulnerable locations may be completely ignored
by all males.

The nesting season at cacique colonies is a protracted affair—it is
dragged out for more than half of the year. At any time, only some of the
females within the colony are actively building or laying—an adaptation
that perhaps helps confound nest predators and reduces the chances that
an entire colony will be wiped out all at once. At the same time, it gives
an especially robust male the opportunity to consort with a large number
of the laying females in the colony.

But life for the dominant male is not all roses, and he may enjoy
only a brief, if promiscuous, fling at the top. The male must stay with
and jealously guard each female closely throughout her egg-laying period
of about three to five days to prevent cuckoldry by rival males whose sexual appetites exceed their dominance standing in the colony. During this
time, the male constantly drives away other males, has to contend with
rivals that disrupt his mating attempts (most copulations occur away
from the colony) and is so harried he has little opportunity to look for
food himself. As soon as one female's egg-laying period is completed, the
male switches immediately to another female, and so on down the line.

For a young male awash in hormones and surrounded by a seemingly endless succession of supplicant females, it would almost seem too
good to be true—and it is. The energetic demands required to maintain
a dominant position and to consort continually with a succession of females, all the while on an empty stomach, soon exact their toll.
Eventually, the dominant male succumbs to weight loss, becomes weaker
and is toppled into positions of successively lower ranking by heavier

males. Unfortunately (or perhaps fortunately), he is only rarely able to mount a successful comeback in succeeding years. According to Robinson, all young males start in the top half of the hierarchy, but in subsequent years, more and more drop into the bottom half where there are few breeding opportunities.

The rate at which males lose their dominance varies greatly. Robinson observed that some males lasted most of a season, others only a few weeks or a few days. Occasionally, after laying out and recuperating for the balance of the breeding season, males are able to make brief comebacks, but by the fifth or sixth year, all are relegated to low status.

Low-ranking males become satellites—stationing themselves at the edge of the colony or in nearby trees. These males occasionally mate with low-ranking females or with females left temporarily unattended by a dominant male, though most live out the balance of their lives in virtual abstinence, relegated to a low-stress, low-dominance position and effectively excluded from the breeding population.

A case history of male W/R, reported by Robinson in *Natural History Magazine,* illustrates the elusiveness of social dominance and sexual access of males to females in a cacique colony:

> In W/R's first year of adulthood, he became the top-ranked male at two colonies. During the year, he consorted with eleven different females, and by season's end he was the second-ranked male in a large colony. Early in his second year of adulthood, W/R reclaimed the top position in the hierarchy of an island colony and had a record of seventeen uncontested consortships after two months. But by the middle of the nesting season, W/R had been bested by five males and consorted with only seven more females. At the end of the season, W/R was behaving like a satellite male. In his third year, he once again rose to top position early in the season, but later dropped to third. When the season ended, W/R had consorted with only four females, twenty fewer than the previous year. In his fourth and fifth year of adulthood, W/R adopted satellite tactics.

When ecological forces such as predation force many females to nest close together, the opportunity for polygyny arises—a few dominant males are able to monopolize most of the females. Polygynous mating systems are relatively common among colonial nesting birds and among many herding mammals, but they rarely occur when females are scattered. But polygyny, in whatever form, can only evolve when it is possible for females to provide almost all of the feeding and parental care without help from the males. Among insect-eating birds, few females alone are able to find enough food for themselves and their nestlings because insects are time-consuming to locate compared with fruit or nectar. For this reason, polygyny is more common in nectar-feeding and fruit-eating birds.

The year-round availability of fruit and nectar may have been an important factor permitting polygyny to evolve as a breeding system in caciques. Caciques occur mainly in humid tropical regions where seasonal differences in the abundances of fruit and insects are not pronounced. Adult females supplement their diet of insects with considerable quantities of nectar and fruit, freeing up time for the more laborious task of searching for insects for their young. But a female cacique's relatively broad diet alone may not be enough to have allowed emancipation of the males from nesting duties.

Female caciques adjust their foraging behavior and speed to the work load imposed upon them. By timing how often the females flew from one branch to another when foraging, Robinson discovered that females feeding nestlings foraged at a much faster rate than non-nesting birds. Furthermore, they moved lower in the forest, spending most of their time in the understory where they captured more large katydids than in the canopy.

Robinson believed that this shift into the more dangerous lower part of the forest by such a conspicuous bird and the simultaneous increase in foraging speed was a sign of stress imposed by the burden of feeding young. Even so, without the availability of fruit and nectar, Robinson doubted that female caciques could catch enough insects to feed themselves and their young. Most females manage to fledge only one of their two young, and still they lose weight during the nesting cycle.

The nests of caciques may also indirectly contribute to the evolution of polygynous behavior. The open-cup nests of many birds offer little protection from predators or the weather, and one member of a pair must usually be in attendance. With both members of a pair sharing in parental chores, opportunities for promiscuous behavioral patterns to develop are minimized. Cacique nests, on the other hand, are very tightly woven and difficult to pull apart, and the nest opening is too small for large predators to enter. They are also almost completely closed, so they provide better insulation from temperature changes than open nests, and this allows the females to be away foraging for longer periods of time, an advantage if she alone feeds the young.

The shift to colonial nesting and polygynous breeding has pushed male and female caciques into strikingly different behavioral roles. Females gain reproductive success with advancing age, despite their declining physical abilities, but for males the reverse is true. Their chance at dominance comes early in life, and once lost, it is seldom regained.

These opposing behavioral paths provide us with a link between the costs and benefits of life in a cacique colony. Watching a vigorous male cacique display and chase rivals, we know he is enjoying the benefits of a breeding system that has been shaped by the pressures of predation and food resources. He benefits by having sexual access to a succession of receptive females, but his enviable stature within the colony is put into perspective by the knowledge that his sexual success is the positive side of a short-lived dominance that will soon be traded for a lifetime of virtual abstinence.

The female, too, is ensnared in a web of costs and benefits imposed by colonial life. She benefits from the security of nesting within the colony, but, unlike her profligate suitor who plays first and pays later, her benefits accumulate much more slowly. They come only after she fights for and gains social acceptance into an elitist circle of older, established females or forms her own coalitions for the purpose of establishing herself in the colony. Her benefit is a form of social security for she reaps her rewards in old age.

The yellow-rumped caciques' breeding system—in technical jargon known as female defense polygyny—is unlike that of any other bird so far known, though oropendolas share some similar features. Oropendolas are the most obvious homologues of caciques, and sometimes both can be seen sharing the same tree for their nesting colonies. They may even feed their young the same kinds of food.

Not surprisingly, polygyny has evolved in oropendolas, too, yet in oropendolas, important behavioral differences have permitted polygyny to proceed along a somewhat different course. Unlike caciques, most oropendolas forage in flocks when they are away from the colony. It isn't known why they do this—perhaps because they are larger and less agile than caciques and thus gain protection from predators by foraging together. In any case, because female oropendolas both nest and feed together, the potential exists for a single dominant male to guard and consort with all of the females of a colony. This option, of course, is not open to male caciques because their females generally forage alone. And the curious habit of oropendolas all leaving their colony together to forage helps explain why giant cowbirds are much more successful in parasitizing oropendola colonies than those of caciques in Peru.

Polygyny in one form or another is especially prevalent among blackbirds, the family to which both caciques and oropendolas belong. For example, males of red-winged blackbirds and tropical dwellers like yellow-hooded and scarlet-hooded blackbirds defend a patch of marsh and try to attract as many females as possible to it. But in such cases, rival males are competing primarily for resources for their females, rather than directly for females, and aggression between males is minimized because they are separated on territories.

Caciques and oropendolas, on the other hand, guard their females directly—a system that often leads to fighting and direct challenges to a male's dominance. Consequently, male caciques and oropendolas are much larger than females. Male crested oropendolas weigh nearly three times as much as females—a size difference that is among the largest known for any bird; male caciques weigh about 50 to 90 percent more than the females.

Because successful defense of a harem of females against rivals is probably a function of size, there is very strong natural selection favoring large size in male oropendolas—more so presumably than among caciques, where males are limited to only one female at a time. The extreme size differences between male and female oropendolas is most likely the result of a polygyny that emphasizes defense of a harem rather than of a sequence of individual females.

When I observe the complexity of organization in a busy cacique colony, I cannot help but wonder how many people must have passed by cacique colonies with scarcely a thought to their existence or an inkling of their marvelous society until Scott Robinson paused to observe and record what he saw in the Manu River Basin. But grand as it is, the caciques' story is only one of many rainforest stories that awaits telling, and perhaps it is not even the grandest or most complex of all. We can only hope that others will continue to search for these yet untold stories.

# Sound Strategies

## Sopranos Should Sing
## From the Treetops

I HEARD THE WHISTLES—an urgent series of rapid piercing notes. There was no mistaking the message. Danger! The messenger was a white-fronted nunbird that had spotted danger—perhaps a hawk overhead or a forest-falcon in the understory—and was sounding the alarm to its mate and family.

The nunbird alarm whistles are heard and understood by virtually every bird in the forest. They also are understood by every brown capuchin monkey. One foraging nearby repeated the whistles of the nunbird almost perfectly. The forest became eerily quiet, but after a minute or two, faint chips and weak singing signaled an all clear. Soon everything was back to normal.

This kind of drama is a daily occurrence in the lives of the nunbirds. Widespread in lowland rainforests, they are large birds, dark gray in color with a white forehead and a big coral bill that is useful for capturing large insects. But nunbirds are slow and clumsy. Perhaps to compensate for their lethargy, they often sit quietly waiting for large but slow-moving prey. As a consequence of this sit-and-watch strategy, the sharp-eyed nunbirds are often quick to spot danger and sound the alarm.

An alarm call is used to warn a mate or offspring of danger, and if it is to work at a distance, it must be easy to hear and unambiguous so there is no chance of mistaking the message. Other birds, including specialized sentinel species like shrike-tanagers and some antshrikes, also have alarm whistles that sound similar to the nunbirds'. There is undeniable value in species giving similar-sounding warning calls because a single call type can be easily recognized by all.

But there is more to an alarm whistle than being easy to recognize. Why, for example, is the alarm sound a whistle at all? Why wouldn't a trill or a rattle or a higher-frequency or lower-frequency sound serve equally well? Would the same kind of vocalization work just as well in open habitats or treetops, or does the environment in which a bird lives limit or shape, through natural selection, the range of sound options that are available to it?

Some sounds travel very well across great distances while others do not. To understand why this happens, it is worth remembering that sound travels in waves. The frequency or pitch of the sound we hear is related to the number of waves per unit of time; the more waves, the higher the pitch and vice versa. And in general, low-pitched sounds travel farther than high ones of similar intensity because the waves are farther apart and travel around solid objects such as trees. This is why the low drumming of a grouse or the low humming song of a curassow travels much farther through the forest than the high, thin call of a warbler.

Natural environments differ greatly in their ability to propagate and absorb sounds. Almost everyone has had the experience of hearing sound waves echo in a rocky canyon. Solid surfaces like rocks reflect most sound waves back toward the listener, but these same sound waves hardly carry at all in a snowstorm because softly falling snowflakes quickly absorb most of the sound. Once, my wife and I were caught by a surprise snowstorm in the Colorado Rockies. With snowfall reducing our visibility to near zero, we temporarily lost the trail and decided to walk in opposite compass directions for an agreed-upon distance to search for the trail. Though we were separated by less than 100 yards and yelled as loudly as possible to maintain contact, the densely falling snow completely absorbed the sound, and we were unable to hear each other.

Forest environments can reflect sounds, amplify, absorb or even alter the properties of a sound before it reaches an intended receiver. Sounds such as the contact calls of a dipper can be readily heard even above the noise of a rushing stream, yet the high-pitched begging calls of young birds in the nest may carry only a few feet.

The alarms used by the nunbirds, capuchins, shrike-tanagers and other species in the rainforest are pure, medium-pitched whistles. They are easily heard in the upper levels of the rainforest. But do they work equally well at ground level in the rainforest or in open grasslands or in the wind? Would another kind of sound transmit better in these habitats?

Eugene Morton, when a graduate student at Yale, was one of the first people to grapple with the problem of how, or whether, environments, particularly tropical ones, influence bird songs. Morton conducted his research in Panama in three kinds of habitats—rainforest, forest edge and grassland. He first broadcast a test tape of randomized sounds in their habitats and rerecorded them at various distances. He then measured the amount of degradation of sound that occurred as they passed through the habitats. Armed with these results, he recorded the songs of 177 different species of birds and began looking for patterns in the physical structure of the bird songs that he could associate with sound transmission in each habitat. His study firmly established a connection between pure-tone bird sounds and the density of the vegetation.

Morton discovered that pure, relatively unvarying tones of low to intermediate frequency—between about 1 kHz and 2.5 kHz—traveled best in the rainforest. Lower frequency sounds didn't travel as well through the rainforest because echoes and reverberations interfered. Higher-pitched sounds attenuated rapidly and were quickly lost amid the vegetation.

When he then examined the bird songs, Morton found a striking correlation. Most of the birds living in the rainforest understory were using song frequencies in this same, relatively low-pitched to medium-pitched range. Their songs were often whistles or other pure tones that didn't vary much in frequency—precisely the kinds of vocalizations that penetrated best through the forest. They are the kinds of sounds that we hear from tinamous, quail-doves, ground-cuckoos, antbirds, antpittas, nightingale-wrens and ant-tanagers—inhabitants of the lower story or floor of the rainforest. Their songs are decidedly lower in frequency than their forest canopy and grassland counterparts.

The song of the chestnut-backed antbird provides a perfect example of the kind of vocalization that is well suited for broadcast from low heights inside the rainforest. Walking along a forest trail at dawn in the lowlands of Costa Rica or Panama, visitors often hear the song of this common and rather conservatively dressed bird whose most distinctive feature is its bare blue eye patch. The song consists of two or three pure whistles at about 2 kHz; the last whistle is downslurred a bit. This pitch falls precisely into the middle of Morton's sound window zone, and it is also about the same pitch that most humans use to whistle. The antbird's song, for this reason, is very easy to imitate.

Besides producing a song that projects well through the forest, there are other advantages to singing notes of similar frequency. By concentrating all of the sound energy into a narrow frequency range, a bird is able to sing louder while using less energy than it would if the energy were spread over a broad frequency band.

But of more interest to naturalists hoping to locate a rare species by its vocalization or to an individual bird hoping to communicate with a mate, pure tones such as whistles are easier to hear than modulated sounds when projected against the spectrum of noise produced by rustling leaves, wind, rain and insects in the forest or along a stream. Dippers, which spend their entire lives along noisy streams, have particularly loud pure-tone contact calls that don't vary much in pitch. Their calls can be easily heard at a distance, even above noisy streams.

In the openness of the canopy, there are few reverberations and echoes because the vegetation is not dense. Consequently, canopy birds are able to sing songs of higher frequency than their neighbors in the understory because there is less attenuation or loss of high-pitched sounds. Rapidly modulated notes—notes that change in frequency (pitch) and amplitude (loudness)—are commonly used by canopy birds. These notes permit more variation in songs, and they still can be heard easily at some distance. Modulated notes sound quavering, even echolike, if the notes

A MUSICIAN WREN SINGS AN UNUSUALLY
COMPLEX SONG IN THE RAINFOREST
UNDERSTORY.

are given slowly, but at the speed they are delivered by most birds, we hear them as trills or buzzes. In the canopy of rainforests in the New World Tropics, songs composed of rapidly modulated notes are sung by trogons, woodcreepers, antwrens, flycatchers, greenlets and some tanagers.

Despite what you might expect, grasslands and other open areas are not necessarily easy environments for sound propagation. Days are often windy, and wind turbulence, as well as variation in wind speed, affects the propagation of sound. Temperatures are likely to fluctuate widely from early morning to midday and from ground level up as well. Because of temperature gradients and air movement, rapid sound loss can occur even over short distances, and this affects a bird's ability to discriminate between songs. On a clear, calm morning or evening in the quiet countryside, voices carry long distances—you might hear the sounds of normal conversation an eighth of a mile or more away. Yet, on a hot, windy day, you probably couldn't yell loudly enough to attract someone's attention at the same distance.

When Eugene Morton measured average song frequencies of tropical grassland birds, he discovered their songs were almost twice the average pitch of those of birds living low inside the rainforest. Furthermore, songs of the grassland birds were composed mostly of modulated sounds that spanned a broad range of frequencies. In other words, the songs contained many trills, buzzes and changes of pitch. The songs of grassland birds resemble a coded message—one that depends more upon the spacing of notes and phrases in time than on the loudness or pitch of the notes. As long as even part of the song can be heard, it will be recognizable, and the singer can be identified. And to be recognized is, after all, what matters most.

Grassland birds everywhere, from the Arctic to Patagonia, usually have complex songs that are sung either in flight or from a prominent perch. Songs like these are seldom found among rainforest birds. The little sliding notes and buzzes of a savanna sparrow, or the complex flight song of a pipit are put into perspective by the knowledge that they represent particular solutions to the problem of communication in the open, often windy environment where they live.

Sounds broadcast at ground level don't carry well in any environment—whether inside the forest or in the open. This explains why birds seek an elevated perch to sing. In the absence of a high perch, many birds simply take to the air and sing in flight. The problem with singing from ground level is that, in the first place, much of the sound energy is absorbed by the ground itself. Secondly, sound waves traveling parallel to the ground tend to be pushed or deflected upward by wind currents and air-temperature gradients. This causes a zone to develop between the rising sound waves and the ground where no sound energy penetrates. Sound engineers call this a sound shadow.

No wonder dickcissels, meadowlarks and other grassland birds readily use man-made perches, such as fences and telephone poles. At a height of only three feet, most of the ground-effect problem disappears, and at 10 to 20 feet, the negative effects of wind currents and temperature gradients largely disappear too. So it should come as no surprise that so many species have evolved flight songs as a means of increasing their ability to broadcast their messages. About 25 percent of Panama's grassland birds have flight songs. In the pampas and Patagonian steppes of Argentina, it is much the same. During a Patagonian spring, it seems as if nearly all birds take to the air—seedsnipes, dotterels, ground-tyrants and pipits alike—in an aerial orchestration of sound as rich and varied as any in the world.

Few people spend much time in the New World Tropics without meeting the friendly little blue-black grassquit. It seems to be common wherever there are neglected pastures and cleared or waste areas, and while its buzzy, unmusical song isn't much to brag about, its comical little jump display is sure to be noticed. Perched on the tops of grass and weed stems or on fences, the grassquit jumps straight up into the air a few feet and then sings as it flips forward and tumbles back to its perch. It may repeat this performance half a dozen times a minute.

Why do grassquits do this? Although thousands of naturalists have watched grassquits leap and sing, few have commented on the possible significance of these acrobatics. Three researchers, Walter Wicynski,

Michael Ryan and Eliot Brenowitz, who studied the grassquit in Panama, produced measurements which indicate that at the top of the leap, the grassquit's song can be heard over an area almost twice as large as that reached when the bird is perched. The larger area corresponds to the territory defended by each male grassquit. For the grassquit, jumping up as it sings accomplishes what a meadowlark does when it flies up to the top of a fence post to sing.

Some nonforest birds use fairly high-pitched songs composed of pure whistled sounds in what seems to be a vocal repudiation of the laws of physics. How do they achieve maximum sound projection and song pattern recognition in these breezy environments using seemingly inappropriate vocalizations? These species seem to have solved the problems associated with air turbulence by singing only early in the morning before the winds and daytime temperature gradients can distort their songs or cause sound loss. For instance, in partially open areas in Panama, the rufous-tailed hummingbird sings for about an hour at dawn using pure tonelike sounds, but the fork-tailed emerald, which sings a buzzy song, is able to continue throughout the day. This pattern is also repeated in the grasslands of South America. In eastern Bolivia, the red-winged tinamou's short song of three or four pure whistled notes can be heard drifting over the grasslands only at dawn or dusk—a time when the air is still and cool.

The convergence of song patterns among birds in similar environments cuts right across species' lines, suggesting that the environment in which a bird sings strongly influences the type of song it should use. Among the oscines, or singing birds, which include about half of all birds in the world, forest dwellers have songs that are significantly lower in frequency than their oscine allies living in edge or open areas. In the Neotropics, most fringillids—finches, seedeaters, grassquits and so on—are forest-edge or grassland species, and they usually sing buzzy songs, or complicated songs composed of both pure tones and modulated sounds. However, two common fringillids, the blue-black grosbeak and slate-colored grosbeak, live inside the forest. Unlike their open-country allies, both species have songs that are mainly pure whistled tones within a narrow and rather low to moderate frequency range typical of forest birds.

Examples of convergence in song type that correlate with the structure of the environment can be found in many groups of birds. Antbirds of the genus *Myrmeciza* include species that inhabit the rainforest interior and others that occur in forest-edge zones. Deep forest dwellers like the chestnut-tailed, white-shouldered and sooty antbirds sing notes that are pure, low-pitched tones in a narrow frequency range. The edge-inhabiting white-bellied, plumbeous and black-throated antbirds sing their songs much faster and have many rapidly modulated notes that span a wider and higher frequency range.

The different vocalizations of four neotropical vireos of the genus *Hylophilus* also parallel the distinct habitats in which each lives. All four occur in central Panama and are similar in plumage. Tawny-crowned greenlets are found in rainforests, usually in the lower half of the forest strata. Their advertising call is a pure-tone whistle almost entirely on one pitch. Scrub greenlets live in open areas with shrubby trees, and their song is a long series of medium-pitched, pulsating whistles that consist of essentially the same note uttered over and over. The lesser greenlet and golden-fronted greenlet are found in rainforest canopy and dense forest-edge zones, respectively, and their songs are the most complex of the greenlets and are also quite similar to each other, as might be expected from the similarity of their habitats.

The songs of nearly all birds throughout the world are sung at pitches at or below about 8 kHz. This level seems to represent an upper limit for effective long-distance sound communication. Above this, sounds are so degraded by the environment that they do not carry well. Over short distances, however, birds do make frequent use of sounds well over 8 kHz, indicating that there is no physiological limit to producing or hearing very high-pitched sounds. Under some circumstances, this can be advantageous, permitting communication between individuals at short distances without alerting possible predators or competitors. Even an alarm call can be very high-pitched if the intended receiver is close by. Nestlings use very high-pitched begging calls, presumably for this reason, and copulatory calls are often very high-pitched as well.

Naturalists have commented upon the beauty and the complexity or simplicity of bird songs for centuries—most without realizing that the beauty or the purity of the song was at least partly molded by the habitat in which the bird lived. The acoustical characteristics of bird habitats are only a framework within which other sources of natural selection, such as territory size, behavior and sexual displays, operate to mold the sounds that we hear. By looking at the structure of an environment, we cannot predict why one bird sings a more beautiful song than another, or why one gets along with only one or two songs while another sings dozens. But we can be relatively sure that the songs they sing have been winnowed through time for their adaptive value.

I can still appreciate the beauty of a bird's song, but now I listen to them a little differently than I used to. The slow, clear whistles of an antpitta somewhere in the rainforest, the clear, pleasing phrases of the wood thrush and the chattering song of a little greenlet or warbler high overhead have new meaning now. I understand that these birds sing the way they do, in part, because of the acoustic stage on which they perform.

# *Perilous Paradise*
## Tropical River Islands

**T**ROPICAL ISLANDS have always beckoned irresistibly to those who seek refuge and shelter—and visions of shimmering coral seas, blue-green lagoons and idyllic adventures lure those of us who dream of freedom from the complexities of life. Robinson Crusoe's mythical existence as well as those of others, real or imagined, was spawned from these dreams. A Castelnau's antshrike owes its existence to the shelter of a tropical island, too, but one of a different kind—a tropical river island in the midst of the churning Amazon.

Tropical river islands are not benign places. They are baked by a burning sun and ravaged by crushing floods that sweep them away overnight or leave them drowned for weeks at a time. So why do antshrikes and other species that live mainly on tropical river islands prefer these high-stakes risks to the methodical predictability of the rainforest?

The first tropical river island I visited was several hours up the Amazon River from the raucous port town of Leticia, Colombia. Little did I know that this island would soon provide me with a pivotal introduction to tropical river-island biology. The island was large—nearly two miles long and half a mile wide. The nearest mainland riverbank lay on the Colombian side about a mile away; the opposite riverbank, claimed by Peru, was even farther away. The upper end of the island was covered by tall forest, mostly composed of figs (*Ficus*), bucare (*Erythrina*) and *Cecropia* trees; the lower end was a succession of sand, grass and shrubs. Almost from the moment I set foot on shore, I was struck by how abundant birds were on the island and how easy many of them were to see.

A small frame cabin with a thatched roof was the only shelter on the island. The cabin was raised up on stilts, almost as high as a person's shoulders, so the twice-annual floodwaters that covered the island could pass harmlessly beneath. A narrow muddy path led past a huge old mango tree and down to the riverbank, but when the water was high, a boat was simply tied to the porch. There was no electricity and cooking was done on a little two-burner kerosene stove—crusty and blackened from years of neglect. There was no bathroom or shower, but the mighty Amazon River itself, barely a stone's throw away, supplied more than enough water to meet the most demanding hygienic needs. I also have memories of mosquitoes, leaky, uncomfortable dugout canoes and calf-deep mud that sucked off boots and turned every trail into an obstacle course.

But to an ornithologist, it was an idyllic place, teeming with birds. The melancholy whistles of undulated tinamous, once likened to the first notes of the barcarolle in Offenbach's opera *The Tales of Hoffmann*, issued round-the-clock from the depths of *Heliconia*-choked fig swamps. Tiger-herons croaked in the predawn darkness as they stalked the shores of the backwater lagoon behind the cabin; hoatzins with radioactive-looking red eyes glared from swampy thickets; and a dozen kinds of parrots, parakeets and macaws squealed overhead in raucous confusion. Barbets, attilas and a parade of colorful honeycreepers and tanagers roamed the clearing. Resident oropendolas and caciques were joined each evening by hundreds from the mainland that came for safety from nocturnal predators. A few antbirds and spinetails skulked around in dark places on the island too.

During those first days of wonderment, just learning the birds on the island and in the tall rainforests on the far riverbanks was a challenge. I hadn't accumulated enough information to begin sorting out groups of species according to the habitats they preferred. It was clear there were a number of birds on the island that I never saw in the adjacent mainland forests, but with more than 500 species of birds in the area, I couldn't be sure that they didn't occur in both places. In all, there were nearly 20 species that I never found on the mainland.

The island where I was staying was large and fairly old as far as Amazonian river islands go. Consequently, it boasted a rather diverse forest and many different kinds of birds. The twice-annual flooding, though, resulted in a turnover of the resident bird species. Terrestrial birds, in particular, and some others whose food resources are affected by flooding, leave the island temporarily during the high-water season. Some species nest here, others arrive from the mainland forests at dusk to roost, and many widespread edge species reach the island from distant locations.

Edge species such as kingbirds, social flycatchers and blue-gray tanagers use island forests as stepping stones for traveling, much as they would the forest border or the top of the canopy on the mainland. There are also some river-island specialists—birds that inhabit certain early vegetation stages on these river islands and are found almost nowhere else. Only much later, after visiting several smaller river islands—ones with simple vegetation communities that are perhaps more vulnerable to the power and fury of the river—did I find this curious group of island specialists to be conspicuous. On these small islands, the specialists are very common and outnumber even widespread species.

Through hindsight, the concept of river-island specialists seems obvious. Why did it take so long for ornithologists to recognize the uniqueness of this fascinating group of birds that live in pioneer plant communities which spring up almost overnight on sandbars and islands left in the wake of floods? These are the gamblers, the species that risk the odds and live in defiance of powerful floods that can create an entire island or destroy it in one cataclysmic burst of liquid energy. Other questions still remain. Why are these interesting birds with the gypsy life-styles so abundant on the islands? Is their fate sealed with the next great flood, or by some premonition do they leave in time to seek other homes?

Islands in the Amazon and other large rivers are created in one of two ways: they form when the river cuts a new channel or they form from sandbars. When a river cuts a new channel, the vegetation, birds and animals isolated on the island are the same as those on the mainland riverbank, though eventually sandbars may form on the downstream end of the island and create opportunities for new plant and animal colonization. More important for the river-island specialists, however, are the islands which start as sandbars that build up behind eddies.

The muddy Amazon carries enormous quantities of silt, and sandy islands, which dot the entire length of the river system, can form almost overnight in its turbulent, swirling waters and silt-laden tributaries. These islands are of great importance to river-island birds because the young shrubby vegetation they prefer occurs most abundantly there. Several stages of pioneering plants rapidly colonize new sandbars, and island-hopping avian specialists are seldom far behind.

Sand builds up along river bends and forms long, sweeping beaches on the inside bank. Sandy beaches are formed on the downstream side of river islands in the same manner. Soon, several plants colonize these beaches and become sorted into distinctive vegetation communities.

Grasses occupy the outermost zone—the one nearest the water—and are followed almost in lockstep by *Tessaria*, a shrubby willowlike tree that belongs to the sunflower, or Composite, family. The fast-growing *Tessaria* matures in three to four years and is rapidly invaded by a tall cane that is itself soon shaded out by spindly and even taller *Cecropia* trees. In five to ten years, the *Cecropia* is overtopped by figs and bucare. So, proceeding from the beach at the lower end of a river island back toward the forest, each vegetation zone, like a chorus on risers, grows a little taller and lasts a little longer than the preceding one.

Eventually, the grass and cane give way in shady places to broadleaved herbs such as *Heliconias*, gingers and amaranths. If the island survives long enough, the figs become tall, and in time, they are joined by other kinds of trees and a more complex forest evolves. This last stage can last for decades if the island isn't washed away during a flood. But most river islands are washed away long before plant succession advances this far.

River islands tend to cycle through a series of stages. The downstream end of an island continues to grow downstream as silt and sand is deposited, and this is where colonizing opportunities abound for fast-growing, pioneering plants. This is also where birds that are island-habitat specialists concentrate. The upstream end of an island—the oldest and most vulnerable—is almost constantly eroded away by floods and river currents. So an island tends to travel downstream.

The time that it takes for an island to completely replace itself—that is to move downstream by a full length—varies from one season to decades. This places an upper limit on the age of trees on a tropical river island, and probably few trees reach the ripe old age of 30. Some islands, even big ones, may simply disappear overnight in one cataclysmic flood, while others are sculpted and reshaped after each high-water season but survive for many years.

The early grass, *Tessaria* forest and *Cecropia* forest are the most important habitats for island-specialist birds. In the Amazon River Basin, these pioneer vegetation communities are usually most extensive on sandy or muddy river islands, though they also occur along riverbanks. Along a few rivers, such as the Río Napo in eastern Ecuador, islands seldom survive long enough to develop much vegetation. There, birds simply shift to zones of grass that grow on the enormous sandbars that develop along the riverbanks.

River-island specialists pose some perplexing biological questions for naturalists. What set of characteristics, for example, could possibly be shared by such a widely divergent group of birds as a parrotlet, a hummingbird and several furnariids, antbirds, flycatchers and honeycreepers? There is even a tiny woodpecker, called a piculet, that occurs on these islands and almost nowhere else.

There isn't much that distinguishes them from their relatives that live along river edges, lakes and streams, except that these habitat specialists confine themselves mainly to the first plant communities that appear on sandbars. Perhaps ancestry brings the pioneers together on tropical river islands. All but two of them are members of genera that are widespread and typical of open and brushy habitats, which is not unlike the young vegetation on a river sandbar. The behavioral traits that permitted the ancestors of these birds to succeed in open habitats would surely have preadapted them for life in similar places on tropical river islands.

Gary Rosenberg, a graduate student at Louisiana State University, was the first person to carry out a study of this curious group of birds. When he looked at where the birds foraged, he found that about half of the island birds occurred in just one of the scrub habitats. One species, for instance might live only in the *Tessaria* trees, while another might live only in the cane and grass and so on. Rosenberg found, for example, that two members of the honeycreeper family, the pearly-breasted and bicolored conebills, spent most of their time in the tops of the *Cecropia* trees, while ash-breasted antbirds skulked in *Heliconia* thickets beneath them.

The *Tessaria* scrub was especially important, and many of the island specialists foraged there at least part of the time. Several, such as the wagtail-tyrant and white-bellied spinetail, spent all of their time in *Tessaria* scrub. This extreme specialization, Rosenberg believes, is the most important distinction between the island scrub birds and other more widespread birds that also occurred on the islands.

Few of the birds found on river islands are also found in the rainforest. One reason for the distinctiveness of river-island birdlife when compared to that of nearby rainforest is the tremendous difference in the structure of the habitats. Only a bird that is an extreme habitat-generalist would be able to inhabit the simple river-edge, scrub and tall-forest habitats. Nevertheless, as old islands, like the one where I stayed near Leticia, develop taller, more complex forest vegetation at their upper ends, they are colonized by some forest birds.

As the structure of the river-island forest matures, it begins to resemble that of the forest on the adjacent river floodplain. The main factor that prevents many species from colonizing these islands is probably their inability to cross large areas of open water. Near Leticia, Colombia, which is still 2,000 miles above the mouth of the Amazon River, the Amazon's banks are nearly five miles apart at their widest point, and an island located somewhere in the middle of the river could be more than two miles from the closest mainland bank. Most raptors, parrots, icterids and aquatic birds can easily cross such distances. So can most toucans, umbrellabirds, fruitcrows and large flycatchers because these birds generally forage in the open forest canopy or in open areas outside the forest.

Birds of the forest interior, however, usually stay near cover and may hesitate even before crossing a forest trail. Such species are rarely found on river islands.

Floods, which cover most river islands twice a year, limit colonization opportunities for terrestrial birds. Nevertheless, some notoriously terrestrial species manage to find their way onto river islands. Tinamous are renowned for their retiring, forest-dwelling habits and reluctance to fly, yet the undulated tinamou forages and breeds on river islands and leaves only when the islands are underwater. The undulated tinamou, in a flurry of rapid wingbeats, simply hurtles itself straight out over the open water of the Amazon River.

It must be a daunting decision for this normally reclusive forest bird to travel to river islands. Standing on the Amazon's banks near Leticia, Colombia, the river is immense, oceanic and intimidating. From one side, you can barely make out the forest—a mere thread on the horizon—crowding the far bank. I once watched a tinamou reach an island that was at least a mile from the nearest riverbank, and I expect the bird could have flown much farther. Because river islands are isolated and relatively inaccessible to many mainland predators such as monkeys, they are safe refuges for nesting and roosting and thus apparently worth the risk of a long overwater flight.

Two other terrestrial birds, the pale-legged hornero and the lesser hornero, also thrive on river islands. These ambitious birds scrape up mud from the edges of pools and riverbanks and carry it to a tree where they construct their ball-like nests that resemble little brick ovens, hence their name, which means oven in Spanish. Horneros sing clattering songs and, when not working on their nests, which are usually placed conspicuously on bare branches, these jaunty little masons roam around on foot and search for food. When the islands are flooded, horneros move up into shrubbery to forage or cross to higher ground on the mainland.

River-island birds are unusual for their ability to quickly build up populations whose numbers far surpass those of related species found in mature forests on the mainland. When Gary Rosenberg began censusing populations on several river islands near Iquitos in northern Peru, he was astonished at how abundant species were. On one island, the commonest species, the white-bellied spinetail, averaged over ten pairs per acre—a density more than ten times higher than that of their relatives on the mainland.

All of the island specialists are insect eaters, and insect populations, like those of the birds that eat them, must build up rapidly on these islands. An abundance of food is important to nesting success, but the virtual lack of nest predators is probably of greater importance to breeding success. With no marauding monkeys or squirrels and few other mammalian or reptilian nest predators, island birds achieve some of the highest breeding success rates anywhere in the American Tropics.

Large, almost unrestricted population growth for a few years is eventually balanced by emigration as individuals fan out in search of suitable new islands or are killed in floods. Even where islands and riverbanks escape the ravages of flooding for a few years, the cane, *Tessaria* and *Cecropia*—the essential habitat ingredients of the specialists—may eventually be shaded out and replaced by a more diverse association of trees, thus limiting birds to only a few generations before having to move. Rapid population buildups and emigration appear to be an essential part of these birds' overall strategy of taking advantage of brief windows of opportunity in an otherwise highly unpredictable environment.

River-island specialists have evolved in Amazonia but not in other large river basins of the world. Ornithologists J. Van Remsen and Ted Parker of Louisiana State University studied river-island birds over a wide area of western Amazonia, and they believe that several factors may have contributed to the emergence and success of this unique group of birds.

Of course, scientists can only speculate as to what these factors may have been and what their importance is. The Amazon and its tributaries make up the largest river system in the world, altogether carrying more than one-fifth of the world's freshwater back to the sea. The Amazon Basin is also one of the flattest places on earth, with a gradient that drops less than an inch per mile for the last 2,000 miles of its journey to the

Atlantic Ocean. This extraordinary flatness contributes to extensive flooding, which occurs twice annually. Each flood creates new islands and destroys old ones in an inexorable cycle—an island is lost and another is gained in a dynamic exchange that sometimes results in radical face-lifts of riverine environments every few months. Season in and season out, the floodwaters leave in their wake a succession of newly emerging microhabitats, each a golden opportunity for fast-reacting colonists.

The tremendous size of the river system not only creates an abundance of habitats but it also acts as a buffer against long-term climatic changes that might result in extinctions. Most river-island specialists are distributed along thousands of miles of river courses—along the Amazon and up and down its large tributaries. Their distributions may span geographical distances much larger than their mainland forest counterparts—a factor that helps insulate their populations during adverse climatic conditions.

Seasonal floods drown vast areas along the Amazon and its tributaries for weeks at a time. The Amazon can rise and fall 30 to 40 feet in a few days and transform vast areas of floodplain forest into tree-filled lakes. Humans live and travel in canoes, fish swim among the trees and most wildlife flees to higher ground or takes to the trees. River-island birds, whether terrestrial or arboreal, must adjust to these floods that may submerge their territories for weeks at a time or completely destroy them.

*Tessaria* trees are usually no more than 10 to 15 feet high and are regularly submerged during high water. As long as they remain rooted in the sand, most emerge from weeks of drowning with little visible damage. Nevertheless, when *Tessaria* and other island vegetation is covered by water, the island birds, unlike their forest relatives that can move higher in trees, must disperse to suitable new areas.

Most tropical birds, especially those that live in the forest understory, are very poor at dispersing across open areas or through different habitats. Several of the riverine shrub specialists belong to families whose members are notoriously poor dispersers. Antbirds are usually considered to be among the most sedentary of all neotropical birds, so it comes as a surprise that four of the nineteen river-island specialists in western Amazonia are antbirds.

Most river islands are colonized quickly. On a tiny island less than a year old and only partially covered with grass and *Tessaria*, Rosenberg found that several specialists, as well as other river-edge birds, were already common. The shortest overwater distance from the mainland to the island was more than half a mile. Islands are often separated by much longer distances—they are sometimes miles apart—and the nearest riverbanks, often a half mile or more away, contain little suitable habitat.

Nothing is known about the dispersal of river-island specialists. Scientists, for example, do not known when they leave, how they search for new islands, how far they go or what kind of mortality they suffer during dispersal. But we do know that at least occasionally they move from island to island by one of the oldest methods known—rafting down the river.

During high-water seasons, the awesome power of the Amazon River is unleashed on the land itself. Everything in the river's path gets swept away. Riverbanks are undercut and acres of forest disappear with the blink of an eye. Floating islands of grass and trees, some as large as ships, are swept downriver. And like the biblical Ark, these floating islands transport many of the Amazon's rainforest creatures, willingly or unwillingly, to new and unfamiliar destinations. Some, such as small mammals and reptiles, have little choice but to go where the currents take them. Others, like birds, may voluntarily hitchhike to new destinations.

Once on the Amazon River, I saw a male chestnut-bellied seedeater cheerfully singing from a little twig as it rafted downriver on a large floating mat of grass. I passed the seedeater in a motorized dugout, but then stopped several kilometers downstream. Some time later, to my amazement, I looked out from the bank and saw this same bird passing me by, still perched atop his precarious raft and singing as cheerfully as ever.

I have seen yellow-hooded blackbirds drifting downriver on miniature islands, too, and suspect that, over time, many birds are transported downstream in this curious manner. Neither the seedeater nor the blackbird are riverine-scrub specialists, but they inhabit the river edges and open habitats of Amazonia and both demonstrate the feasibility of dispersing in one direction—downstream—without really having to leave cover.

Compared to the size of the Amazon Basin, the total area of river-island and river-edge scrub is minuscule. The populations of most river-island specialists, even though they are very dense on the islands, are still quite small in comparison with those of mainland birds. By their very nature, river-island species are dependent upon the continued formation of river islands. Perhaps never before, not even during epochs of Pleistocene aridity, have the birds been as vulnerable as they are today to a complete collapse of the ecological machinery that is responsible for forming river islands.

Deforestation in the Andes has the potential to greatly alter flood cycles hundreds, even thousands, of miles away in the Amazon Basin—and it is already doing so. Without forests to retard the runoff, every heavy rain in the mountains has the potential to become a dangerous flood. While a flood in one small valley is not likely to affect water levels far downriver on the Amazon, the combined floods from many watersheds may. Already, residents near Iquitos, for example, say that floods are occurring more frequently and cresting at higher levels than they have ever experienced. They point to deforestation in the Andes as the culprit.

High rates of flooding interfere with the normal creation and destruction of sandbars and river islands and result in a loss of island vegetation. Additionally, frequent flooding interferes with the normal breeding cycles of island birds, which out of necessity must confine their activities to low-water periods. New hydroelectric plants on tributaries in the lower Amazon Basin could further disrupt river-island communities by virtually eliminating floods and resulting in the complete cessation of normal river-island formation. Sandbar plants and their avian colonists will find fewer and fewer opportunities for colonization, and the ecological machinery that keeps the river-island ecosystem viable could grind to a halt.

River-island specialists owe their existence to the interaction of a complex set of physical and biological conditions that are virtually unique to the Amazon Basin. I cannot help but marvel at how these small birds cope with the demands of an environment whose physical structure is altered after almost every flood. I wonder about the ways in which such a demanding environment molds everyday activities like breeding, territorial behavior and dispersal. We can learn much from these birds. Perhaps this unique little community of birds will one day help us to better understand the greatest river system in the world.

# In Search of a Season
## When Do Tropical Birds Nest?

O NE OF THE surest signs of spring in northern latitudes is the return of migrant birds and the explosion of song and activity that accompanies their arrival. They come fresh from exotic tropical lands and, between April and July, nothing is so urgent as the business of reproduction; many raise two broods during this brief but frantically productive time. In south-temperate latitudes, spring arrives between September and November, and the changes there—from the dreary browns and grays of winter to the exhilarating greens of spring—are equally dramatic.

All across southern Brazil and Argentina, migrating birds arrive from wintering grounds in the Amazon Basin or northern South America. Their annual pilgrimage southward prompted W. H. Hudson, in his classic *The Naturalist in La Plata* to write of spring on his beloved Argentine pampas:

> When, in July and August, I watched for the coming spring, it was the migrants, the birds that came annually to us from the far north, that chiefly attracted me. Before their arrival the bloom was gone from the peach trees, and the choir of countless little finches broken up and scattered all over the plain.

Inside tropical latitudes, however, discrete nesting seasons, like those in temperate latitudes, aren't always easy to recognize. Spring in the temperate zone, with its lengthening days, warmer temperatures and resurgence of insect activity, is the anchor to which the reproductive activities of so many plants and animals are tied. This anchor is lost in the perpetual warmth of the Tropics. Years may pass in a charmed but unchanging way with no predictable climatic events to mark the passage of time. There is no rejoicing the bursting life of spring's renewal nor lamenting the cold bare landscape of winter.

In the Western Andes of Colombia, I once lived in a valley where the rainfall averaged more than 14 feet a year; no month would ever be called dry, yet this wasn't the wettest valley in the area. Some nearby areas reported annual rainfall averages of twice that amount. Moreover, at about three degrees above the equator, there was only a small difference in day length between the longest days in June and the shortest in December.

As part of my research, I kept records of all bird breeding activity, but finding the nests of rainforest birds can be challenging. They tend to be well hidden and therefore difficult to locate. Predation on eggs and nestlings in the tropical rainforest is high, and a bird's best defense against predation is making their nests difficult to find. For the naturalist interested in finding nests there is another challenge, too, for most tropical birds become extremely furtive and quiet when they are nesting, and this only adds to the difficulty of finding them.

Over a 15-month period, I found nests of about 40 species—less than 15 percent of all the species that occurred there, but I did not always have to find nests to be sure that breeding was in progress. Other clues may be birds carrying nest material, food and fecal sacs and adults with fledged young. Sometimes the activities of hole-nesting birds are betrayed by telltale signs of bent and frayed tails—the result of incubating and spending much time in the cramped confines of a nest chamber. I also mist-netted birds and examined them for the presence of brood patches—a sign that incubation is in progress.

Mist-netted birds permit naturalists to record molt and this, too, provides clues to breeding seasons, though in a negative sort of way. Birds normally do not molt while they are nesting because both activities require a great deal of energy—too much for both to be carried out simultaneously. The start of the annual molt, then, signals the end of a breeding season.

JABIRUS AND MANY WADERS BEGIN NESTING IN
THE RAINY SEASON IN THE LLANOS
(GRASSLANDS) OF NORTHERN SOUTH AMERICA.

In the perennially wet environment of western Colombia, I didn't expect much breeding synchrony, but that hypothesis proved to be naive. True, birds were nesting during every month of the year, but there was increased nesting activity during the first six months of the year. More surprising still, nearly half of all nesting occurred from March through June. This agrees with a broad, generally acknowledged pattern in regions of the Neotropics north of the equator. The peak nesting season for many birds of this region seems to be squeezed as much as possible into a relatively short period of time just before and during the beginning of the rainy season. A little south of the equator, the pattern is reversed. Nevertheless, because of the great variety of breeding patterns found within any tropical bird community, broad statements about tropical breeding seasons are, at best, of limited usefulness, and close to the equator few patterns are evident.

There are no simple answers that explain when tropical birds nest or how their rhythms are maintained from one year to the next. Nor is there an easy answer as to why birds in the relatively aseasonal climate of the Anchicayá Valley in Colombia still follow a breeding pattern that is broadly similar to seasonal areas in the northern part of the Neotropics. Certainly western Colombia does not look like a seasonal environment. No one that lives there would ever mistake the endless afternoons and nights of rain, month in and month out, for the more seasonal changes that mark the passage of time in the northern part of the country, and certainly no one would mistake it for the changes that occur in a temperate-latitude landscape. Yet there is a clear annual rhythm to the breeding behavior of the birds there.

Nesting seasons come with no great rush in tropical lands. Only with close scrutiny does one note that changes are under way. In most tropical land bird communities, birds can be found nesting during every month of the year. The breeding season of each species may last well over half of the year. During the annual peak of breeding, some individuals may be finishing, others just starting and the remainder perhaps somewhere in the middle of their nesting cycle.

Much of what is known about breeding seasons in Central American birds comes from a lifetime of meticulous recordkeeping by Alexander Skutch in Costa Rica. Skutch found that the greatest number of birds in Costa Rica nest from April through June—about the same time that nesting is taking place in northern latitudes. David and Barbara Snow compiled a large number of nesting records during a residence of four and a half years on the tiny island of Trinidad, which lies at about the same latitude as Costa Rica. The main nesting season was broadly similar to that in Costa Rica, though the Snows found considerably more year-to-year variation in the onset of breeding. White-bearded manakins, for example, began nesting as early as December one year and as late as May another. The drab and unassuming little ocher-bellied flycatcher varied its nesting times almost as much, and oilbirds began nesting as much as three months earlier in some years.

There may be good reasons for the lack of punctuality in the onset of nesting in tropical environments. Most naturalists believe that food abundance is ultimately the most important factor affecting the timing of nesting among tropical land birds because it is a good indication of favorable breeding conditions. But food levels can vary greatly from year to year. This differs somewhat from temperate latitudes, where changes in day length set the breeding process in motion. Biologists have generally ruled out the likelihood of day length as an important regulator of breeding seasons in low tropical latitudes. One reason for this is that, even though daylight and light intensity do change somewhat at low latitudes, tropical bird communities do not show a single breeding season, as in temperate regions, but instead show a variety of breeding patterns.

In the Tropics, the abundance of both insects and fruit is greatly affected by rainfall. Even the wettest rainforests show some year-to-year variation in these resources, and if the patterns seem insignificant or indistinguishable to humans, they are clearly seen by its inhabitants. All of the rhythms of tropical rainforests, savannas and deserts are ultimately affected by the common denominator of food.

The white-bearded manakins studied by David Snow were especially sensitive to levels of small fruits and berries—their primary food source. They begin breeding anywhere from late December to May—the period

when small berries and fruits are ripening and becoming increasingly numerous. But the fruit increase is not necessarily steady. Some years, fruit
abundance is irregular, and Snow felt that the great variability in the onset of breeding by the manakins was the result of these birds tracking the
changing levels of food.

Fruit is generally most abundant just before the onset of the rainy
season, and many kinds of insects are most numerous shortly after the
rainy season begins. This, also, is when the greatest number of tropical
birds begin nesting. Visitors new to the rainforest may find it odd that
the beginning of the rains is the time of greatest nesting activity. After
all, warm dry days should mean more rain-free time to forage and less
risk of soaking rains harming nestlings.

But there is more to a successful nesting than warm, pleasant days.
Food must be abundant enough for adult birds to feed themselves and
their young efficiently. Minimizing the time spent foraging is also an important component of the nesting equation in tropical birds. The dry
season is pleasant for well-fed human visitors, but it is often the leanest
season of the year for birds—the time when fruits and insects are least
abundant, and the time when birds have to work the hardest to find
food. The added expenditure of energy and risk associated with the
greater amount of time needed to find food in the dry season apparently
does not translate into more successfully fledged young.

In terrestrial insect-eating birds, breeding is tied to the abundance of
leaf-litter insects. As the wet season progresses, leaf-litter insects show a
gradual increase in abundance, which is associated with a softening of
the soil and more rapid decay and turnover of leaf litter. Consequently,
terrestrial and ant-following birds often have prolonged breeding seasons
that overlap most of the wet season.

Some individuals may not begin breeding until the latter half of the
wet season when leaf-litter insect populations are high and relatively stable. Leaftossers follow this strategy. These small brownish members of
the ovenbird, or furnariid, family forage by walking on the floor of tropical forests and incessantly flipping over leaves with their long bills. The
objects of their intense scrutiny are arthropods, which hide beneath

leaves. Consequently, these birds are affected by the same peaks and declines in leaf-litter insect abundance that affect other terrestrial insect eaters.

In Trinidad and northern Venezuela, the gray-throated leaftosser nests late in the year. Breeding does not begin until the last three months of the wet season—the peak of the rains—and it is in full swing when the rains end in December. Even leaftosser nests, dug deep into the sides of steep banks, seem to be an adaptation designed to deal with the heaviest downpours of the year, for their young, snug and dry at the upper end of these nest tunnels, are unaffected by rains or temperature changes.

The seed crops of tropical grasses provide naturalists with another example of a seasonal food resource that synchronizes breeding. Few tropical habitats provide such a marked seasonal contrast as the grasslands in northern and south-central South America. Roads through the llanos and pantanal are billowing clouds of dust during the dry season and wallows of axle-gripping mud in the rainy season. Grasses that lie parched and brown during the searing heat of the dry season quickly revive with the rains, sending up green shoots at the rate of an inch a day. Following a month or so of growth they flower, and grass-seed production peaks around the middle of the rainy season.

Seed-eating birds like *Sporophila* delay breeding, waiting until well into the rainy season to take advantage of the increased seed abundance. At this time of year, wandering flocks of seedeaters, searching for areas of maximum seed production, descend upon grassy fields and flutter to reach grass seeds, all the while clinging precariously to long, flexible stems that bend under their insignificant weight. Soon, grassy places everywhere are serenaded with the sweet songs of seedeater courtship.

In Venezuela and Colombia, lined and Lesson's seedeaters appear almost magically in June, some having just completed a trans-Amazonian migration perfectly timed to the rainy season abundance of the northern Tropics. We have only the merest inkling of the mental chemistry that compels them to cross thousands of miles of Amazonian rainforests in search of a season of seeds.

Marshes and lagoons pulse with life during the rainy season, but dry seasons rob wetlands of much of their life-sustaining water and the aquatic life that they support. Yellow-chinned spinetails, water-tyrants and marsh-tyrants are rarely found away from marshes, but their nesting seasons ebb and flow with the cyclic productivity of these wetlands.

During the dry season, shallow marshes and lagoons become parched and are almost devoid of the small-insect prey these birds seek. After the rainy season begins, these marshes fill up with water and the number of aquatic breeding insects increases. Only then, perhaps a month or more after the rainy season begins, do the tyrants and spine-tails begin to construct their bulky nests.

Large wading birds face increasingly lean times during the rainy season as rivers overflow their banks and floods seep across a thirsty land. The flat grasslands are transformed into vast, shallow seas, and fish and other aquatic life upon which large waders depend disperse far and wide. Yet in the midst of famine and flooding and with rains at their peak, the immense water bird communities of the Venezuelan and Colombian grasslands begin to assemble for the annual rites of courtship and nest-ing. How can this be? What rhythms orchestrate the onset of the year's most demanding activities at a time when food resources are least accessible?

Breeding in a rookery is a protracted affair, often stretching over nearly half the year. Large nests must be built or repaired, incubation may last a month or more and it is many months before nestlings take flight. Wading birds must anticipate far in advance the largess of the dry seasons because it is then, when water holes and lagoons are drying up, that fish and other prey are most concentrated and easiest to capture. By the time nestlings are demanding the greatest amount of food, thunder-clouds will be traded for blue skies and grasslands will be shimmering beneath a merciless sun that licks up every drop of moisture. Somehow these birds know that the leanness of August will give way to the abundance of January.

The breeding seasons of hummingbirds resist facile classifications. In high-Andean páramos, the main flowering season occurs during the latter half of the rainy season—usually around September—and it is at this time, when temperatures are moderated and nectar is abundant among carpets of colorful flowers covering Andean meadows, that tropical alpine hummingbirds conduct the business of reproduction. But in tropical lowland forests, this may be one of the leanest times of the year for nectar production, and relatively few species breed at this time.

The somber-plumaged hermits, which live out their lives whirring from one distant flower to another in the shady understory of humid lowland rainforests, may have the longest breeding seasons of any hummingbird. The long flowering seasons of understory vines and shrubs, upon which they depend, make it possible for nesting to take place over much of the year. Once in western Colombia, I recorded white-whiskered hermits singing all year long at a lek—a good indication that breeding, as well, was spread over the entire year. The breeding seasons of their brightly attired counterparts of forest edges and canopies are more constrained by unpredictable or brief flowering periods. Yet even in the humid and relatively unvarying environment of the rainforest understory, hermits usually suspend their amorous singing and abandon their leks for a few months in the latter part of the rainy season, perhaps for just long enough to undergo an annual molt.

Naturalists accustomed to the predictable rhythms of breeding seasons in temperate latitudes may find themselves confounded by the complexity and irregularity that characterize many tropical bird communities. Seasonal changes in food abundance, for example, may differ only a little from one month to the next. But the variable onset and intensity of rainy and dry seasons from year to year can be striking, resulting in widely fluctuating food levels. Consequently, breeding seasons timed precisely from one year to the next are not likely to be as critical in tropical as in temperate latitudes; they may even be counterproductive in an environment where food abundance varies markedly between years.

This complexity of tropical breeding patterns is well displayed even on the tiny island of Trinidad. There, the Snows found that, in general, breeding seasons were longer for species of open and semiopen regions than for forest species. Ruddy ground-doves, striped cuckoos, smooth-billed anis, house wrens and palm and blue-gray tanagers fit this category. They are also among the commonest species in towns, gardens and waste areas throughout the Neotropics. In some areas, they can be found nesting during almost any month of the year. Typically they are opportunists—capable of breeding whenever conditions permit, and if resources are abundant, a pair may raise several broods in succession.

In Trinidad, David and Barbara Snow found ruddy ground-doves nesting during every month of the year near the town of Sangre Grande. But a few miles to the west, in the Arima Valley, the rainfall is lower and more seasonal and no breeding occurs after the end of the rather long dry season. Trinidadian house wrens display a similar pattern, breeding all year long at Sangre Grande but suspending their breeding activities in the middle of the dry season and again in the middle of the wet season in the Arima Valley.

Forest birds may also show striking differences in breeding synchrony over short distances. White-bearded manakins occur almost throughout Trinidad's northern mountain range. As a consequence of the heavier rainfall in the east, many trees and shrubs fruit earlier in the year there than in Arima, which is located in the central part of the mountains. The Snows noticed that manakins begin nesting up to six weeks earlier in the east than in Arima—a remarkable difference over a geographical distance of only about 15 miles. If breeding changes of this magnitude can be found in tiny Trinidad, naturalists can only guess at the variation and complexity of breeding strategies that occur in countries as large and diverse as nearby Venezuela.

The timing of a nesting season is not the only energy-demanding process that must be factored into the annual cycle of every bird. Most naturalists consider a bird's complete molt, which occurs once a year in all birds, to be a time of high metabolic demand. Like breeding, molt usually takes place during a period of the year when food is plentiful. Both processes are inextricably linked and usually occur back to back, with molt immediately following breeding, during the most favorable time of the year. This link between molt and the average time of the year when food is most abundant is strengthened by the fact that no matter when young birds are hatched in the Tropics, most are well synchronized with the molting cycle of the adult population in the area within a year or two.

Even for scientists, interpreting molt and its various stages can be tricky business because it does not always proceed in an identical fashion in each species nor at a constant rate. Often, differences between the sexes and ages of a bird affect the timing of molt. Generally molt begins about one or two months after the last egg-laying attempt for species in which both the male and female care for the young. Males that do not take part in any nesting activities begin to molt earlier than females, sometimes at almost the same time that egg-laying begins.

The rufous piha, a familiar bird of Central American rainforests, illustrates this compression of breeding and molting. The males gather in small, loosely associated groups in the forest where they give loud whistles to attract females, but they take no part in the nesting activities. In Costa Rica, piha females nest from about March through July, and some males may begin molting by late February, even slightly before egg-laying begins. Females, on the other hand, don't even begin to molt until April—up to two months later than the males, whose molting peak occurs in June, and only after the breeding season is nearly over.

It may seem odd that molting, rather than breeding, is better synchronized with the time of the year when food is most abundant, especially when breeding is more energy-demanding and presumably more critical to the survival of the species. But there is an important difference between the two processes. The annual molt takes a more or less fixed length of time to complete, whereas the breeding season is variable in length. In a year with abundant resources, several broods may be raised in succession over many months, while in poor years, a single breeding attempt may last less than two weeks. Because the two events—breeding and molting—cannot take place at the same time, it is advantageous for the event of fixed length to take place at the same time each year because the variable process of nesting can vary in length according to environmental conditions.

A study of molt is, in a sense, like a study of the end of the breeding season. And because the timing of molt in tropical birds is less variable from year to year than breeding, a few records of molt may turn out to be a better indication of tropical breeding seasons—at least the end of them—than the same number of nesting records.

Without doubt, the greatest progress in understanding this fascinating area of avian biology will come not from large-scale surveys but from the work of biologists studying discrete guilds or small groups of birds in great detail. Whether we ever fully understand the complexities of tropical bird breeding seasons or not may be less important than the enjoyment we receive from observing them and thinking about them each time we go afield.

# Bibliography

## AVIAN ADDRESSES

Gentry, A. H. (Ed.). (1990). *Four neotropical forests.* New Haven, Connecticut: Yale University Press.

Karr, J. A. (1980). Geographical variation in the avifaunas of tropical forest undergrowth. *Auk, 97,* 283-298.

Terborgh, J., Robinson, S. K., Parker III, T. A., Munn, C. A., & Pierpont, N. (1990). Structure and organization of an Amazonian forest bird community. *Ecological Monographs, 60,* 213-238.

## TROPICAL DIVERSITY

Nadkarni, N., & Matelson, T. (1989). Bird use of epiphyte resources in neotropical trees. *Condor, 91,* 891-907.

Remsen Jr., J. V., & Parker III, T. A. (1984). Arboreal dead-leaf-searching birds of the Neotropics. *Condor, 86,* 36-41.

Terborgh, J. (1992). *Diversity and the tropical rain forest.* New York: W. H. Freeman & Company.

Terborgh, J. (1985). Habitat selection in Amazonian birds. In M. L. Cody (Ed.), *Habitat selection in birds.* New York: Academic Press.

## GHOSTS OF RAINFORESTS PAST

Capparella, A. P. (1990). Neotropical avian diversity and riverine barriers. *V Acta XX Congressus Internationalis Ornithologici.*

Cracraft, J. (1985). Historical biogeography and patterns of differentiation within the South American avifauna: Areas of endemism. In P. A. Buckley, M. S. Foster, E. S. Morton, R. S. Ridgely & F. G. Buckley (Eds.), *Neotropical ornithology.* Washington, D.C.: Ornithological Monographs, *36.*

Endler, J. (1982). Pleistocene forest refuges: Fact or fancy? In G. T. Prance (Ed.), *Biological diversification in the Tropics.* New York: Columbia University Press.

Haffer, J. (1974). Avian speciation in tropical South America. *Nuttall Ornithological Club, No. 14.* Cambridge, Massachusetts.

Haffer, J. (1993). Time's cycle and time's arrow in the history of Amazonia. *Biogeographica, 69,* 15-45.

## HIGH-ANDEAN GENEALOGY

Fjeldsa, J. (1985). Origin, evolution and status of the avifauna of Andean wetlands. In P. A. Buckley, M. S. Foster, E. S. Morton, R. S. Ridgely & F. G. Buckley (Eds.), *Neotropical ornithology.* Washington, D.C.: Ornithological Monographs, *36.*

Vuilleumier, F. (1981). The origin of high Andean birds. *Natural History, 90,* pp. 50-56.

Vuilleumier, F., & Monasterio, M. (Eds.). (1986). *High altitude tropical biogeography.* Oxford, New York: Oxford University Press & The American Museum of Natural History.

Wright Jr., H. E., Seltzer, G. O., & Hansen, B. C. S. (1989). Glacial and climatic history of the central Peruvian Andes. *National Geographic Research, 5,* 439-445.

## TROPICAL TRAVELERS

Bates, J. M., Parker III, T. A., Capparella, A. P., & Davis, J. (1992). Observations on the campo, cerrado and forest avifaunas of dpto. Santa Cruz, Bolivia, including 21 species new to the country. *Bulletin of the British Ornithologists' Club, 111,* 86-98.

Levey, D. J., & Stiles, F. G. (1992). Evolutionary precursors of long-distance migration: Resource availability and movement patterns in neotropical latitudes. *American Naturalist, 140 ,* 447-476.

Loiselle, B. A., & Blake, J. G. (1991). Temporal variation in birds and fruits along an elevational gradient in Costa Rica. *Ecology, 72,* 180-193.

O'Neill, J. P., & Parker III, T. A. (1978). Responses of birds to a snowstorm in the Andes of southern Peru. *Wilson Bulletin, 90,* 446-449.

Stiles, F. G. (1988). Altitudinal movements of birds on the Caribbean slope of Costa Rica: Implications for conservation. In F. Almeda & C. M. Pringle (Eds.), *Tropical rainforests: Diversity and conservation.* San Francisco: California Academy of Sciences, *Memoir No. 12.*

## THE CLUBBIEST OF CLUBS

Buskirk, W. (1976). Social systems in a tropical forest avifauna. *American Naturalist, 110,* 293-310.

Gill, F. B. (1990). Flocking: To eat or be eaten. In F. M. Gill (Ed.), *Ornithology.* New York: W. H. Freeman & Company.

Munn, C. (1984, November). Birds of different feather also flock together. *Natural History*, pp. 34-42.

Munn, C. (1986). Birds that cry wolf. *Nature, 319*, 143-145.

Munn, C. (1985). Permanent canopy and understory flocks in Amazonia: Species composition and population density. In P. A. Buckley, M. S. Foster, E. S. Morton, R. S. Ridgely & F. G. Buckley (Eds.), *Neotropical ornithology*. Washington, D.C.: Ornithological Monographs, *36*.

## ANTBIRDS DON'T EAT ANTS

Willis, E. O. (1967). The behavior of bicolored antbirds. *University of California Publications in Zoology, 79*, 1-132.

Willis, E. O. (1972). The behavior of spotted antbirds. Washington, D. C.: Ornithological Monographs, *10*.

Willis, E. O. (1973). The behavior of ocellated antbirds. *Smithsonian Contributions to Zoology, 144*, 1-57.

## WHO IS THE FAIREST?

Bailey, S. F. (1978). Latitudinal gradients in colors and patterns of passerine birds. *Condor, 80*, 372-381.

Endler, J. A. (1990). On the measurement and classification of colour in studies of animal colour patterns. *Biological Journal of the Linnaean Society, 41*, 315-352.

Forsyth, A. (1988). *The nature of birds*. Ontario, Canada: Camden House.

Snow, D. W. (1976). *The web of adaptation: Bird studies in the American Tropics*. New York: Quadrangle/The New York Times Book Co.

Willson, M. F., & von Neumann, R. A. (1972). Why are neotropical birds more colorful than North American birds? *Aviculture Magazine, 78*, pp. 141-147.

## FRUIT OF THE LAND

Howe, H., & Smallwood, J. (1982). Ecology of seed dispersal. *Annual Review of Ecology and Systematics, 13*, 210-228.

McKey, D. (1975). The ecology of coevolved seed dispersal systems. In L. Gilbert & P. Raven (Eds.), *Coevolution of animals and plants*. Austin: University of Texas Press.

Roca, R. (1991, September/October). Fine feathered foresters. *Wildlife Conservation, 94*, 78-87.

Wheelwright, N. T. (1988). Fruit-eating birds and bird-dispersed plants in the Tropics and temperate zone. *Trends in Ecology and Evolution, 3*, 270-274.

## ANATOMY OF A FRUIT EATER

Levy, D. (1987). Seed size and fruit-handling techniques of avian frugivores. *American Naturalist, 129,* 471-485.

Loiselle, B., & Blake, J. G. (1990). Diets of understory fruit-eating birds in Costa Rica: Seasonality and resource abundance. *Studies in Avian Biology, 13,* 91-103.

Moermond, T., & Denslow, J. (1983). Fruit choice in neotropical birds: Effects of fruit type and accessibility on selectivity. *Journal of Animal Ecology, 52* , 407-420.

Moermond, T., & Denslow, J. (1985). Neotropical frugivores: Patterns of behavior, morphology, and nutrition with consequences for fruit selection. Washington, D.C.: Ornithological Monographs, *36,* 865-897.

## A GOOD SONG AND DANCE

Beeler, B., & Foster, M. S. (1988). Hotshots, hotspots, and female preference in the organization of lek mating systems. *American Naturalist, 131,* 203-219.

Bradbury, J., & Gibson, R. (1985). Leks and mate choice. In P. Bateson (Ed.), *Mate choice.* Cambridge: Cambridge University Press.

Emlin, S. T., & Oring, L. W. (1977). Ecology, sexual selection, and the evolution of mating systems. *Science, 197* (4300), 213-223.

Trail, P. (1985). A lek's icon: The courtship display of a Guianan cock-of-the-rock. *American Birds, 39,* 235-240.

Trail, P. (1985). Territoriality and dominance in the lek-breeding Guianan cock-of-the-rock. *National Geographic Research, 1,* 112-123.

## TERRITORIES OR TRAPLINES?

Feinsinger, P. (1987). Approaches to nectarivore-plant interactions in the New World. *Revista Chilena de Historia Natural, 60,* 285-319.

Feinsinger, P., & Colwell, R. (1978). Community organization among neotropical nectar-feeding birds. *American Zoologist, 18,* 779-795.

Stiles, F. G. (1975). Ecology, flowering, and hummingbird pollination of some Costa Rican *Heliconia* species. *Ecology, 56,* 285-301.

Stiles, F. G. (1981). Geographical aspects of bird-flower coevolution, with particular reference to Central America. *Annals of the Missouri Botanical Garden, 68,* 323-351.

## COLD REALITY

Feinsinger, P., Colwell, R. K., Terborgh, J., & Chaplin, S. B. (1979). Elevation and the morphology, flight energetics and foraging ecology of tropical hummingbirds. *American Naturalist, 113,* 481-497.

Snow, D. W. (1983). The use of *Espeletia* by páramo hummingbirds in the eastern Andes of Colombia. *Bulletin of the British Ornithologists' Club, 103*, 89-94.

Snow, D. W., & Snow, B. K. (1980). Relationships between hummingbirds and flowers in the Andes of Colombia. *Bulletin of the British Museum, Zoology Series, 38*, 105-139.

Wolf, L. L., & Gill, F. B. (1983). Physiological and ecological adaptation of high montane sunbirds and hummingbirds. In W. P. Aspey & S. I. Lustick (Eds.), *Behavioral energetics: The cost of survival in vertebrates.* Columbus: Ohio State University Press.

## SALLYING FORTH

Fitzpatrick, J. W. (1980). Foraging behavior of neotropical tyrant flycatchers. *Condor, 82,* 43-57.

Fitzpatrick, J. (1980). Wintering of North American tyrant flycatchers in the Neotropics. In A. Keast & E. S. Morton (Eds.), *Migrant birds in the Neotropics: Ecology, behavior, distribution and conservation.* Washington, D.C.: Smithsonian Institution Press.

Morton, E. S. (1977). Intratropical migration in the yellow-green vireo and piratic flycatcher. *Auk, 94,* 97-106.

Sherry, T. W. (1984). Comparative dietary ecology of sympatric, insectivorous neotropical flycatchers (Tyrannidae). *Ecological Monographs, 54,* 313-338.

Traylor, M. A., & Fitzpatrick, J. W. (1982). A survey of the tyrant flycatchers. *The Living Bird, 19,* 7-50.

## FINDING A NEEDLE IN THE HAYSTACK

Houston, D. (1985). Evolutionary ecology of afrotropical and neotropical vultures in forests. In P. A. Buckley, M. S. Foster, E. S. Morton, R. S. Ridgely & F. G. Buckley (Eds.), *Neotropical ornithology.* Washington, D.C.: Ornithological Monographs, *36.*

Lemon, W. C. (1991). Foraging behavior of a guild of neotropical vultures. *Wilson Bulletin, 103,* 698-703.

Wallace, M. P., & Temple, S. A. (1987). Competitive interactions within and between species in a guild of avian scavengers. *Auk, 104,* 290-295.

## THE COSTS AND BENEFITS OF GROWING OLD

Robinson, S. K. (1986). Competitive and mutualistic interactions among females in a neotropical oriole. *Animal Behavior, 34,* 113-122.

Robinson, S. K. (1986, March). Social security for birds. *Natural History,* pp. 38-47.

Robinson, S. K. (1986). The evolution of social behavior and mating systems in the blackbirds (Icterinae). In D. I. Rubenstein & R. A. Wrangham (Eds.), *Ecological aspects of social evolution*. Princeton, N.J.: Princeton University Press.

## SOUND STRATEGIES

Morton, E. S. (1975). Ecological sources of selection on avian sounds. *American Naturalist, 109*, 17-34.

Richards, D. G., & Wiley, R. H. (1980). Reverberations and amplitude fluctuations in the propagation of sound in a forest: Implications for animal communication. *American Naturalist, 115*, 381-399.

Wilczynski, W., Ryan, M. J., & Brenowitz, E. A. (1989). The display of the blue-black grassquit: The acoustic advantage of getting high. *Ethology, 80*, 218-222.

## PERILOUS PARADISE

Remsen Jr., J. V., & Parker III, T. A. (1983). Contribution of river-created habitats to bird species richness in Amazonia. *Biotropica, 15*, 223-231.

Rosenberg, G. (1990). Habitat specialization and foraging behavior by birds of Amazonian river islands in northeastern Peru. *Condor, 92*, 427-443.

Salo, J., Kalliola, R., Hakkinen, I., Makinen, Y., Niemela, P., Puhakka, M., & Coley, P. D. (1986). River dynamics and the diversity of Amazon lowland forest. *Nature, 322*, 254-258.

## IN SEARCH OF A SEASON

Cruz, A., & Andrews, R. W. (1989). Observations on the breeding biology of passerines in a seasonally flooded savanna in Venezuela. *Wilson Bulletin, 101*, 62-76.

Skutch, A. F. (1950). The nesting seasons of Central American birds in relation to climate and food supply. *Ibis, 92*, 185-222.

Snow, D. W. (1976). The relationship between climate and annual cycles in the Cotingidae. *Ibis, 118*, 366-401.

Snow, D. W., & Snow, B. K. (1964). Breeding seasons and annual cycles of Trinidad landbirds. *Zoologica, 49*, 1-39.

# Index